German Fairy Tales

The German Library: Volume 29

Volkmar Sander, General Editor

Jakob and Wilhelm Grimm and Others

GERMAN FAIRY TALES

Edited by Helmut Brackert and Volkmar Sander

Foreword by Bruno Bettelheim
Illustrations by Otto Ubbelodhe

CONTINUUM · NEW YORK

1985

The Continuum Publishing Company
370 Lexington Avenue, New York, NY 10017

The German Library
is published in cooperation with Deutsches Haus,
New York University.
This volume has been supported by a grant
of Mercedes-Benz of North America, Inc.

Printed in the United States of America

Library of Congress Cataloging in Publication Data
Main entry under title:
German fairy tales.

(The German library ; v. 29)
1. Fairy tales—Germany.   I. Grimm, Jacob,
1785–1863.   II. Grimm, Wilhelm, 1786–1859.
III. Brackert, Helmut.   IV. Sander, Volkmar.
V. Series.
PT921.G45   1984   398.2"1"0943   84-21369
ISBN 0-8264-0288-7
ISBN 0-8264-0289-5 (pbk.)

Acknowledgments will be found on page 284,
which constitutes an extension of the copyright page.

Contents

Contents · vii

Foreword

All fairy tales are folktales, but not all folktales are fairy tales, since in most folktales neither fairies nor wizards appear. Folktales are part of the most ancient literature. They were told and retold everywhere, since the beginning of time, all over the world. Only during the Enlightenment were these tales shunned in educated circles, although even there they continued to be enjoyed by children and ordinary people. All this changed practically overnight when the brothers Grimm published their *Kinder und Hausmärchen (Children's and Household Tales)* in 1812. The success of their collection was so great and immediate that ever since then the folktales of all nations have been and still are collected, studied, and, most important, appreciated for their poetic merit. Without their pioneering effort, for example, Bechstein, some of whose tales are included in this volume, would not have embarked on his collection of folktales.

The brothers Grimm, however, were not the first to collect and publish folktales. As early as 1637, Gianbattista Basile's *Pentamerone* appeared which contained, for example, a Neapolitan version of Snow White. His collection remained virtually unknown until modern times because very few people understood the Neapolitan dialect in which the tales Basile collected were told. At the end of the seventeenth century Charles Perrault published a number of French tales, and so did Mme. d'Aulnoy in her *Contes nouvelles ou les fées à la mode*. Both authors, while basing their stories on then well-known French tales, did indeed rework them *à la mode*. They moralized and prettified them and in doing so did tort to their true spirit. At the beginning of the eighteenth century

Abbé Antoine Galland translated *Thousand and One Nights* into French, but in such orientalizing fashion that they found attention only as strange curiosities which fitted well into the period's fascination with chinoiseries.

This early interest in collecting and publishing folktales evaporated during the following period of the Enlightenment, when it was thought that such fantastic tales did not merit the attention of educated persons, that the irrational and supernatural features of which many of these tales abound are offensive to the intelligent person who was supposed to be interested only in what was rational. When any attention was paid to these tales, it was only after they had been changed beyond recognition, after their original themes had been trivialized and adapted to what was the current style of polite literature. Even Musäus, who published the *Volksmärchen der Deutschen* in five volumes from 1782 to 1787 retold them to conform to the literary taste of the educated classes of his day. None of these early collectors of folktales considered them worthy of publication in the form in which they were told; they all felt the need to edit them in polite language and as if they contained only lofty ideas.

The attitude with which Jakob Grimm, born in 1785, and his brother Wilhelm, born a year later, approached the task of collecting and publishing fairy tales was an entirely different one. The Napoleonic wars had aroused their nationalistic feelings, while the Romantic movement had stimulated their interest in the German past. While their *Kinder und Hausmärchen* established their worldwide reputation which since then has increased from year to year, and while they created German folklore as a discipline, it was possibly their *German Dictionary* that was their *magnum opus*. It represents a new departure in lexicography, incomparable in its day. Without the Grimms' efforts in pioneering modern lexicography, the *Oxford English Dictionary* might never have come into being, or in a quite different form, since it was their *German Dictionary* which broke entirely new scholarly ground.

It was their respect for the German past which induced them to try to retell these ancient tales the way they had been told and retold in the past. In their introduction to the first volume of these tales, published in 1812, they stated their intentions: "We have taken pains to record these tales as untouched as was possible. . . . No situation has been added, or prettified, or altered, for we hesitated to expand tales that were already so rich in their own analogies and reminiscences. . . . There is no other collection in this manner existent in Germany, for people have almost always used the tales only as narrative material in order to make larger stories out of them which, arbitrarily expanded and changed, may still have some value but took from children what was properly theirs and gave them nothing in return. Even those who took thought in the matter could not help mixing in mannerisms which were supplied by the poetic mode of the time; almost always there has been a lack of diligence in collecting."

It is not that the brothers did not take some liberties with the tales when they published them. They often tightened the plot or clarified it to obtain a more closely knit tale. It was their genius that out of several versions of the same tale they wove one which in the end was truer to the spirit of the folktale, as later research taught us to recognize, than was the particular way in which their informers, such as "Old Marie," the housekeeper of their neighbors, the Wild family, or Gretchen Wild, one of the daughters, told them. Thanks to the brothers' poetic and historic genius they recognized what in the versions they were told was the product of the imagination of the person who told the story and what was the essential tale that lay behind it, and this they created or rather re-created by the small changes they introduced into the tale they had been told.

The German poet Ludwig Uhland said that the brothers Grimm "had spun a golden thread of poetry which, thanks to them, runs through all of German life." The brothers succeeded in lifting a veil which up to their time had obscured most of the German folk literature of the past. Not only that, due to the enormous success of their collection, fairy tales captured the imagination of all of Europe, and eventually of all continents, and brought about a recognition of the importance of the fairy tales of all people.

When Achim von Arnim, another German Romantic poet, objected to Jakob Grimm that not all tales were truly children's stories, he replied that it was wrong to distinguish between the interests of adults and children, stressing that all ages can enjoy these tales, that they have much to offer to anyone who opens himself to their beauty, that they have meaning to young and old alike, although on different levels of appreciation.

On various occasions both brothers emphasized that children

could learn a great deal from these stories. Jakob Grimm, in his dedication of their book to a friend, wrote that he hoped that his child would learn a great deal from it, because "it is our firm intention that the book be regarded as an educational book." And Wilhelm wrote to their friend and mentor Friedrich Karl von Savigny, in whose library they had first become acquainted with German literary antiquities, "We really wished the tales to be an educational book, since I know nothing that is more nourishing, more innocent and refreshing for childlike powers and nature."

When the brothers Grimm spoke of the education children can derive from these tales, they had not school learning in mind, but education in the best, the highest humanistic sense, an education that, as it nourishes the child's mind, teaches him much about his very nature, aspects of which he can understand only when these are presented to him in the symbolic language of art which speaks directly to his deepest longings, relieves his anxieties, kindles his hopes so that he can meet the vagaries of life with greater confidence.

Every person can discover only in his own way what appeals to him of the literary, the poetic qualities of these stories, and he can do so only by listening to or reading the stories, letting sink in what they tell about the child in all of us. For this reason I shall try in the following remarks to illustrate, by means of one well-known story, what some of the "educational" merits of these stories are, how they indeed help the child to become more deeply aware of his very nature.

The poet Rainer Maria Rilke, at the beginning of the first of the *Duino Elegies,* reveals what forms the essence of great art: "Beauty is nothing but the beginning of terror we are still just able to bear, and why we adore it so is because it serenely disdains to destroy us." This certainly is true for most fairy tales. Their beauty is inextricably interwoven with the terror they arouse and the hero's— and with it our—rescue at the happy ending. Fairy tales present to us this essence of beauty in a most concise manner, and in ways in which it can be comprehended even by the most naive peruser of this literature, even by the young child.

Beginning in a setting akin to our most ordinary existence, fairy tales take us in a short and dramatic move to the very edge of the abyss, as does any true exploration of the meaning of life, of its deeper purpose, as does any serious effort to know ourselves that penetrates beyond the surface of our being and reaches into the darker recesses of our mind, particularly those which we desire not to recognize. These are the aspects of our existence which threaten us most, which are likely to cause our troubles, but which also endow our existence with some of its deepest meaning. This darkness within ourselves is what we need most to become acquainted with if we want to know ourselves. The fairy tale, after having made us tremble by taking us to the edge of the abyss, after having forced us to face evil and all the darkness within man, after having acquainted us with what we rather wish to avoid, serenely rescues us. In the course of the story, as we identify with its hero, we gain the ability to live a richer and more meaningful life on a much higher plane than the one on which we found ourselves at the story's beginning, where the hero, who is our mirror image, was forced to embark on his perilous voyage of self-discovery.

Hänsel and Gretel are two very ordinary children when we meet them at the beginning of their story. Like most children, they are assailed in the darkness of the night by anxious fantasies about their parents' plans to get rid of them, are beset by starvation anxiety. Convinced that they cannot take care of themselves, they know only one way to be safe: to hang on most determinedly to what they are most familiar with: their home, their mother's apron strings. But it will no longer do. Like all children, Hänsel and Gretel must learn not only to become able to fend for themselves but also to meet the dark aspects of life. Most of all they must learn to combat their primitive anxieties about being starved and devoured, which are closely connected with their deep oral cravings tempting them to eat even what seems to offer most pleasant shelter, symbolized by the gingerbread house. They will not be able to be themselves nor to meet the world successfully unless they have first courageously faced their anxious fantasy of the archetypical bad, devouring mother. It is an image which every child creates out of his experience of wishing to eat up his mother so that she will never be able to desert him even for a moment, and of his fear that, in retaliation, the mother will eat him up. It is an image as old as the child's nursing experience when, as he sucks from the breast—or from the bottle which he experiences as a poor substitute for the breast—he imagines himself as incorporating the mother. It is the fear of the bad mother which is the inescapable reverse image of the all-loving mother, the counterpart of the giving and protective mother whose image is replaced when she makes demands, criticizes, and even occasionally punishes the infant. It is the consequence of the infant's utter dependence on an all-powerful person, whose intentions the infant cannot fathom and which therefore may be evil. All of this is symbolically expressed in the fairy tale by the replacement of the all-good mother, who gave birth to her infant but soon disappears, by the demanding and frustrating stepmother, as in Cinderella and Snow White.

Hänsel and Gretel encounter their own fantasies about the devouring mother in the form of the witch. This witch hides within or behind the alluring, wish-fulfilling oral fantasy of the gingerbread house, which has its origin in the earliest phase of the child's development when he experiences everything in terms of his orality. At the beginning of the story, we met the archetypical image of the bad mother in its more ordinary form of the depriving and rejecting stepmother, who is intent on forcing the children to learn to shift for themselves, to stop being a burden to their parents, to begin to become masters of their fate. As reluctant as the children are to become their own masters, the fairy tale tells that they will perish unless they do so. Harsh events force them to learn to defeat evil incarnate: the witch. In destroying her they free themselves at the same time from dependence on their orality, and learn to recognize and activate the forces within them of self-protection. This they do as they overcome their fear of the all-destructive figure of the witch, outwit her, and in the end overcome her.

Because Hänsel and Gretel were able to gain control over their nightmarish terror—given tangible form in the figure of the witch—they gained confidence in their own strength to defeat evil and to rescue themselves. Because they succeeded in their battle against the primordial oral anxiety about being devoured, their lives are as if miraculously enriched. This is symbolically expressed in their gaining the witches' jewels which henceforth provide them with a secure livelihood. Having found their own strength and gained the ability to exercise it, they no longer need to live in fear, nor to depend on others for their well being. Life will be good for them forever after.

It was their experience in the dark and pathless forest, it was their encounter with terror, that did all this for them. Finding one-self in a dark impenetrable forest is an ancient literary image for man in need of self-knowledge. Dante evoked it at the beginning of the *Divine Comedy*, but long before him it served as image of man in search of himself, of man caught in a moral crisis, of man having to negotiate a developmental impasse, as he wishes to move from a lower to a higher level of self-consciousness. It is the am-bience in which Hänsel and Gretel meet the witch. It is the ambi-ence into which the knight errant rides, seeking the greatest adven-ture man can encounter: to meet and find himself, as he does battle against the forces of evil. This evil, this darkness that surrounds him in the forest, is but a projection of the darkness that resides in himself, and so is the dragon against which he does battle. The dragon is a figment of his imagination onto which he projects all that he cannot accept in himself. By defeating the dragon he wins a moral victory over himself, symbolized by his rescuing the dragon's victim. His victory is gaining permanent access to his higher self which up to then had been held captive, inoperative, by the pow-ers of darkness. Because of their encounter with the witch, Hänsel and Gretel's childish naïvete and utter dependence on others is re-placed by a proud maturity which permits them not only to rescue themselves but also their father, who had despaired of his ability to take care of his children. The children, who at the story's be-ginning had felt themselves the helpless pawns of their parents and of fate, are at its end masters of their destiny and able to take care of their parent. What happier ending to a story can there be?

Comprehending what a fairy tale reveals in symbolic form about how one must organize one's life to master its invariable difficul-ties requires not only repeated listening but also the chance to ponder the tale's meaning to one's heart's delight. Only then can the child begin to understand that the story tries to tell him that he cannot remain forever dependent, cannot expect to be taken care of by others all his life. Only then does the child comprehend the shortcomings of relying for his security on his parents, recognize the advantages of becoming a person in his own right. Only then does he gain the hope that however nightmarishly difficult it may seem to him to dare to become truly himself, it is a task that he can master and be much the better for it. It is a lesson that many fairy tales teach, each in its own and different form, by means of different images and in an esthetic rendering suitable to its content.

Typically, in Hänsel and Gretel as in many other fairy tales, the child protagonists have to meet fearful dangers and to engage in actions requiring great valor before they can gain their just rewards. However the story's hero may have been threatened as the story unfolds, in the end he is rescued. The eventual rescue, complete restoration, and elevation of the hero to a superior existence is characteristic of fairy tales because as works of art their purpose is to acquaint us with the fact not only that life is difficult and often entails dangerous struggles but also that only through the mastery of succeeding crises in our existence can we eventually find our true self. Having achieved this, we then no longer need to live in fear of our childish anxieties.

One might even say that the stories tell the child that he will succeed only because hardships force him to develop his ingenuity, initiative, and independence. There are no fairy tales telling of a child growing into a self-reliant, successful person whose original mother continued to take marvelous care of him all through his growing-up years. Painful as is the process of separation and individuation, fairy tales assure the child that it is a necessary and inescapable developmental task, and one that turns out to be for the best. Cinderella's stepsisters, who are indulged all their lives by their mother who demands nothing of them, come to a very bad end because they never learned to cope with frustration.

Since it has been objected that fairy tales, with their monsters, giants, and witches, scare children unnecessarily, in ending I might mention that every child, all on his own, invents scary figures such as the bogeyman. But also all on his own he feels helpless to cope with them and the anxieties they create in him. The fairy tale shows him that it is not just he who is terrified by such figures but that these stand for universal anxieties, and while on his own the child fears he can never get the better of these terrifying figures of his imagination, fairy tales assure him that the good are always helped and rewarded, and in the end victorious, as even little Gretel can push the evil witch into the oven where she meets her well-deserved fate.

BRUNO BETTELHEIM

Introduction

When Margaret Hunt's translation of the Grimm Fairy Tales first appeared in 1944, W. H. Auden said in his review, "It is hardly too much to say that these tales rank next to the Bible in importance." That was perhaps always true, but it was the Grimms' scholarship and classic style that popularized the folktale.

Jakob Grimm (1785–1863) and his brother Wilhelm (1786–1859) started their collection in 1806. They never imagined that their fairy tales would be reprinted in countless editions and turn up as source material for everyone from poets and scholars to cartoonists, advertisers, and film makers. They never grew rich from their endeavor. But it was not, after all, material interest that induced them to scour their native Hessian countryside, seeking out informants who could tell them the old tales still circulating among the people. The Grimms were driven rather by a burning, almost obsessive passion for the folk tradition, a passion born out of the historical moment.

An interest in folklore had already been awakened by Herder's collection of folk songs (1778–79), and by the turn of the century the poets Arnim and Brentano in Heidelberg had begun assembling the material for a "popularly priced book of folk songs," the first volume of which, *Des Knaben Wunderhorn* appeared in 1805. But toward the end of that same year, a new impulse added fuel to the fire, an impulse forged in the heat of the political developments of the day. Consider the following: when Arnim appealed to a wider public to join the ranks of the folklore collectors, his argument was manifestly patriotic. At a time when the German nation was divided into more than a hundred small and minuscule independent principalities (a Germany both politically and militarily powerless in the face of the growing threat of Napoleon's France), any such reminder of a common German heritage, of a nation and culture once united, served to spur on the popular will to resist. The Grimms were wholeheartedly receptive to Arnim's appeal, as it bespoke both the spirit of the times, and their own long-standing sense of the significance of folklore. But it was a side interest of Arnim's, an afterthought, as it were, that caught their fancy: "Old legends and fairy tales from the oral tradition will be published as a sequel to this collection."

And so they set to work and began systematically the task of collecting tales, a formidable task, to be sure. As the Grimms note in their foreword, there were very few individuals left who still knew the original old tales and had the knack to tell them. Also, informants were not always easy to persuade. They were usually simple people, accustomed to telling their tales at intimate family gatherings, or to children, and were ashamed to do so in front of two cultured gentlemen. Not by the farthest stretch of imagination could these simple women comprehend that grown men really wanted to hear about such things. They thought for sure they'd laugh at them, if they set about telling children's stories to educated people. But others told eagerly and at great length.

It was not only the painstaking search for informants that complicated their work, but also the conditions under which they sought to record what they had collected: technical aids of the sort that modern folklorists have at their disposal were not available then. There were no tape recorders to preserve a faithful facsimile, true to voice inflection and the peculiarities of dialect; stenography had not yet been invented, and everything had to be taken down in longhand. No wonder then that the task of collecting took so many years, and that it wasn't until 1812 that the first volume finally appeared. The second volume was published in 1815, the third in 1822. This last volume contained variations and annotated notes and, with its astonishingly wide range of material, constituted the beginning of a brand new field of inquiry: comparative folklore.

We should, however, not compare their methods with our modern scientific standards of exact reproduction, not only because of today's more precise technological tools but, above all, because an exact reproduction of what they heard was not at all what the

Grimms were after. They sought rather to record an impression taken from the living, ever-changing oral tradition, a rough sketch, from which, so they believed, the true original version would have to be hammered out.

By a lucky turn of events, we are in a position to compare the 1812 edition (in which the more meticulous Jakob Grimm still had a hand), not only with the 1837 edition, revised by Wilhelm Grimm, but also with the original handwritten manuscript which Brentano had borrowed from his friends. This so-called Oelenberg Collection gives us the opportunity to study somewhat more closely the method applied by the brothers Grimm in finalizing their material for print.

Let us consider the beginning of the famous fairy tale Hänsel and Gretel. Evidently the brothers must have heard it the way it appears in the Oelenberg Collection:

> Once upon a time there was a poor woodcutter who lived beside a big forest. Things went so badly for him that he could hardly feed his wife and children. Then it came to pass that he had no more bread left and he grew very frightened; so his wife spoke to him that evening in bed: "take both children tomorrow morning and lead them into the big forest, give them the bread that's left and build them a big fire and then go away and leave them there." For a long time the man would not listen, but his wife gave him no peace untill he finally gave in.

The first printed version of 1812, in comparison, is already far more delineated, more articulate and thus longer, more logical in sentence sequence, more complex in syntax. The straight narrative style has been replaced with dialogue, a conversation between father and mother in which the parents' behavior is given psychological motivation:

> Beside a great forest there lived a poor woodcutter, who earned little more than a mouthfull to eat, and hardly enough to feed his wife and two children, Hänsel and Gretel. Then one day he could not bring home even that much, and he didn't know what to do. That evening as he tossed anxiously about in bed, his wife said to him: "Listen, husband, tomorrow morning you must take both children, give each of them a crust of bread, then lead them deep into the middle of the

forest, to its darkest part, build them a fire, and then go away and leave them there. We can't feed them any longer," "No, woman," said the man, "I haven't the heart to take my own dear children to the wild animals in the forest, where they'll be torn to shreds." "If you won't," said the woman, "we'll all die of hunger," and she gave him no peace till he said yes.

The second edition which became the source of all subsequent reprints takes far greater liberties still. It is pointless then even to speak of a faithfulness to the oral rendition, or any pretense of exact replication. Arnim sensed something of this truth when he wrote the Grimms in 1812: "I'll never again believe you (even if you believe it yourselves), that you wrote down these fairy tales just the way you heard them." ·

One might well impute a certain arbitrariness to the Grimms' methodology. But Wilhelm Grimm would have vehemently objected to any such implication; he would have contended that his revisions—his simplification of sentence structure, his insertion of word repetition and stock phrases, his vivid descriptions and poignant emotional shading—all served to make the fairy tales more childlike, more folklike, more magical: in short, more like a fairy tale. The subsequent popular success of his versions seems only to confirm the soundness of his approach. Wilhelm Grimm's interpretations insured for the fairy tale a permanent place in the heritage of children's literature. Whoever speaks of the fairy tale today, thinks first and foremost of these texts, and the genre Grimm as distinct from all other folk fairy tales. And yet in tailoring his versions to suit the special needs of children, in excizing objectionable passages, in holding up proper middle class manners for praise and condemning any deviation from the norm, in seeking, as such, to impose a didactic moral, Wilhelm Grimm seriously distorted the function of the fairy tale. For as his brother Jakob had already noted, "This fairy tale book was by no means written for children," though he did admit, "But children take to the fairy tale, and that makes me very happy."

According to the brothers Grimm, the child's affinity for the fairy tale harkens back to the simple, natural, primitive magical beliefs of an earlier stage of human development. It is still an open issue whether and to what extent the marked similarities and sometimes even identical plot structures and motif patterns found in folktales of diverse cultures can be traced back to this one common source.

In the nineteenth century, with the beginning of a systematic study of fairy tales, a study initiated by the collections and historical research of the Grimm brothers, scholarly interest focused largely on the question of the origin of the fairy tale. The more international material became known (attesting to an astonishing structural similarity between fairy tales from different countries and even continents), the more pressing grew this question of origin. The discovery that in numerous motifs and motif patterns Irish fairy tales correspond point for point to Russian tales, German tales bear an uncanny resemblance to the Scandinavian, the Hungarian, and even the Indian tales—this discovery demanded further explanation, raising issues, the dynamic of which provided the key thrust to the study of comparative folklore as we know it today. Some researchers contend that the question of origin is still the central issue.

The comparative linguistic method, likewise a product of nineteenth-century thought, gave rise to the concept of an ancient Indogermanic family of nations. Proponents of the so-called Indogermanic Theory saw the fairy tale as a mythological vestige of the world view once held by this primordial Indogermanic clan, whose daughter nations altered and modified their cultural inheritance over time. But the theory proved untenable. The legendary clan turned out to be an imaginary fabrication, the contours of its alleged wide ethnic range were never more clearly defined; moreover, the similarities and analogies were by no means limited to fairy tales of this supposed linguistic family. Another theory claimed that the fairy tales were passed on from mouth to mouth, that they traveled between countries, and that each nation participated in the process both as bearer and recipient, the result being an international exchange: a narrative fabric woven of the diverse ethnic strands of all peoples.

But difficulties arose even here, for how, according to this theory, could one explain the striking similarities between stories of peoples geographically far removed from each other? Wilhelm Grimm had already proposed another possible explanation, one that has since been further refined and now constitutes an important working hypothesis, namely that of the polygenesis of the fairy tale. In 1856 he wrote in his annotated notes to the *Kinder- und Haus*

Märchen: "There are situations so simple and natural that they reappear everywhere, just as there are thoughts that seem to invent themselves. It is possible then that the same or strikingly similar fairy tales might have originated quite independently of one another in different countries."

These anthropological theories, that sought to trace back the origin of identical fairy tales to identical primitive forms of human society and consciousness, were supported by a host of diverse contentions. Fairy tales were alternately associated with cannibalism and animism, with ritual customs and practices, with magic and shamanism, with seasonal and puberty rites. The fairy tale was identified with mythological conceptions of the sort still common to the "primitive" peoples of today and once held in the distant past by the "civilized" nations. But whatever its hypothetical context, we can come to some general conclusions about the nature of the world that the fairy tales depict. It is a world governed by secret magical forces, a world in which inanimate objects also have souls, in which anything can transform itself into anything else, a world in which animals can speak, and the very elements act to help or hinder man. In the fairy-tale world, language has the power to invoke spirits, water and air are inhabited by good and evil spirits, dwarves and fairies, nymphs and giants, dragons and witches. More abstractly, the fairy tale knows no separation between subject and object, between the perceived and the imagined; in its logical substructure these realms are still identical.

To facilitate a discussion in literary terms of the fairy-tale realm of experience (a realm so different from our own), certain descriptive categories were developed: one-dimensionality, shallowness, abstractness, isolation and interconnectedness, sublimation and here-and-nowness. The fairy tale knows no differentiation between the real and the imaginary; all characters experience life on one and the same plane; space is limitless and time irrelevant; individual objects are never clearly delineated, everything is named, nothing described; all characters remain isolated from each other, learning nothing, experiencing nothing, and yet able, nonetheless, to commune with all that exists. Though free of any attachments, the fairy-tale protagonist can at any time establish a tie. Magic is the dominant force, and the hero effortlessly commands magical tools and helpers. Only seldom do objects serve their ostensible purpose, but the fairy tale is infinitely inventive in finding extraordinary applications. There are also certain formal hallmarks of the fairy tale, characteristic of its typology: the preference for formulaic repetition, the significance of the number three, and the importance of passwords in plot structure and for the presentation of character.

Let us confine our attention to the most important category, that of one-dimensionality. It is congruent with other aspects of the fairy tale: the fact that internal and external are as yet undifferentiated, that all lies under a magic spell, that time plays no part, that characters seem isolated from each other. Without undergoing any psychological development, learning and experiencing nothing, fairy-tale characters are nonetheless able to enter into a spontaneous communion with all that is, with people and animals, with plants and even with stones.

The oral tradition of storytelling is still alive today. Storytellers can be found telling the old tales in the market place or at family gatherings in many parts of the world. But with the spread of civilization, the tradition is dying out. Research into the oral tradition has, at any rate, made one thing eminently clear: the storyteller does not tell a fixed unchanging text but rather addresses himself each time anew to a specific audience, always keeping them in mind. The same storyteller will vary his tale on different occasions, depending on the spirit of the gathering and the mood of his listeners. His only given is a general, as yet undeveloped idea of plot and certain motif combinations; the rest is improvised on the spot. This explains how the host of storytelling occasions that entered into the fabric of the tales over time can likely be traced back to diverse eras.

Grimms' fairy tales, written down and revised as they were by 1812, took on their final definitive form relatively early, historically speaking—that is, they stopped evolving. Before being written down, they still belonged to that living, ever-changing stock of lore, tapped and reactivated every time a social occasion called for a fairy tale. One scholar described such social occasions: "In the past, fairy tales were told both to bolster the spirit, during work hours, and to entertain after work. At basketmaking, charcoal burning, tobacco bolting, quill splitting, corn husking, chestnut pealing, fishnet repair and weaving—any collective work effort was a fitting occasion. Fairy tales were also told at wakes, and during leisure hours at harvest time. Soldiers liked to tell them, as did lumberjacks and journeymen. It was a favorite pastime on walking trips to market, on pilgrimages, on ocean voyages and at country fairs" (Max Luethi). Thus it is clear that fairy tales were by no means conceived as mere children's stories. They once had a definite place in the adult world, although we can't really say for sure what made them so appealing, why fairy tales in particular were told on the job and after work, on holidays and trips. Were these stories, in their simple imagery, expressions of the social condition? Were the solutions sought after, the wishes granted, the longing fulfilled—were these all issues with which storyteller and audience could identify?

There is little definite evidence to help answer such questions. One can say with assurance, however, that the popular reception of Grimms' fairy tales once they appeared in book form centered largely around the realm of the nursery: the book was welcomed above all for its pedagogical value. Of course, the book was also well received in learned circles. Scholars and a good many amateur enthusiasts took up the discussion of origin and history. They sought to trace the existence of original versions, to isolate structural laws, and to study the sociological and psychological ramifications of the genre. But scholarly response proved quantitatively negligible compared to the immeasurable influence the fairy tales had as elementary forms of amusement and edification for children.

Edification in what sense? A contemporary of the brothers Grimm, the well-known theologian Friedrich Schleiermacher, held that an early encounter with these simple literary texts would fortify the child's imagination; in this vein he declared enthusiastically: "There is no other poetry for children but the fairy tale."

Often however, edification had an altogether different meaning, particularly so just after the failed revolution of 1848. In that time of the ever tightening grip of middle-class values, fairy tales came to be viewed as model stories whose simple morals could be used to mold the "proper" attitude: by praising the good, reprimanding the bad, rewarding moderation, and punishing extravagance— tendencies which could easily be highlighted by means of judicious adaptation and selection. In short, by the middle of the nineteenth century, at the very latest, fairy tales took on a key function in the insidious process whereby the grownups of one generation try to inflict their ideals on their children.

Ludwig Bechstein (1801–1860) deserves mention in this connection: a noted fairy-tale collector and scholar, his adaptations place him very much in the tradition of the brothers Grimm. He envisioned his fairy-tale collections as children's books right from the start. True to his pedagogical purpose, "the edification and good breeding of children," Bechstein laid heavy emphasis on the moral message. He added touches of folk humor to his fairy tales and tried generally to smooth over, to muffle harsh passages, and to beautify the whole. At times his more innocuous versions (which tended to neutralize the conflicts inherent in the fairy tale), were more popular than those of the brothers Grimm.

But Bechstein's popularity was limited to Germany. In other countries Grimms' fairy tales became paradigms of the form within a short time after their appearance. In the English-speaking world and particularly in North America, the term fairy tale came practically to be used as a synonym for the genre Grimm.

American receptivity to the fairy tale began to take root from 1835 to 1839, with the reissuance of the two-volume edition of the first English translation of Grimms' fairy tales, entitled *German Popular Stories.* The book contained some fifty-five tales and was illustrated by George Cruikshank. (Here, as in the following, I borrow heavily from the research findings of Linda Degh.)

In the course of the nineteenth century, thirty to thirty-five editions of Grimms' fairy tales appeared; around 1900 there were forty-five editions in print; by 1927 the number had increased to two hundred and seventy-five; and in 1938, when Walt Disney brought out his animated movie *Snow White,* ninety more editions followed. During and after World War II the number of editions in print dropped rapidly. Till then the term fairy tale had automatically and inextricably been associated in the popular consciousness (and favorably so) with the tales of the brothers Grimm. Henceforth, opinion changed: fairy tales were considered brutal, and they were now associated with the political developments in Germany. And yet there were always defenders of the fairy tale, particularly among child psychologists and analysts, who saw its value precisely in the fact that it helped children to cope with the brutalities of everyday life. Bruno Bettelheim's *The Uses of En-*

chantment (1977) is to date the most important expression of this viewpoint.

According to Linda Degh, bookstores are not the only source of the widespread dissemination of Grimms' fairy tales in America, storytellers and children's libraries also play a significant role. A 1975 survey of the children's libraries in five American cities found over a hundred-thirty different editions of Grimms' fairy tales and two hundred picture books based on individual tales. In the last ten to fifteen years, so-called Storytelling Guilds have been formed, organizations of storytellers who get together annually at festivals devoted exclusively to the art. Of late, however, fairy tales are being squeezed out of the picture by the more modern "grassroots" storytellers, who take their material from the homegrown tradition or spin their yarns around current events. Other storytellers prefer science fiction, horror stories, and soap opera; the old fairy tales are slowly being forgotten.

There are at any rate only a very few of Grimms' fairy tales that have become firmly anchored in the American consciousness, albeit, in a rather rudimentary abridgement, removed from their original context. These fairy tale fragments derive in large part from the media: from advertising, comics, and cartoons. Apparently, we have more use for fairy-tale metaphors than for the fairy tale itself.

Psychologists, psychoanalysts, and teachers, among others, have lamented the great loss that the disappearance of the fairy tale implies. But "children need fairy tales," says Bruno Bettelheim, a man who has rightfully been hailed a pioneer in the movement to bring them back. The fairy tale, so argue its defenders, is particularly well suited to give focus to the child's boundless fear, to give it a concrete form. The fairy tale helps the child learn to endure fear and to overcome it. For normal children, fairy tales, like games, provide an opportunity to master fear by means of play. In his identification with the fairy-tale hero (who braves dangers and kills monsters), the child also gains confidence in his own ability to win out over the forces of evil. The naive world view of the fairy tale demands the victory of good and the defeat of evil, thereby strengthening the child's moral fiber. Here are dramatized the experiences and threatening situations of the sort that every growing person must face in real life. The only difference is that the fairy tale demonstrates how the critical, and most often unconsciously experienced crises of growing up can be mastered step by step and without fear.

Some educators underline the significance of the fairy tale from an altogether different perspective. They point out that the very idea that this literary genre was ever intended for children is a fallacy which led to its misrepresentation. According to this school of thought, the fairy tale's true meaning can only be revealed by isolating its original spirit of protest, and by digging away the sediment of values imposed by nineteenth-century interpretation. To be emphasized above all is the social function of a literary genre that originally belonged to the lower classes and reflected their dreams of emancipation, their optimism, their longing for an end to the oppression of person and class.

The objection has rightfully been raised that the child, to whom the fairy tale is either read or told, cannot yet possess any historical consciousness or critical perspective. The child thus runs the risk of adapting archaic modes of behavior derived from the constraints of the social and economic conditions of another era.

In fact, there is a danger here, not to be underestimated, which the German political scientist Iring Fetscher (b. 1922) points out in his *Märchenverwirrbuch* ("Book of Fairy Tale Confusion"). Fetscher writes, in reference to the Cinderella story: "The message is self-evident, the story is meant to sooth: Just be patient, you poor and oppressed, you downtrodden and despised soul; for the day will come when you will be surrounded by silver and gold, and when, with the aid of a handsome and powerful prince, you will triumph over your oppressors. That will be the day when deception and wickedness are no more, and the whole of nature will celebrate its reawakening and the victory of good people everywhere. It is indeed a beautiful dream, but it deters from action and permits the dreamer to endure his miserable reality. If the fairy tale is to emancipate, it must first be activated."

This may very well be true. But it appears highly questionable whether Fetscher's postscript to the tale offers a tenable solution. According to his version, Cinderella turns activist, mobilizing the serving girls in the surrounding district to take part in a joint action to fight their exploitation. A successful strike is held, and Cinderella opens an office of the maids and servants' union. The prince, who is sympathetic to the cause, takes a liking to Cinderella, but his father, the power-conscious king reacts with retaliatory measures: "One fine day the king's soldiers marched into the city and arrested Cinderella. The servants' union was dissolved, and judges and preachers everywhere proclaimed it a sin for any class to unite and rise up against another. The high-flown word on everyone's lips was freedom, and after doing time for offenses against the king and refractions of the servants' code, Cinderella emigrated to America, where there were no kings and princes, and where she believed all people were truly free and equal."

One should not underestimate the enlightening intent of such creative license. A valid skepticism grounded in reality is here set against the unreal fabric of the fairy tale. Yet such an act of rationalization robs the fairy tale of one of its intrinsic qualities. For the free and easy interplay of the magical and the mundane, a quality so characteristic of the fairy tale, is thus reduced to the ordinary—whose standard measure is the here and now, not "Once upon a time."

To the philosopher Ernst Bloch, the standard fairy tale opening, "Once upon a time," signals a brighter, sweeter elsewhere. By the end of each tale, the hero overcomes all obstacles and troubles in his path, and for him the golden age has come. The wise man (always here synonymous with the poor man) arrives at that blessed state of peace and harmony. Fairies and other well-intentioned powers fulfill his deepest desire: they grant him the necessities of life and enable him to accomplish effortlessly the most difficult tasks. All distances draw near, all time dissolves into the now and forever of a golden paradise. And unlike the age-old promises of ecclesiastical and secular authorities, this paradise is not a heavenly then-and-there to compensate for the miserable here and now: this paradise is here.

Look over the abundance of fairy tales and you will doubtless find that many do not follow in tone and content the standard pattern of the folk fairy tale. Not even all folktales constitute a unified body. And yet in all fairy tales there is something of that longing for a better world, that playful dream-sketch of paradise, free of the limitations of everyday life. The fairy tale translates "things could be better" into "once upon a time," and thereby dissolves the empirical laws of reality in a glorious halo of hope: "And they lived happily ever after." Material good fortune takes on an eternal form; redemption and harmony are destined to last forever.

Herein lies the clue to the survival of the fairy tale genre. For what it expresses again and again in poetic form is a fundamental human possibility: the fairy tale playfully evokes a sense of freedom—freedom not of the world as it is but as it might be. We realize that fairy tale in essence means return: return to the familiar, to childhood, to paradise. The fairy tale is a whispered promise: you're here at last, you're home again.

H.B.

Of the 210 tales of the standard edition of 1819, 57 of the most familiar ones are reprinted here; one more (Puss-in-Boots), not included in the standard version, was taken from the first edition of 1812. As token examples of later developments, there are three fairy tales by Ludwig Bechstein (1857) and one anti-fairy tale by Iring Fetscher (1972).

Parallel to their collection of *Volksmärchen,* the Grimms also gathered *Deutsche Sagen,* legends and sagas, which appeared in two volumes in 1816. Only one, but perhaps the best known in this country, is included here, "The Pied Piper of Hamelin." It is, of course, not a fairy tale but a popular legend with a basis in historic fact, most probably the story of recruiting officers who enticed young people away to do battle or to colonize in the East.

The popularity and lure of the genre is also attested to by the fact that apart from *Volksmärchen,* a great many *Kunstmärchen* were written in German since the Grimm brothers first captured the imagination. For a collection of these, from Goethe to Franz Kafka and Hermann Hesse, see *German Literary Fairy Tales,* Volume 30 in this series.

V.S.

Jakob and Wilhelm Grimm

GERMAN
FAIRY TALES

Translated by Margaret Hunt

The Frog-King, or Iron Henry

In olden times when wishing still helped one, there lived a king whose daughters were all beautiful, but the youngest was so beautiful that the sun itself, which has seen so much, was astonished whenever it shone in her face. Close by the King's castle lay a great dark forest, and under an old lime-tree in the forest was a well, and when the day was very warm, the King's child went out into the forest and sat down by the side of the cool fountain; and when she was bored she took a golden ball, and threw it up on high and caught it; and this ball was her favorite plaything.

Now it so happened that on one occasion the princess's golden ball did not fall into the little hand which she was holding up for it, but onto the ground beyond, and rolled straight into the water. The King's daughter followed it with her eyes, but it vanished, and the well was deep, so deep that the bottom could not be seen. At this she began to cry, and cried louder and louder, and could not be comforted. And as she thus lamented, someone said to her: "What ails you, King's daughter? You weep so that even a stone would show pity." She looked round to the side from whence the voice came, and saw a frog stretching forth its big, ugly head from the water. "Ah! old croaker, is it you?" said she; "I am weeping for my golden ball, which has fallen into the well."

"Be quiet, and do not weep," answered the frog, "I can help you, but what will you give me if I bring your plaything up again?" "Whatever you will have, dear frog," said she— "my clothes, my pearls and jewels, and even the golden crown which I am wearing."

The frog answered: "I do not care for your clothes, your pearls and jewels, nor for your golden crown; but if you will love me and let me be your companion and play-fellow, and sit by you at your little table, and eat off your little golden plate, and drink out of your little cup, and sleep in your little bed—if you will promise me this I will go down below, and bring you your golden ball up again."

"Oh, yes," said she, "I promise you all you wish, if you will but bring me my ball back again." But she thought: "How the silly frog does talk! All he does is to sit in the water with the other frogs, and croak! He can be no companion to a human being!"

But the frog when he had received this promise, put his head into the water and sank down, and in a short while came swimming up again with the ball in his mouth, and threw it on the grass. The King's daughter was delighted to see her pretty plaything once more, and picking it up, ran away with it. "Wait, wait," said the frog. "Take me with you. I can't run as you can." But what did it avail him to scream his croak, croak, after her, as loudly as he could? She did not listen to it, but ran home and soon forgot the poor frog, who was forced to go back into his well again.

The next day when she had seated herself at table with the King and all the courtiers, and was eating from her little golden plate, something came creeping splish splash, splish splash, up the marble staircase, and when it had got to the top, it knocked at the door and cried: "Princess, youngest princess, open the door for me." She ran to see who was outside, but when she opened the door, there sat the frog in front of it. Then she slammed the door to, in great haste, sat down to dinner again, and was quite frightened. The King saw plainly that her heart was beating violently, and said: "My child, what are you so afraid of? Is there perchance a giant outside who wants to carry you away?" "Ah, no," replied she, "it is no giant, but a disgusting frog."

"What does the frog want with you?" "Ah, dear father, yesterday as I was in the forest playing by the well, my golden ball fell into the water. And because I cried so, the frog brought it out again for me; and because he so insisted, I promised him he should be my companion, but I never thought he would be able to come out of his water! And now he is outside there, and wants to come in to me."

In the meantime it knocked a second time, and cried:

"Princess! youngest princess!
Open the door for me!
Do you not know what you said to me
Yesterday by the cool waters of the well?
Princess, youngest princess!
Open the door for me!"

Then said the King: "That which you have promised must you perform. Go and let him in." She went and opened the door, and the frog hopped in and followed her, step by step, to her chair. There he sat and cried: "Lift me up beside you." She delayed, until at last the King commanded her to do it. Once the frog was on the chair he wanted to be on the table, and when he was on the table he said: "Now, push your little golden plate nearer to me that we may eat together." She did this, but it was easy to see that she did not do it willingly. The frog enjoyed what he ate, but almost every mouthful she took choked her. At length he said: "I have eaten and am satisfied; now I am tired. Carry me into your little room and make your little silken bed ready, and we will both lie down and go to sleep."

The King's daughter began to cry, for she was afraid of the cold frog which she did not like to touch, and which was now to sleep in her pretty, clean little bed. But the King grew angry and said: "He who helped you when you were in trouble ought not afterwards to be despised by you." So she took hold of the frog with two fingers, carried him upstairs, and put him in a corner. But when she was in bed he crept to her and said: "I am tired, I want to sleep as well as you; lift me up or I will tell your father." At this she was terribly angry, and took him up and threw him with all her might against the wall. "Now, will you be quiet, odious frog," said she. But when he fell down he was no frog but a king's son with kind and beautiful eyes. He by her father's will was now her dear companion and husband. Then he told her how he had been bewitched by a wicked witch, and how no one could have delivered him from the well but herself, and that to-morrow they would ride together to his kingdom. Then they went to sleep, and next morning when the sun awoke them, a carriage came driving up with eight white horses, which had white ostrich feathers on their heads, and were harnessed with golden chains, and behind stood the young King's servant, faithful Henry. Faithful Henry had been so unhappy when his master was changed into a frog, that he had caused three iron bands to be laid round his heart, lest it should burst with grief and sadness. The carriage was to conduct the young King into his kingdom. Faithful Henry helped them both in, and placed himself behind again, and was full of joy because of this deliverance. And when they had driven a part of the way, the King's son heard a cracking behind him as if something had broken. So he turned round and cried: "Henry, the carriage is breaking."

"No, master, it is not the carriage. It is a band from my heart, which was put there in my great pain when you were a frog and imprisoned in the well." Again and once again while they were on their way something cracked, and each time the King's son thought the carriage was breaking; but it was only the bands which were springing from the heart of faithful Henry because his master was set free and was happy.

Cat and Mouse in Partnership

A certain cat had made the acquaintance of a mouse, and had said so much to her about the great love and friendship she felt for her, that at length the mouse agreed that they should live and keep house together. "But we must make a provision for winter, or else we shall suffer from hunger," said the cat; "and you, little mouse, cannot venture everywhere, or you will be caught in a trap some day." The good advice was followed, and a pot of fat was bought, but they did not know where to put it. At length, after much consideration, the cat said: "I know no place where it will be better stored up than in the church, for no one dares take anything away from there. We will set it beneath the altar, and not touch it until we are really in need of it." So the pot was placed in safety, but it was not long before the cat had a great yearning for it, and said to the mouse: "I want to tell you something, little mouse; my cousin has brought a little son into the world, and has asked me to be godmother; he is white with brown spots, and I am to hold him over the font at the christening. Let me go out to-day, and you look after the house by yourself." "Yes, yes," answered the mouse, "by all means go, and if you get anything very good to eat, think of me, I should like a drop of sweet red christening wine myself." All this, however, was untrue; the cat had no cousin, and had not been asked to be godmother. She went straight to the church, stole to the pot of fat, began to lick at it, and licked the top of the fat off. Then she took a walk upon the roofs of the town, looked out for opportunities, and then stretched herself in the sun, and licked her lips whenever she thought of the pot of fat, and not until it was evening did she return home. "Well, here you are again," said the mouse, "no doubt you have had a merry day." "All went off well," answered the cat. "What name did they give the child?" "Top off!" said the cat quite coolly. "Top off!" cried the mouse, "that is a very odd and uncommon name, is it a usual one in your family?" "What does that matter," said the cat, "it is no worse than Crumb-stealer, as your god-children are called."

Before long the cat was seized by another fit of yearning. She said to the mouse: "You must do me a favor, and once more manage the house for a day alone. I am again asked to be godmother, and, as the child has a white ring round its neck, I cannot refuse." The good mouse consented, but the cat crept behind the town walls to the church, and devoured half the pot of fat. "Nothing ever seems so good as what one keeps to oneself," said she, and was quite satisfied with her day's work. When she went home the mouse inquired: "And what was this child christened?" "Half-done," answered the cat. "Half-done! What are you saying? I never heard the name in my life, I'll wager anything it is not in the calendar!"

The cat's mouth soon began to water for some more licking. "All good things go in threes," said she, "I am asked to stand godmother again. The child is quite black, only it has white paws, but with that exception, it has not a single white hair on its whole body; this only happens once every few years, you will let me go, won't you?" "Top-off! Half-done!" answered the mouse, "they are such odd names, they make me very thoughtful." "You sit at home," said the cat, "in your dark-grey fur coat and long tail, and are filled with fancies, that's because you do not go out in the daytime." During the cat's absence the mouse cleaned the house, and put it in order, but the greedy cat entirely emptied the pot of fat. "When everything is eaten up one has some peace," said she to herself, and well filled and fat she did not return home till night. The mouse at once asked what name had been given to the third child. "It will not please you more than the others," said the cat. "He is called All-gone." "All-gone," cried the mouse, "that is the most suspicious name of all! I have never seen it in print. All-gone; what can that mean?" and she shook her head, curled herself up, and lay down to sleep.

From this time forth no one invited the cat to be godmother, but when the winter had come and there was no longer anything to be found outside, the mouse thought of their provision, and said: "Come, cat, we will go to our pot of fat which we have stored up for ourselves—we shall enjoy that." "Yes," answered the cat, "you will enjoy it as much as you would enjoy sticking that dainty tongue of yours out of the window." They set out on their way, but when they arrived, the pot of fat certainly was still in its place, but it was empty. "Alas!" said the mouse, "now I see what has happened, now it comes to light! You a true friend! You have devoured all when you were standing godmother. First top off, then half done, then—" "Will you hold your tongue," cried the cat, "one word more, and I will eat you too." "All gone" was already on the poor mouse's lips; scarcely had she spoken it before the cat sprang on her, seized her, and swallowed her down. Verily, that is the way of the world.

The Story of the Youth Who Went Forth to Learn What Fear Was

A certain father had two sons, the elder of whom was smart and sensible, and could do everything, but the younger was stupid and could neither learn nor understand anything, and when people saw him they said: "There's a fellow who will give his father some trouble!" When anything had to be done, it was always the elder who was forced to do it; but if his father bade him fetch anything when it was late, or in the night-time, and the way led through the churchyard, or any other dismal place, he answered; "Oh, no, father, I'll not go there, it makes me shudder!" for he was afraid. Or when stories were told by the fire at night which made the flesh creep, the listeners sometimes said: "Oh, it makes us shudder!" The younger sat in a corner and listened with the rest of them, and could not imagine what they could mean. "They are always saying: 'It makes me shudder, it makes me shudder!' It does not make me shudder," thought he. "That, too, must be an art of which I understand nothing!"

Now it came to pass that his father said to him one day: "Hearken to me, you fellow in the corner there, you are growing tall and strong, and you too must learn something by which you can earn your bread. Look how your brother works, but you do not even earn your salt." "Well, father," he replied, "I am quite willing to learn something—indeed, if it could but be managed, I should like to learn how to shudder. I don't understand that at all yet." The elder brother smiled when he heard that, and thought to himself: "Good God, what a blockhead that brother of mine is! He will never be good for anything as long as he lives! He who wants to be a sickle must bend himself betimes."

The father sighed, and answered him: "You shall soon learn what it is to shudder, but you will not earn your bread by that."

Soon after this the sexton came to the house on a visit, and the father bewailed his trouble, and told him how his younger son was so backward in every respect that he knew nothing and learnt nothing. "Just think," said he, "when I asked him how he was going to earn his bread, he actually wanted to learn to shudder." "If that be all," replied the sexton, "he can learn that with me. Send him to me, and I will soon polish him." The father was glad to do it, for he thought: "It will train the boy a little." The sexton therefore took him into his house, and he had to ring the church bell. After a day or two, the sexton awoke him at midnight, and bade him arise and go up into the church tower and ring the bell. "You shall soon learn what shuddering is," thought he, and secretly went there before him; and when the boy was at the top of the tower and turned round, and was just going to take hold of the bell rope, he saw a white figure standing on the stairs opposite the sounding hole. "Who is there?" cried he, but the figure made no reply, and did not move or stir. "Give an answer," cried the boy, "or take yourself off, you have no business here at night."

The sexton, however, remained standing motionless that the boy might think he was a ghost. The boy cried a second time: "What do you want here?—speak if you are an honest fellow, or I will throw you down the steps!" The sexton thought: "He can't mean to be as bad as his words," uttered no sound and stood as if he were made of stone. Then the boy called to him for the third time, and as that was also to no purpose, he ran against him and pushed the ghost down the stairs, so that it fell down ten steps and remained lying there in a corner. Thereupon he rang the bell, went home, and without saying a word went to bed, and fell asleep. The sexton's wife waited a long time for her husband, but he did not come back. At length she became uneasy, and wakened the boy, and asked: "Do you not know where my husband is? He climbed up the tower before you did." "No, I don't know," replied the boy, "but someone was standing by the sounding hole on the other side of the steps, and as he would neither give an answer nor go away, I took him for a scoundrel, and threw him downstairs. Just go there and you will see if it was he. I should be sorry if it were." The woman ran away and found her husband, who was lying moaning in the corner, and had broken his leg.

She carried him down, and then with loud screams she hastened to the boy's father. "Your boy," cried she, "has been the cause of a great misfortune! He has thrown my husband down the steps so that he broke his leg. Take the good-for-nothing fellow out of our house." The father was terrified, and ran thither and scolded the boy. "What wicked tricks are these?" said he, "the devil must have put them into your head." "Father," he replied, "do listen to me I am quite innocent. He was standing there by night like one intent on doing evil. I did not know who it was, and I entreated him three times either to speak or to go away." "Ah," said the father, "I have nothing but unhappiness with you. Go out of my sight. I will see you no more."

"Yes, father, right willingly, wait only until it is day. Then will I go forth and learn how to shudder, and then I shall, at any rate, understand one art which will support me." "Learn what you will," spoke the father, "it is all the same to me. Here are fifty talers for you. Take these and go into the wide world, and tell no one from whence you come, and who is your father, for I have reason to be ashamed of you." "Yes, father, it shall be as you will. If you desire nothing more than that, I can easily keep it in mind."

When day dawned, therefore, the boy put his fifty talers into his pocket, and went forth on the great highway, and continually said to himself: "If I could but shudder! If I could but shudder!" Then a man approached who heard this conversation which the youth was holding with himself, and when they had walked a little farther to where they could see the gallows, the man said to him: "Look, there is the tree where seven men have married the rope-maker's daughter, and are now learning how to fly. Sit down beneath it, and wait till night comes, and you will soon learn how to shudder." "If that is all that is wanted," answered the youth, "it is easily done; but if I learn how to shudder as fast as that, you shall have my fifty talers. Just come back to me early in the morning." Then the youth went to the gallows, sat down beneath it, and waited till evening came. And as he was cold, he lighted himself a fire, but at midnight the wind blew so sharply that in spite of his fire, he could not get warm. And as the wind knocked the hanged men against each other, and they moved backwards and forwards, he thought to himself: "If you shiver below by the fire, how those up above must freeze and suffer!" And as he felt pity for them, he raised the ladder, and climbed up, unbound one of them after the other, and brought down all seven. Then he stoked the fire, blew it, and set them all round it to warm themselves. But they sat there and did not stir, and the fire caught their clothes. So he said: "Take care, or I will hang you up again." The dead men, however, did not hear, but were quite silent, and let their rags go on burning. At this he grew angry, and said: "If you will not take care, I cannot help you, I will not be burnt with you," and he hung them up again each in his turn. Then he sat down by his fire and fell asleep, and the next morning the man came to him and wanted to have the fifty talers, and said: "Well, do you know how to shudder?" "No," answered he, "how should I know? Those fellows up there did not open their mouths, and were so stupid that they let the few old rags which they had on their bodies get burnt." Then the man saw that he would not get the fifty talers that day, and went away saying: "Such a youth has never come my way before."

The youth likewise went his way, and once more began to mutter to himself: "Ah, if I could but shudder! Ah, if I could but shudder!" A waggoner who was striding behind him heard this and asked: "Who are you?" "I don't know," answered the youth. Then the waggoner asked: "From whence do you come?" "I know not." "Who is your father?" "That I may not tell you." "What is it that you are always muttering between your teeth?" "Ah," replied the youth, "I do so wish I could shudder, but no one can teach me how." "Enough of your foolish chatter," said the waggoner. "Come, go with me, I will see about a place for you." The youth went with the waggoner, and in the evening they arrived at an inn where they wished to pass the night. Then at the entrance of the parlor the youth again said quite loudly: "If I could but shudder! If I could but shudder!" The host who heard this, laughed and said: "If that is your desire, there ought to be a good opportunity for you here." "Ah, be silent," said the hostess, "so many prying persons have already lost their lives, it would be a pity and a shame if such beautiful eyes as these should never see the daylight again."

But the youth said: "However difficult it may be, I will learn it.

For this purpose indeed have I journeyed forth." He let the host have no rest, until the latter told him, that not far from thence stood a haunted castle where anyone could very easily learn what shuddering was, if he would but watch in it for three nights. The King had promised that he who would venture should have his daughter to wife, and she was the most beautiful maiden the sun shone on. Likewise in the castle lay great treasures, which were guarded by evil spirits, and these treasures would then be freed, and would make a poor man rich enough. Already many men had gone into the castle, but as yet none had come out again. Then the youth went next morning to the King, and said: "If it be allowed, I will willingly watch three nights in the haunted castle." The King looked at him, and as the youth pleased him, he said: "You may ask for three things to take into the castle with you, but they must be things without life." Then he answered: "Then I ask for a fire, a turning lathe, and a cutting-board with the knife."

The King had these things carried into the castle for him during the day. When night was drawing near, the youth went up and made himself a bright fire in one of the rooms, placed the cutting-board and knife beside it, and seated himself by the turning-lathe. "Ah, if I could but shudder!" said he, "but I shall not learn it here either." Towards midnight he was about to poke his fire, and as he was blowing it, something cried suddenly from one corner: "Au, miau! how cold we are!" "You fools!" cried he, "what are you crying about? If you are cold, come and take a seat by the fire and warm yourselves." And when he had said that, two great black cats came with one tremendous leap and sat down on each side of him, and looked savagely at him with their fiery eyes. After a short time, when they had warmed themselves, they said: "Comrade, shall we have a game of cards?" "Why not?" he replied, "but just show me your paws." Then they stretched out their claws. "Oh," said he, "what long nails you have! Wait, I must first cut them for you." Thereupon he seized them by the throats, put them on the cutting-board and screwed their feet fast. "I have looked at your fingers," said he, "and my fancy for card-playing has gone," and he struck them dead and threw them out into the water. But when he had made away with these two, and was about to sit down again by his fire, out from every hole and corner came black cats and black dogs with red-hot chains, and more and more of them came until

he could no longer move, and they yelled horribly, and got on his fire, pulled it to pieces, and tried to put it out. He watched them for a while quietly, but at last when they were going too far, he seized his cutting-knife, and cried: "Away with you, vermin," and began to cut them down. Some of them ran away, the others he killed, and threw out into the fish-pond. When he came back he fanned the embers of his fire again and warmed himself. And as he thus sat, his eyes would keep open no longer, and he felt a desire to sleep. Then he looked round and saw a great bed in the corner. "That is the very thing for me," said he, and got into it. When he was just going to shut his eyes, however, the bed began to move of its own accord, and went over the whole of the castle. "That's right," said he, "but go faster." Then the bed rolled on as if six horses were harnessed to it, up and down, over thresholds and stairs, but suddenly hop, hop, it turned over upside down, and lay on him like a mountain. But he threw quilts and pillows up in the air, got out and said: "Now anyone who likes, may drive," and lay down by his fire, and slept till it was day. In the morning the King came, and when he saw him lying there on the ground, he thought the evil spirits had killed him and he was dead. Then said he: "After all it is a pity,—for so handsome a man." The youth heard it, got up, and said: "It has not come to that yet." Then the King was astonished, but very glad, and asked how he had fared. "Very well indeed," answered he; "one night is past, the two others will pass likewise." Then he went to the innkeeper, who opened his eyes very wide, and said: "I never expected to see you alive again! Have you learnt how to shudder yet?" "No," said he, "it is all in vain. If someone would but tell me!"

The second night he again went up into the old castle, sat down by the fire, and once more began his old song: "If I could but shudder!" When midnight came, an uproar and noise of tumbling about was heard; at first it was low, but it grew louder and louder. Then it was quiet for a while, and at length with a loud scream, half a man came down the chimney and fell before him. "Hullo!" cried he, "another half belongs to this. This is not enough!" Then the uproar began again, there was a roaring and howling, and the other half fell down likewise. "Wait," said he, "I will just stoke up the fire a little for you." When he had done that and looked round again, the two pieces were joined together, and a hideous man was sitting in his place. "That is no part of our bargain," said the youth, "the bench is mine." The man wanted to push him away; the youth, however, would not allow that, but thrust him off with all his strength, and seated himself again in his own place. Then still more men fell down, one after the other; they brought nine dead men's legs and two skulls, and set them up and played at nine-pins with them. The youth also wanted to play and said: "Listen you, can I join you?" "Yes, if you have any money." "Money enough," replied he, "but your balls are not quite round." Then he took the skulls and put them in the lathe and turned them till they were round. "There, now they will roll better!" said he. "Hurrah! now we'll have fun!" He played with them and lost some of his money, but when it struck twelve, everything vanished from his sight. He lay down and quietly fell asleep. Next morning the King came to inquire after him. "How has it fared with you this time?" asked he. "I have been playing at nine-pins," he answered, "and have lost a couple of farthings." "Have you not shuddered then?" "What?" said he, "I have had a wonderful time! If I did but know what it was to shudder!"

The third night he sat down again on his bench and said quite sadly: "If I could but shudder." When it grew late, six tall men came in and brought a coffin. Then said he: "Ha, ha, that is certainly my little cousin, who died only a few days ago," and he beckoned with his finger, and cried: "Come, little cousin, come." They placed the coffin on the ground, but he went to it and took the lid off, and a dead man lay therein. He felt his face, but it was cold as ice. "Wait," said he, "I will warn you a little," and went to the fire and warmed his hand and laid it on the dead man's face, but he remained cold. Then he took him out, and sat down by the fire and laid him on his breast and rubbed his arms that the blood might circulate again. As this also did no good, he thought to himself: "When two people lie in bed together, they warm each other," and carried him to the bed, covered him over and lay down by him. After a short time the dead man became warm too, and began to move. Then said the youth, "See, little cousin, have I not warmed you?" The dead man, however, got up and cried: "Now will I strangle you."

"What!" said he, "is that the way you thank me? You shall at once go into your coffin again," and he took him up, threw him into it, and shut the lid. Then came the six men and carried him away again. "I cannot manage to shudder," said he. "I shall never learn it here as long as I live."

Then a man entered who was taller than all others, and looked terrible. He was old, however, and had a long white beard. "You wretch," cried he, "you shall soon learn what it is to shudder, for you shall die." "Not so fast," replied the youth. "If I am to die, I shall have to have a say in it." "I will soon seize you," said the fiend. "Softly, softly, do not talk so big. I am as strong as you are, and perhaps even stronger." "We shall see," said the old man. "If you are stronger, I will let you go—come, we will try." Then he led him by dark passages to a smith's forge, took an axe, and with one blow struck an anvil into the ground. "I can do better than that," said the youth, and went to the other anvil. The old man placed himself near and wanted to look on, and his white beard hung down. Then the youth seized the axe, split the anvil with one blow, and in it caught the old man's beard. "Now I have you,"

said the youth. "Now it is your turn to die." Then he seized an
iron bar and beat the old man till he moaned and entreated him
to stop, when he would give him great riches. The youth drew out
the axe and let him go. The old man led him back into the castle,
and in a cellar showed him three chests full of gold. "Of these,"
said he, "one part is for the poor, the other for the king, the third
yours." In the meantime it struck twelve, and the spirit disappeared, so that the youth stood in darkness. "I shall still be able
to find my way out," said he, and felt about, found the way into
the room, and slept there by his fire. Next morning the King came
and said: "Now you must have learnt what shuddering is?" "No,"
he answered; "what can it be? My dead cousin was here, and a
bearded man came and showed me a great deal of money down
below, but no one told me what it was to shudder." "Then," said
the King, "you have saved the castle, and shall marry my daughter." "That is all very well," said he, "but still I do not know what
it is to shudder!"

Then the gold was brought up and the wedding celebrated; but
howsoever much the young King loved his wife, and however happy
he was, he still said always: "If I could but shudder—if I could but
shudder." And this at last angered her. Her waiting-maid said: "I
will find a cure for him; he shall soon learn what it is to shudder."
She went out to the stream which flowed through the garden, and
had a whole bucketful of gudgeons brought to her. At night when
the young King was sleeping, his wife was to draw the clothes off
him and empty the bucketful of cold water with the gudgeons in
it over him, so that the little fishes would sprawl about him. Then
he woke up and cried: "Oh, what makes me shudder so?—what
makes me shudder so, dear wife? Ah! now I know what it is to
shudder!"

The Wolf and the Seven Little Kids

There was once upon a time an old goat who had seven little kids,
and loved them with all the love of a mother for her children. One
day she wanted to go into the forest and fetch some food. So she
called all seven to her and said: "Dear children, I have to go into

the forest, be on your guard against the wolf; if he comes in, he will devour you all—skin, hair, and everything. The wretch often disguises himself, but you will know him at once by his rough voice and his black feet." The kids said: "Dear mother, we will take good care of ourselves; you may go away without any fear." Then the old one bleated, and went on her way with an easy mind.

It was not long before someone knocked at the house-door and called: "Open the door, dear children; your mother is here, and has brought something back with her for each of you." But the little kids knew that it was the wolf, by the rough voice. "We will not open the door," cried they, "you are not our mother. She has a soft, pleasant voice, but your voice is rough; you are the wolf!" Then the wolf went away to a shopkeeper and bought himself a great lump of chalk, and ate it to make his voice soft. Then he came back, knocked at the door of the house, and called: "Open the door, dear children, your mother is here and has brought something back with her for each of you." But the wolf had laid his black paws against the window, and the children saw them and cried: "We will not open the door, our mother has not black feet like you: you are the wolf!" Then the wolf ran to a baker and said: "I have hurt my feet, rub some dough over them for me." And when the baker had rubbed his feet over, he ran to the miller and said: "Strew some white meal over my feet for me." The miller thought to himself: "The wolf wants to deceive someone," and refused; but the wolf said: "If you will not do it, I will devour you." Then the miller was afraid, and made his paws white for him. Truly, this is the way of mankind.

So now the wretch went for the third time to the house-door, knocked at it and said: "Open the door for me, children, your dear little mother has come home, and has brought every one of you something back from the forest with her." The little kids cried: "First show us your paws that we may know if you are our dear little mother." Then he put his paws in through the window, and when the kids saw that they were white, they believed that all he said was true, and opened the door. But who should come in but the wolf! They were terrified and wanted to hide themselves. One sprang under the table, the second into the bed, the third into the stove, the fourth into the kitchen, the fifth into the cupboard, the sixth under the washing-bowl, and the seventh into the clock-case.

But the wolf found them all, and used no great ceremony; one after the other he swallowed them down his throat. The youngest, who was in the clock-case, was the only one he did not find. When the wolf had satisfied his appetite he took himself off, laid himself down under a tree in the green meadow outside, and began to sleep. Soon afterwards the old goat came home again from the forest. Ah! what a sight she saw there! The house-door stood wide open. The table, chairs, and benches were thrown down, the washing-bowl lay broken to pieces, and the quilts and pillows were pulled off the bed. She sought her children, but they were nowhere to be found. She called them one after another by name, but no one answered. At last, when she came to the youngest, a soft voice cried: "Dear mother, I am in the clock-case." She took the kid out, and it told her that the wolf had come and had eaten all the others. Then you may imagine how she wept over her poor children.

At length in her grief she went out, and the youngest kid ran with her. When they came to the meadow, there lay the wolf by the tree, snoring so loudly that the branches shook. She looked at him on every side and saw that something was moving and struggling in his gorged belly. "Ah, heavens," she said, "is it possible that my poor children whom he has swallowed down for his supper, can be still alive?" Then the kid had to run home and fetch scissors, and a needle and thread, and the goat cut open the monster's stomach, and hardly had she made one cut than one little kid thrust its head out, and when she had cut farther, all six sprang

out one after another, and were all still alive, and had suffered no injury whatever, for in his greediness the monster had swallowed them down whole. What rejoicing there was! They embraced their dear mother, and jumped like a tailor at his wedding. The mother, however, said: "Now go and look for some big stones, and we will fill the wicked beast's stomach with them while he is still asleep." Then the seven kids dragged the stones thither with all speed, and put as many of them into his stomach as they could get in; and the mother sewed him up again in the greatest haste, so that he was not aware of anything and never once stirred.

When the wolf at length had had his fill of sleep, he got on his legs, and as the stones in his stomach made him very thirsty, he wanted to go to a well to drink. But when he began to walk and to move about, the stones in his stomach knocked against each other and rattled. Then cried he:

> "What rumbles and tumbles
> Against my poor bones?
> I thought 'twas six kids,
> But it feels like big stones."

And when he got to the well and stooped over the water to drink, the heavy stones made him fall in, and he drowned miserably. When the seven kids saw that, they came running to the spot and cried aloud: "The wolf is dead! The wolf is dead!" and danced for joy round about the well with their mother.

Faithful John

There was once upon a time an old king who was ill, and thought to himself: "I am lying on what must be my deathbed." Then said he: "Tell Faithful John to come to me." Faithful John was his favorite servant, and was so called, because he had for his whole life long been so true to him. When therefore he came beside the bed, the King said to him: "Most faithful John, I feel my end approaching, and have no anxiety except about my son. He is still of tender age, and cannot always know how to guide himself. If you do not promise me to teach him everything that he ought to know, and to be his foster-father, I cannot close my eyes in peace." Then answered Faithful John: "I will not forsake him, and will serve him with fidelity, even if it should cost me my life." At this, the old King said: "Now I die in comfort and peace." Then he added: "After my death, you shall show him the whole castle: all the chambers, halls, and vaults, and all the treasures which lie therein, but the last chamber in the long gallery, in which is the picture of the princess of the Golden Dwelling, shall you not show. If he sees that picture, he will fall violently in love with her, and will drop down in a swoon, and go through great danger for her sake, therefore you must protect him from that." And when Faithful John had once more given his promise to the old King about this, the King said no more, but laid his head on his pillow, and died.

When the old King had been carried to his grave, Faithful John told the young King all that he had promised his father on his deathbed, and said: "This will I assuredly keep, and will be faithful to you as I have been faithful to him, even if it should cost me my life." When the mourning was over, Faithful John said to him: "It is now time that you should see your inheritance. I will show you your father's palace." Then he took him about everywhere, up and down, and let him see all the riches, and the magnificent apartments, only there was one room which he did not open, that in which hung the dangerous picture. The picture, however, was so placed that when the door was opened you looked straight on it, and it was so admirably painted that it seemed to breathe and live, and there was nothing more charming or more beautiful in the whole world. The young King noticed, however, that Faithful John always walked past this one door, and said: "Why do you never open this one for me?" "There is something within it," he replied, "which would terrify you." But the King answered: "I have seen all the palace, and I want to know what is in this room also," and he went and tried to break open the door by force. Then Faithful John held him back and said: "I promised your father before his death that you should not see that which is in this chamber, it might bring the greatest misfortune on you and on me." "Ah, no," replied the young King, "if I do not go in, it will be my certain destruction. I should have no rest day or night until I had seen it with my own eyes. I shall not leave the place now until you have unlocked the door.''

Then Faithful John saw that there was no help for it now, and with a heavy heart and many sighs, sought out the key from the great bunch. When he had opened the door, he went in first, and thought by standing before him he could hide the portrait so that the King should not see it in front of him. But what good was this? The King stood on tip-toe and saw it over his shoulder. And when he saw the portrait of the maiden, which was so magnificent and shone with gold and precious stones, he fell fainting to the ground. Faithful John took him up, carried him to his bed, and sorrowfully thought: ''The misfortune has befallen us, Lord God, what will be the end of it?'' Then he strengthened him with wine, until he came to himself again. The first words the King said were: ''Ah, the beautiful portrait! whose is it?'' ''That is the princess of the Golden Dwelling,'' answered Faithful John. Then the King continued: ''My love for her is so great, that if all the leaves on all the trees were tongues, they could not declare it. I will give my life to win her. You are my most faithful John, you must help me.''

The faithful servant considered within himself for a long time how to set about the matter, for it was difficult even to obtain a sight of the King's daughter. At length he thought of a way, and said to the King: ''Everything which she has about her is of gold— tables, chairs, dishes, glasses, bowls, and household furniture. Among your treasures are five tons of gold; let one of the gold-smiths of the kingdom fashion these into all manner of vessels and utensils, into all kinds of birds, wild beasts and strange animals, such as may please her, and we will go there with them and try our luck.''

The King ordered all the goldsmiths to be brought to him, and they had to work night and day until at last the most splendid things were prepared. When everything was stowed on board a ship, Faithful John put on the dress of a merchant, and the King was forced to do the same in order to make himself quite unrecogniz-able. Then they sailed across the sea, and sailed on until they came to the town wherein dwelt the princess of the Golden Dwelling.

Faithful John bade the King stay behind on the ship, and wait for him. ''Perhaps I shall bring the princess with me,'' said he, ''therefore see that everything is in order; have the golden vessels set out and the whole ship decorated." Then he gathered together in his apron all kinds of golden things, went on shore and walked straight to the royal palace. When he entered the courtyard of the palace, a beautiful girl was standing there by the well with two golden buckets in her hand, drawing water with them. And when she was just turning round to carry away the sparkling water she saw the stranger, and asked who he was. So he answered: "I am a merchant," and opened his apron, and let her look in. Then she cried: "Oh, what beautiful golden things!" and put her pails down and looked at the golden wares one after the other. Then said the girl: "The princess must see these, she has such great pleasure in golden things, that she will buy all you have." She took him by the hand and led him upstairs, for she was the waiting-maid. When the King's daughter saw the wares, she was quite delighted and said: "They are so beautifully worked, that I will buy them all from you." But Faithful John said: "I am only the servant of a rich merchant. The things I have here are not to be compared with those my master has in his ship. They are the most beautiful and valuable things that have ever been made in gold." When she wanted to have everything brought up to her, he said: "There are so many of them that it would take a great many days to do that, and so many rooms would be required to exhibit them, that your house is not big enough." Then her curiosity and longing were still more excited, until at last she said: "Conduct me to the ship, I will go there myself, and behold the treasures of your master."

At this Faithful John was quite delighted, and led her to the ship, and when the King saw her, he perceived that her beauty was even greater than the picture had represented it to be, and thought no other than that his heart would burst in twain. Then she boarded the ship, and the King led her within. Faithful John, however, remained with the helmsman, and ordered the ship to be pushed off, saying: "Set all sail, till it fly like a bird in the air." Within, the King showed her the golden vessels, every one of them, also the wild beasts and strange animals. Many hours went by whilst she was seeing everything, and in her delight she did not observe that the ship was sailing away. After she had looked at the last, she thanked the merchant and wanted to go home, but when she came to the side of the ship, she saw that it was on the high seas far from land, and hurrying onwards with all sail set. "Ah," cried she in her alarm, "I am betrayed! I am carried away and have fallen into the power of a merchant—I would rather die!" The King, however, seized her hand, and said: "I am not a merchant. I am a king, and of no meaner origin than you are, and if I have carried you away with subtlety, that has come to pass because of my exceeding great love for you. The first time that I looked on your portrait, I fell fainting to the ground." When the princess of the Golden Dwelling heard this, she was comforted, and her heart was drawn to him, so that she willingly consented to be his wife.

It so happened, while they were sailing onwards over the deep sea, that Faithful John, who was sitting on the fore part of the vessel, making music, saw three ravens in the air, which came flying towards them. At this he stopped playing and listened to what they were saying to each other, for that he well understood. One cried: "Oh, there he is carrying home the princess of the Golden Dwelling." "Yes," replied the second, "but he has not got her yet." Said the third: "But he has got her, she is sitting beside him in the ship." Then the first began again, and cried: "What good will that do him? When they reach land a chestnut horse will leap forward to meet him, and the prince will want to mount it, but if he does that, it will run away with him, and rise up into the air, and he will never see his maiden more." Spoke the second: "But is there no escape?"

"Oh, yes, if someone else mounts it swiftly, and takes out the pistol which he will find in its holster, and shoots the horse dead, the young King is saved. But who knows that? And whosoever does know it, and tells it to him, will be turned to stone from the toe to the knee." Then said the second: "I know more than that; even if the horse be killed, the young King will still not keep his bride. When they go into the castle together, a wrought bridal garment will be lying there in a dish, and looking as if it were woven of gold and silver; it is, however, nothing but sulphur and pitch, and if he put it on, it will burn him to the very bone and marrow." Said the third: "Is there no escape at all?"

"Oh, yes," replied the second, "if anyone with gloves on seizes the garment and throws it into the fire and burns it, the young King will be saved. But what good will that do? Whosoever knows it and tells it to him, half his body will become stone from the knee to the heart."

Then said the third: "I know still more; even if the bridal garment be burnt, the young King will still not have his bride. After the wedding, when the dancing begins and the young Queen is dancing, she will suddenly turn pale and fall down as if dead, and if someone does not lift her up and draw three drops of blood from her right breast and spit them out again, she will die. But if anyone who knows that were to declare it, he would become stone from the crown of his head to the sole of his foot." When the ravens had spoken of this together, they flew onwards, and Faithful John had well understood everything, but from that time forth he became quiet and sad, for if he concealed what he had heard from his master, the latter would be unfortunate, and if he disclosed it to him, he himself must sacrifice his life. At length, however, he said to himself: "I will save my master, even if it bring destruction on myself."

When therefore they came to shore, all happened as had been foretold by the ravens, and a magnificent chestnut horse sprang forward. "Good," said the King, "he shall carry me to my palace," and was about to mount it when Faithful John got before him, jumped quickly on it, drew the pistol out of the holster, and shot the horse. Then the other attendants of the King, who were not very fond of Faithful John, cried: "How shameful to kill the beautiful animal, that was to have carried the King to his palace!" But the King said: "Hold your peace and leave him alone, he is my most faithful John. Who knows what good may come of this!" They went into the palace, and in the hall there stood a dish, and therein lay the bridal garment looking no otherwise than as if it were made of gold and silver. The young king went towards it and was about to take hold of it, but Faithful John pushed him away, seized it with gloves on, carried it quickly to the fire and burnt it. The other attendants again began to murmur, and said: "Behold, now he is even burning the King's bridal garment!" But the young King said: "Who knows what good he may have done, leave him alone, he is my most faithful John."

And now the wedding was solemnized: the dance began, and the bride also took part in it; then Faithful John was watchful and looked into her face, and suddenly she turned pale and fell to the ground as if she were dead. On this he ran hastily to her, lifted her up and bore her into a chamber—then he laid her down, and knelt and sucked the three drops of blood from her right breast, and spat them out. Immediately she breathed again and recovered herself, but the young King had seen this, and being ignorant why Faithful John had done it, was angry and cried: "Throw him into a dungeon." Next morning Faithful John was condemned, and led to the gallows, and when he stood on high, and was about to be executed, he said: "Everyone who has to die is permitted before his end to make one last speech; may I too claim the right?" "Yes," answered the King, "it shall be granted unto you." Then said Faithful John: "I am unjustly condemned, and have always been true to you," and he related how he had hearkened to the conversation of the ravens when on the sea, and how he had been obliged to do all these things in order to save his master. Then cried the King: "Oh, my most faithful John. Pardon, pardon—bring him down." But as Faithful John spoke the last word he had fallen down lifeless and become a stone.

Thereupon the King and the Queen suffered great anguish, and the King said: "Ah, how ill I have requited great fidelity!" and ordered the stone figure to be taken up and placed in his bedroom beside his bed. And as often as he looked on it he wept and said: "Ah, if I could bring you to life again, my most faithful John."

Some time passed and the Queen bore twins, two sons who grew fast and were her delight. Once when the Queen was at church and the father was sitting with his two children playing beside him, he looked at the stone figure again, sighed, and full of grief he said: "Ah, if I could but bring you to life again, my most faithful John." Then the stone began to speak and said: "You can bring me to life again if you will use for that purpose what is dearest to you." Then cried the King: "I will give everything I have in the world for you." The stone continued: "If you will cut off the heads of your two children with your own hand, and sprinkle me with their blood, I shall be restored to life."

The King was terrified when he heard that he himself must kill his dearest children, but he thought of Faithful John's great fidelity, and how he had died for him, drew his sword, and with his own hand cut off the children's heads. And when he had smeared the stone with their blood, life returned to it, and Faithful John stood once more safe and healthy before him. He said to the King: "Your truth shall not go unrewarded," and took the heads of the children, put them on again, and rubbed the wounds with their blood, at which they became whole again immediately, and jumped about, and went on playing as if nothing had happened. Then the King was full of joy, and when he saw the Queen coming he hid Faithful John and the two children in a great cupboard. When she entered, he said to her: "Have you been praying in the church?" "Yes," answered she, "but I have constantly been thinking of

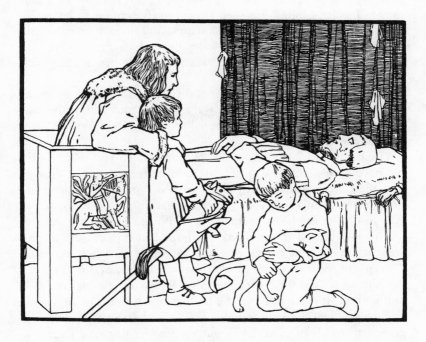

Faithful John and what misfortune has befallen him through us." Then said he: "Dear wife, we can give him his life again, but it will cost us our two little sons, whom we must sacrifice." The Queen turned pale, and her heart was full of terror, but she said: "We owe it to him, for his great fidelity." Then the King was rejoiced that she thought as he had thought, and went and opened the cupboard, and brought forth Faithful John and the children, and said: "God be praised, he is delivered, and we have our little sons again also," and told her how everything had occurred. Then they dwelt together in much happiness until their death.

The Twelve Brothers

There were once upon a time a King and a Queen who lived happily together and had twelve children, but they were all boys. Then said the King to his wife: "If the thirteenth child which you are about to bring into the world, is a girl, the twelve boys shall die, in order that her possessions may be great, and that the kingdom may fall to her alone." He even caused twelve coffins to be made, which were already filled with shavings, and in each lay the little death pillow, and he had them taken into a locked-up room, and then he gave the Queen the key of it, and bade her not to speak of this to anyone.

The mother, however, now sat and lamented all day long, until the youngest son, who was always with her, and whom she had named Benjamin, from the Bible, said to her: "Dear mother, why are you so sad?"

"Dearest child," she answered, "I may not tell you." But he let her have no rest until she went and unlocked the room, and showed him the twelve coffins ready filled with shavings. Then she said: "My dearest Benjamin, your father has had these coffins made for you and for your eleven brothers, for if I bring a little girl into the world, you are all to be killed and buried in them." And as she wept while she was saying this, the son comforted her and said: "Weep not, dear mother, we will save ourselves, and go hence." But she said: "Go forth into the forest with your eleven brothers, and let one sit constantly on the highest tree which can be found, and keep watch, looking towards the tower here in the castle. If I give birth to a little son, I will put up a white flag, and then you may venture to come back. But if I bear a daughter, I will hoist a red flag, and then fly hence as quickly as you are able, and may the good God protect you. And every night I will rise up and pray for you—in winter that you may be able to warm yourself at a fire, and in summer that you may not faint away in the heat."

After she had blessed her sons therefore, they went forth into the forest. They each kept watch in turn, and sat on the highest oak and looked towards the tower. When eleven days had passed and the turn came to Benjamin, he saw that a flag was being raised. It was, however, not the white, but the blood-red flag which announced that they were all to die. When the brothers heard that, they were very angry and said: "Are we all to suffer death for the sake of a girl? We swear that we will avenge ourselves—wheresoever we find a girl, her red blood shall flow."

Thereupon they went deeper into the forest, and in the midst of it, where it was the darkest, they found a little bewitched hut, which was standing empty. Then said they: "Here we will dwell, and you Benjamin, who are the youngest and weakest, you shall stay at home and keep house, we others will go out and fetch food." Then they went into the forest and shot hares, wild deer, birds and pigeons, and whatsoever there was to eat; this they took to Benjamin, who had to dress it for them in order that they might appease their hunger. They lived together ten years in the little hut, and the time did not appear long to them.

The little daughter which their mother the Queen had given birth to, was now grown up; she was good of heart, and fair of face, and had a golden star on her forehead. Once, on a great washing, she saw twelve men's shirts among the things, and asked her mother: "To whom do these twelve shirts belong, for they are far too small for father?" Then the Queen answered with a heavy heart: "Dear child, these belong to your twelve brothers." Said the maiden: "Where are my twelve brothers, I have never yet heard of them?" She replied: "God knows where they are, they are wandering about the world." Then she took the maiden and opened the chamber for her, and showed her the twelve coffins with the shavings, and the death pillows. "These coffins," said she, "were destined for your brothers, who went away secretly before you were born," and she related to her how everything had happened; then said the maiden: "Dear mother, weep not, I will go and seek my brothers."

So she took the twelve shirts and went forth, and straight into the great forest. She walked the whole day, and in the evening she came to the bewitched hut. Then she entered it and found a young boy, who asked: "From whence do you come, and whither are you bound?" and was astonished that she was so beautiful, and wore royal garments, and had a star on her forehead. And she answered: "I am a king's daughter, and am seeking my twelve brothers, and I will walk as far as the sky is blue until I find them." And she showed him the twelve shirts which belonged to them. Then Benjamin saw that she was his sister, and said: "I am Benjamin, your youngest brother." And she began to weep for joy, and Benjamin wept also, and they kissed and embraced each other with the greatest love. But after this he said: "Dear sister, there is still one difficulty. We have agreed that every maiden whom we meet shall die, because we have been obliged to leave our kingdom on account of a girl." Then said she: "I will willingly die, if by so doing I can save my twelve brothers."

"No," answered he, "you shall not die. Seat yourself beneath this tub until our eleven brothers come, and then I will soon come to an agreement with them."

She did so, and when it was night the others came from hunting, and their dinner was ready. And as they were sitting at table, and eating, they asked: "What news is there?" Said Benjamin: "Don't you know anything?" "No," they answered. He continued: "You have been in the forest and I have stayed at home, and yet I know more than you do." "Tell us then," they cried. He answered: "But promise me that the first maiden who meets us shall not be killed." "Yes," they all cried, "she shall have mercy, only do tell us."

Then said he: "Our sister is here," and he lifted up the tub, and the King's daughter came forth in her royal garments with the golden star on her forehead, and she was beautiful, delicate, and fair. Then they were all rejoiced, and fell on her neck, and kissed and loved her with all their hearts.

Now she stayed at home with Benjamin and helped him with the work. The eleven went into the forest and caught game, and deer, and birds, and wood-pigeons that they might have food, and the little sister and Benjamin took care to make it ready for them. She sought for the wood for cooking and herbs for vegetables, and put the pans on the fire so that the dinner was always ready when the eleven came. She likewise kept order in the little house, and put beautifully white clean coverings on the little beds, and the brothers were always contented and lived in great harmony with her.

Once upon a time the two at home had prepared a wonderful feast, and when they were all together, they sat down and ate and drank and were full of gladness. There was, however, a little garden belonging to the bewitched house wherein stood twelve lily flowers, which are likewise called student-lilies. She wished to give her brothers pleasure, and plucked the twelve flowers, and thought she would present each brother with one while at dinner. But at the self-same moment that she plucked the flowers the twelve brothers were changed into twelve ravens, and flew away over the forest, and the house and garden vanished likewise. And now the poor maiden was alone in the wild forest, and when she looked around, an old woman was standing near her who said: "My child, what have you done? Why did you not leave the twelve white flowers growing? They were your brothers, who are now for evermore changed into ravens." The maiden said, weeping: "Is there no way of saving them?"

"No," said the woman, "there is but one in the whole world, and that is so hard that you will not save them by it, for you must be dumb for seven years, and may not speak or laugh, and if you speak one single word, and only an hour of the seven years is wanting, all is in vain, and your brothers will be killed by the one word."

Then said the maiden in her heart: "I know with certainty that I shall set my brothers free," and went and sought a high tree and seated herself in it and spun, and neither spoke nor laughed. Now it so happened that a King was hunting in the forest, who had a great greyhound which ran to the tree on which the maiden was sitting, and sprang about it, whining, and barking at her. Then the King came by and saw the beautiful King's daughter with the golden star on her brow, and was so charmed with her beauty that he called to ask her if she would be his wife. She made no answer, but nodded a little with her head. So he climbed up the tree himself, carried her down, placed her on his horse, and bore her home. Then the wedding was solemnized with great magnificence and rejoicing, but the bride neither spoke nor smiled. When they had lived happily together for a few years, the King's mother, who was a wicked woman, began to slander the young Queen, and said to the King: "This is a common beggar girl whom you have brought back with you. Who knows what wicked tricks she practises secretly! Even if she be dumb, and not able to speak, she still might laugh for once; but those who do not laugh have bad consciences." At first the King would not believe it, but the old woman urged this so long, and accused her of so many evil things, that at last the King let himself be persuaded and sentenced her to death.

And now a great fire was lighted in the courtyard in which she was to be burnt, and the King stood above at the window and looked on with tearful eyes, because he still loved her so much. And when she was bound fast to the stake, and the fire was licking at her clothes with its red tongue, the last instant of the seven years expired. Then a whirring sound was heard in the air, and twelve ravens came flying towards the place, and sank downwards, and when they touched the earth they were her twelve brothers, whom she had saved. They tore the fire asunder, extinguished the flames, set their dear sister free, and kissed and embraced her. And now as she dared to open her mouth and speak, she told the King why she had been dumb, and had never laughed. The King rejoiced when he heard that she was innocent, and they all lived in great unity until their death. The wicked step-mother was taken before the judge, and put into a barrel filled with boiling oil and venomous snakes, and died an evil death.

Brother and Sister

Little brother took his little sister by the hand and said: "Since our mother died we have had no happiness; our step-mother beats us every day, and if we come near her she kicks us away with her foot. Our meals are the hard crusts of bread that are left over; and the little dog under the table is better off, for she often throws it a choice morsel. God pity us, if our mother only knew! Come, we will go forth together into the wide world."

They walked the whole day over meadows, fields, and stony places; and when it rained the little sister said: "Heaven and our hearts are weeping together." In the evening they came to a large forest, and they were so weary with sorrow and hunger and the long walk, that they lay down in a hollow tree and fell asleep.

The next day when they awoke, the sun was already high in the sky, and shone down hot into the tree. Then the brother said: "Sister, I am thirsty; if I knew of a little brook I would go and just take a drink; I think I hear one running." The brother got up and took the little sister by the hand, and they set off to find the brook.

But the wicked step-mother was a witch, and had seen how the two children had gone away, and had crept after them secretly, as witches creep, and had bewitched all the brooks in the forest.

Now when they found a little brook leaping brightly over the stones, the brother was going to drink out of it, but the sister heard how it said as it ran: "Who drinks of me will be a tiger; who drinks of me will be a tiger." Then the sister cried: "Pray, dear brother, do not drink, or you will become a wild beast, and tear me to pieces." The brother did not drink, although he was so thirsty, but said: "I will wait for the next spring."

When they came to the next brook the sister heard this also say: "Who drinks of me will be a wolf; who drinks of me will be a wolf." Then the sister cried out: "Pray, dear brother, do not drink, or you will become a wolf, and devour me." The brother did not drink, and said: "I will wait until we come to the next spring, but then I must drink, say what you like; for my thirst is too great."

And when they came to the third brook the sister heard how it said as it ran: "Who drinks of me will be a roebuck; who drinks of me will be a roebuck." The sister said: "Oh, I pray you, dear brother, do not drink, or you will become a roebuck, and run away from me." But the brother had knelt down at once by the brook, and had bent down and drunk some of the water, and as soon as the first drops touched his lips he lay there in the form of a young roebuck.

And now the sister wept over her poor bewitched brother, and the little roe wept also, and sat sorrowfully near to her. But at last the girl said: "Be quiet, dear little roe, I will never, never leave you."

Then she untied her golden garter and put it round the roe-buck's neck, and she plucked rushes and wove them into a soft cord. This she tied to the little animal and led it on, and she walked deeper and deeper into the forest.

And when they had gone a very long way they came at last to a little house, and the girl looked in; and as it was empty, she thought: "We can stay here and live." Then she sought for leaves and moss to make a soft bed for the roe; and every morning she went out and gathered roots and berries and nuts for herself, and brought tender grass for the roe, who ate out of her hand, and was content and played round about her. In the evening, when the sister was tired, and had said her prayer, she laid her head upon the roebuck's back: that was her pillow, and she slept softly on it. And if only the brother had had his human form it would have been a delightful life.

For some time they were alone like this in the wilderness. But it happened that the King of the country held a great hunt in the forest. Then the blasts of the horns, the barking of dogs, and the merry shouts of the huntsmen rang through the trees, and the roebuck heard all, and was only too anxious to be there. "Oh," said he to his sister, "let me be off to the hunt, I cannot bear it any longer"; and he begged so much that at last she agreed. "But," said she to him, "come back to me in the evening; I must shut my door for fear of the rough huntsmen, so knock and say: 'My little sister, let me in!' that I may know you; and if you do not say that, I shall not open the door." Then the young roebuck sprang away; so happy was he and so merry in the open air.

The King and the huntsmen saw the lovely animal, and started after him, but they could not catch him, and when they thought that they surely had him, away he sprang through the bushes and vanished. When it was dark he ran to the cottage, knocked, and said: "My little sister, let me in." Then the door was opened for him, and he jumped in, and rested himself the whole night through upon his soft bed.

The next day the hunt began again, and when the roebuck once more heard the bugle-horn, and the ho! ho! of the huntsmen, he had no peace, but said: "Sister, let me out, I must be off." His sister opened the door for him, and said: "But you must be here again in the evening and say your pass-word."

When the King and his huntsmen again saw the young roebuck with the golden collar, they all chased him, but he was too quck and nimble for them. This lasted the whole day, but by the evening the huntsmen had surrounded him, and one of them wounded him a little in the foot, so that he limped and ran slowly. Then a hunter crept after him to the cottage and heard how he said: "My little sister, let me in," and saw that the door was opened for him, and was shut again at once. The huntsman took notice of it all, and went to the King and told him what he had seen and heard. Then the King said: "To-morrow we will hunt once more."

The little sister, however, was dreadfully frightened when she saw that her fawn was hurt. She washed the blood off him, laid herbs on the wound, and said: "Go to your bed, dear roe, that you may get well again." But the wound was so slight that the roebuck, next morning, did not feel it any more. And when he again heard the sport outside, he said: "I cannot bear it, I must be there; they shall not find it so easy to catch me." The sister cried, and said: "This time they will kill you, and here am I alone in the forest and forsaken by all the world. I will not let you out." "Then you will have me die of grief," answered the roe; "when I hear the bugle-horns I feel as if I must jump out of my skin." Then the sister could not do otherwise, but opened the door for him with a heavy heart, and the roebuck, full of health and joy, bounded into the forest.

When the King saw him, he said to his huntsmen: "Now chase him all day long till night-fall, but take care that no one does him any harm."

As soon as the sun had set, the King said to the huntsman: "Now come and show me the cottage in the wood"; and when he was at the door, he knocked and called out: "Dear little sister, let me in." Then the door opened, and the King walked in, and there stood a maiden more lovely than any he had ever seen. The maiden was frightened when she saw, not her little roe, but a man come in who wore a golden crown upon his head. But the King looked kindly at her, stretched out his hand, and said: "Will you go with me to my palace and be my dear wife?" "Yes, indeed," answered the maiden, "but the little roe must go with me, I cannot leave him." The King said: "It shall stay with you as long as you live, and shall want nothing." Just then he came running in, and the sister again tied him with the cord of rushes, took it in her own hand, and went away with the King from the cottage.

The King took the lovely maiden upon his horse and carried her to his palace, where the wedding was held with great pomp. She was now the Queen, and they lived for a long time happily together; the roebuck was tended and cherished, and ran about in the palace-garden.

But the wicked step-mother, because of whom the children had gone out into the world, had never thought but that the sister had been torn to pieces by the wild beasts in the wood, and that the brother had been shot for a roebuck by the huntsmen. Now when she heard that they were so happy, and so well off, envy and jealousy rose in her heart and left her no peace, and she thought of nothing but how she could bring them again to misfortune. Her own daughter, who was as ugly as night, and had only one eye, reproached her and said: "A Queen! that ought to have been my luck." "Just be quiet," answered the old woman, and comforted her by saying: "when the time comes I shall be ready."

As time went on, the Queen had a pretty little boy, and it happened that the King was out hunting; so the old witch took the form of the chamber-maid, went into the room where the Queen lay, and said to her: "Come, the bath is ready; it will do you good, and give you fresh strength; make haste before it gets cold."

Her daughter also was close by; so they carried the weakly Queen into the bath-room, and put her into the bath; then they shut the door and ran away. But in the bath-room they had made a fire of such hellish heat that the beautiful young Queen was soon suffocated.

When this was done the old woman took her daughter, put a nightcap on her head, and laid her in bed in place of the Queen. She gave her too the shape and the look of the Queen, only she could not make good the lost eye. But in order that the King might not see it, she was to lie on the side on which she had no eye.

In the evening when he came home and heard that he had a son he was heartily glad, and was going to the bed of his dear wife to see how she was. But the old woman quickly called out: "For your life leave the curtains closed; the Queen ought not to see the light yet, and must have rest." The King went away, and did not find out that a false Queen was lying in the bed.

But at midnight, when all slept, the nurse, who was sitting in the nursery by the cradle, and who was the only person awake, saw the door open and the true Queen walk in. She took the child out of the cradle, laid it on her arm, and suckled it. Then she shook up its pillow, laid the child down again, and covered it with the little quilt. And she did not forget the roebuck, but went into the corner where it lay, and stroked its back. Then she went quite silently out of the door again. The next morning the nurse asked the guards whether anyone had come into the palace during the night, but they answered: "No, we have seen no one."

She came thus many nights and never spoke a word: the nurse always saw her, but she did not dare to tell anyone about it.

When some time had passed in this manner, the Queen began to speak in the night, and said:

> "How fares my child, how fares my roe?
> Twice shall I come, then never more."

The nurse did not answer, but when the Queen had gone again, went to the King and told him all. The King said: "Ah, God! what is this? To-morrow night I will watch by the child." In the evening he went into the nursery, and at midnight the Queen again appeared and said:

> "How fares my child, how fares my roe?
> Once will I come, then never more."

And she nursed the child as she was wont to do before she disappeared. The King dared not speak to her, but on the next night he watched again. Then she said:

> "How fares my child, how fares my roe?
> This time I come, then never more."

Then the King could not restrain himself; he sprang towards her, and said: "You can be none other than my dear wife." She answered: "Yes, I am your dear wife," and at the same moment she received life again, and by God's grace became fresh, rosy, and full of health.

Then she told the King the evil deed which the wicked witch and her daughter had been guilty of towards her. The King ordered both to be led before the judge, and judgment was delivered against them. The daughter was taken into the forest where she was torn to pieces by wild beasts, but the witch was cast into the fire and miserably burnt. And as soon as she was burnt to ashes, the roebuck changed his shape, and received his human form again, so the sister and brother lived happily together all their lives.

Rapunzel

There were once a man and a woman who had long in vain wished for a child. At length the woman hoped that God was about to grant her desire. These people had a little window at the back of their house from which a splendid garden could be seen, which was full of the most beautiful flowers and herbs. It was, however, surrounded by a high wall, and no one dared to go into it because it belonged to an enchantress, who had great power and was dreaded by all the world. One day the woman was standing by this window and looking down into the garden, when she saw a bed which was planted with the most beautiful rampion (rapunzel), and it looked so fresh and green that she longed for it, and had the greatest desire to eat some. This desire increased every day, and as she knew that she could not get any of it, she quite pined away, and began to look pale and miserable. Then her husband was alarmed, and asked: "What ails you, dear wife?" "Ah," she replied, "if I can't eat some of the rampion, which is in the garden, behind our house, I shall die." The man, who loved her, thought: "Sooner than let your wife die, bring her some of the rampion yourself, let it cost what it will." At twilight, he clambered down over the wall into the garden of the enchantress, hastily clutched a handful of rampion, and took it to his wife. She at once made herself a salad of it, and ate it greedily. It tasted so good to her— so very good, that the next day she longed for it three times as much as before. If he was to have any rest, her husband must once more descend into the garden. In the gloom of evening, therefore, he let himelf down again; but when he had clambered down the wall he was terribly afraid, for he saw the enchantress standing before him. "How can you dare," said she with an angry look, "descend into my garden and steal my rampion like a thief? You shall suffer for it!" "Ah," answered he, "let mercy take the place of justice, I only made up my mind to do it out of necessity. My wife saw your rampion from the window, and felt such a longing for it that she would have died if she had not got some to eat." Then the enchantress allowed her anger to be softened, and said to him: "If the case be as you say, I will allow you to take away with you as much rampion as you will, only I make one condition,

you must give me the child which your wife will bring into the
world; it shall be well treated, and I will care for it like a mother."
The man in his terror consented to everything, and when the woman
was brought to bed, the enchantress appeared at once, gave the
child the name of Rapunzel, and took it away with her.

Rapunzel grew into the most beautiful child under the sun. When she was twelve years old, the enchantress shut her into a tower, which lay in a forest, and had neither stairs nor door, but quite at the top was a little window. When the enchantress wanted to go in, she placed herself beneath it and cried:

> "Rapunzel, Rapunzel,
> Let down your hair to me."

Rapunzel had magnificent long hair, fine as spun gold, and when she heard the voice of the enchantress she unfastened her braided tresses, wound them round one of the hooks of the window above, and then the hair fell twenty ells down, and the enchantress climbed up by it.

After a year or two, it came to pass that the King's son rode through the forest and passed by the tower. Then he heard a song, which was so charming that he stood still and listened. This was Rapunzel, who in her solitude passed her time in letting her sweet voice resound. The King's son wanted to climb up to her, and looked for the door of the tower, but none was to be found. He rode home, but the singing had so deeply touched his heart, that every day he went out into the forest and listened to it. Once when he was thus standing behind a tree, he saw that an enchantress came there, and he heard how she cried:

> "Rapunzel, Rapunzel,
> Let down your hair."

Then Rapunzel let down the braids of her hair, and the enchantress climbed up to her. "If that is the ladder by which one mounts, I too will try my fortune," said he, and the next day when it began to grow dark, he went to the tower and cried:

> "Rapunzel, Rapunzel,
> Let down your hair."

Immediately the hair fell down and the King's son climbed up.

At first Rapunzel was terribly frightened when a man, such as her eyes had never yet beheld, came to her; but the King's son began to talk to her quite like a friend, and told her that his heart had been so stirred that it had let him have no rest, and he had been forced to see her. Then Rapunzel lost her fear, and when he asked her if she would take him for her husband, and she saw that he was young and handsome, she thought: "He will love me more than old Dame Gothel does"; and she said yes, and laid her hand in his. She said: "I will willingly go away with you, but I do not know how to get down. Bring with you a skein of silk every time that you come, and I will weave a ladder with it, and when that is ready I will descend, and you will take me on your horse." They agreed that until that time he should come to her every evening, for the old woman came by day. The enchantress remarked nothing of this, until once Rapunzel said to her: "Tell me, Dame Gothel, how it happens that you are so much heavier for me to draw up than the young King's son—he is with me in a moment." "Ah! you wicked child," cried the enchantress. "What do I hear you say! I thought I had separated you from all the world, and yet you have deceived me!" In her anger she clutched Rapunzel's beautiful tresses, wrapped them twice round her left hand, seized a pair of scissors with the right, and snip, snap, they were cut off, and the lovely braids lay on the ground. And she was so pitiless that she took poor Rapunzel into a desert where she had to live in great grief and misery.

On the same day that she cast out Rapunzel, however, the enchantress fastened the braids of hair, which she had cut off, to the hook of the window, and when the King's son came and cried:

"Rapunzel, Rapunzel,
Let down your hair,"

she let the hair down. The King's son ascended, but instead of finding his dearest Rapunzel, he found the enchantress, who gazed at him with wicked and venomous looks. "Aha!" she cried mockingly, "you would fetch your dearest, but the beautiful bird sits no longer singing in the nest; the cat has got it, and will scratch out your eyes as well. Rapunzel is lost to you; you will never see her again." The King's son was beside himself with pain, and in his despair he leapt down from the tower. He escaped with his life, but the thorns into which he fell pierced his eyes. Then he wandered quite blind about the forest, ate nothing but roots and berries, and did naught but lament and weep over the loss of his dearest wife. Thus he roamed about in misery for some years, and at length came to the desert where Rapunzel, with the twins to which she had given birth, a boy and a girl, lived in wretchedness. He heard a voice, and it seemed so familiar to him that he went towards it, and when he approached, Rapunzel knew him and fell on his neck and wept. Two of her tears wetted his eyes and they grew clear again, and he could see with them as before. He led her to his kingdom where he was joyfully received, and they lived for a long time afterwards, happy and contented.

Hänsel and Gretel

Hard by a great forest dwelt a poor wood-cutter with his wife and his two children. The boy was called Hänsel and the girl Gretel. He had little to bite and to break, and once when great dearth fell on the land, he could no longer procure even daily bread. Now when he thought over this by night in his bed, and tossed about in his anxiety, he groaned and said to his wife: "What is to become of us? How are we to feed our poor children, when we no longer have anything even for ourselves?" "I'll tell you what, husband," answered the woman, "early to-morrow morning we will take the children out into the forest to where it is the thickest; there we will light a fire for them, and give each of them one more piece of bread, and then we will go to our work and leave them alone. They will not find the way home again, and we shall be rid of them." "No, wife," said the man, "I will not do that; how can I bear to leave my children alone in the forest?—the wild animals would soon come and tear them to pieces." "O, you fool!" said she, "then we must all four die of hunger, you may as well plane the planks for our coffins," and she left him no peace until he consented. "But I feel very sorry for the poor children, all the same," said the man.

The two children had also not been able to sleep for hunger, and had heard what their step-mother had said to their father. Gretel wept bitter tears, and said to Hänsel: "Now all is over with us."

"Be quiet, Gretel," said Hänsel, "do not distress yourself, I will soon find a way to help us." And when the old folks had fallen asleep, he got up, put on his little coat, opened the door below, and crept outside. The moon shone brightly, and the white pebbles which lay in front of the house glittered like real silver pennies. Hänsel stooped and stuffed the little pocket of his coat with as many as he could get in. Then he went back and said to Gretel: "Be comforted, dear little sister, and sleep in peace, God will not forsake us," and he lay down again in his bed. When day dawned, but before the sun had risen, the woman came and awoke the two children, saying: "Get up, you sluggards! we are going into the forest to fetch wood." She gave each a little piece of bread, and said: "There is something for your dinner, but do not eat it up before then, for you will get nothing else." Gretel took the bread under her apron, as Hänsel had the pebbles in his pocket. Then they all set out together on the way to the forest. When they had walked a short time, Hänsel stood still and peeped back at the house, and did so again and again. His father said: "Hänsel, what are you looking at there and staying behind for? Pay attention, and do not forget how to use your legs." "Ah, father," said Hänsel, "I am looking at my little white cat, which is sitting up on the roof, and wants to say good-bye to me." The wife said: "Fool, that is not your little cat, that is the morning sun which is shining on the chimney." Hänsel, however, had not been looking back at the cat, but had been constantly throwing one of the white pebble-stones out of his pocket on the road.

When they had reached the middle of the forest, the father said: "Now, children, pile up some wood, and I will light a fire that you may not be cold." Hänsel and Gretel gathered brushwood together, as high as a little hill. The brushwood was lighted, and when the flames were burning very high, the woman said: "Now, children, lay yourselves down by the fire and rest, we will go into the forest and cut some wood. When we have done, we will come back and fetch you away."

Hänsel and Gretel sat by the fire, and when noon came, each ate a little piece of bread, and as they heard the strokes of the wood-axe they believed that their father was near. It was not the axe, however, but a branch which he had fastened to a withered tree which the wind was blowing backwards and forwards. And as they had been sitting such a long time, their eyes closed with fatigue, and they fell fast asleep. When at last they awoke, it was already dark night. Gretel began to cry and said: "How are we to get out of the forest now?" But Hänsel comforted her and said: "Just wait a little, until the moon has risen, and then we will soon find the way." And when the full moon had risen, Hänsel took his little sister by the hand, and followed the pebbles which shone like newly-coined silver pieces, and showed them the way.

They walked the whole night long, and by break of day came once more to their father's house. They knocked at the door, and when the woman opened it and saw that it was Hänsel and Gretel,

she said: "You naughty children, why have you slept so long in the forest?—we thought you were never coming back at all!" The father, however, rejoiced, for it had cut him to the heart to leave them behind alone.

Not long afterwards, there was once more great dearth throughout the land, and the children heard their mother saying at night to their father: "Everything is eaten again, we have one half loaf left, and that is the end. The children must go, we will take them farther into the wood, so that they will not find their way out again; there is no other means of saving ourselves!" The man's heart was heavy, and he thought: "It would be better for you to share the last mouthful with your children." The woman, however, would listen to nothing that he had to say, but scolded and reproached him. He who says A must say B, likewise, and as he had yielded the first time, he had to do so a second time also.

The children, however, were still awake and had heard the conversation. When the old folks were asleep, Hänsel again got up, and wanted to go out and pick up pebbles as he had done before, but the woman had locked the door, and Hänsel could not get out. Nevertheless he comforted his little sister, and said: "Do not cry, Gretel, go to sleep quietly, the good Lord will help us."

Early in the morning came the woman, and took the children out of their beds. Their piece of bread was given to them, but it was still smaller than the time before. On the way into the forest Hänsel crumbled his in his pocket, and often stood still and threw a morsel on the ground. "Hänsel, why do you stop and look round?" said the father, "go on." "I am looking back at my little pigeon which is sitting on the roof, and wants to say good-bye to me," answered Hänsel. "Fool!" said the woman, "that is not your little pigeon, that is the morning sun that is shining on the chimney." Hänsel, however, little by little, threw all the crumbs on the path.

The woman led the children still deeper into the forest, where they had never in their lives been before. Then a great fire was again made, and the mother said: "Just sit there, you children, and when you are tired you may sleep a little; we are going into the forest to cut wood, and in the evening when we are done, we will come and fetch you away." When it was noon, Gretel shared her piece of bread with Hänsel, who had scattered his by the way. Then they fell asleep and evening passed, but no one came to the poor children. They did not awake until it was dark night, and Hänsel comforted his little sister and said: "Just wait, Gretel, until the moon rises, and then we shall see the crumbs of bread which I have strewn about, they will show us our way home again." When the moon came they set out, but they found no crumbs, for the many thousands of birds which fly about in the woods and fields had picked them all up. Hänsel said to Gretel: "We shall soon find the way," but they did not find it. They walked the whole night and all the next day too from morning till evening, but they did not get out of the forest, and were very hungry, for they had nothing to eat but two or three berries, which grew on the ground. And as they were so weary that their legs would carry them no longer, they lay down beneath a tree and fell asleep.

It was now three mornings since they had left their father's house. They began to walk again, but they always came deeper into the forest, and if help did not come soon, they must die of hunger and weariness. When it was mid-day, they saw a beautiful snow-white bird sitting on a bough, which sang so delightfully that they stood still and listened to it. And when its song was over, it spread its wings and flew away before them, and they followed it until they reached a little house, on the roof of which it alighted; and when they approached the little house they saw that it was built of bread and covered with cakes, but that the windows were of clear sugar. "We will set to work on that," said Hänsel, "and have a good meal. I will eat a bit of the roof, and you Gretel, can eat some of the window, it will taste sweet." Hänsel reached above, and broke off a little of the roof to try how it tasted, and Gretel leant against the window and nibbled at the panes. Then a soft voice cried from the parlor:

> "Nibble, nibble, gnaw,
> Who is nibbling at my little house?"

The children answered:

> "The wind, the wind,
> The heaven-born wind,"

and went on eating without disturbing themselves. Hänsel, who liked the taste of the roof, tore down a great piece of it, and Gretel pushed out the whole of one round window-pane, sat down, and enjoyed herself with it. Suddenly the door opened, and a woman as old as the hills, who supported herself on crutches, came creeping out. Hänsel and Gretel were so terribly frightened that they let fall what they had in their hands. The old woman, however, nodded her head, and said: "Oh, you dear children, who has brought you here? Do come in, and stay with me. No harm shall happen to you." She took them both by the hand, and led them into her little house. Then good food was set before them, milk and pancakes, with sugar, apples, and nuts. Afterwards two pretty little beds were covered with clean white linen, and Hänsel and Gretel lay down in them, and thought they were in heaven.

The old woman had only pretended to be so kind; she was in reality a wicked witch, who lay in wait for children, and had only built the little house of bread in order to entice them there. When a child fell into her power, she killed it, cooked and ate it, and that was a feast day with her. Witches have red eyes, and cannot see far, but they have a keen scent like the beasts, and are aware when human beings draw near. As Hänsel and Gretel drew closer and closer, she laughed with malice, and said mockingly: "I have them, they shall never get away!" Early in the morning before the children were awake, she was already up, and when she saw both of them sleeping and looking so pretty, with their plump and rosy cheeks, she muttered to herself: "That will be a dainty mouthful!" Then she seized Hänsel with her shrivelled hand, carried him into a little stable, and locked him in behind a grated door. Scream as he might, it would not help him. Then she went to Gretel, shook her till she awoke, and cried: "Get up, lazy thing, fetch some water, and cook something good for your brother, he is in the stable outside, and is to be made fat. When he is fat, I will eat him." Gretel began to weep bitterly, but it was all in vain, for she was forced to do what the wicked witch commanded.

And now the best food was cooked for poor Hänsel, but Gretel got nothing but crab-shells. Every morning the woman crept to the little stable, and cried: "Hänsel, stretch out your finger that I may feel if you will soon be fat." Hänsel, however, stretched out a little bone to her, and the old woman, who had dim eyes, could not see it, and thought it was Hänsel's finger, and was astonished that there was no way of fattening him. When four weeks had gone by, and Hänsel still remained thin, she was seized with impatience and would not wait any longer. "Now, then, Gretel," she cried to the girl, "stir yourself, and bring some water. Let Hänsel be fat or lean, to-morrow I will kill him, and cook him." Ah, how the poor little sister did lament when she had to fetch the water, and how her tears did flow down her cheeks! "Dear God, do help us," she cried. "If the wild beasts in the forest had but devoured us, we should at any rate have died together." "Just keep your noise to yourself," said the old woman, "it won't help you at all."

Early in the morning, Gretel had to go out and hang up the

cauldron with the water, and light the fire. "We will bake first," said the old woman, "I have already heated the oven, and kneaded the dough." She pushed poor Gretel out to the oven, from which flames of fire were already darting. "Creep in," said the witch, "and see if it is properly heated, so that we can put the bread in." And once Gretel was inside, she intended to shut the oven and let her bake in it, and then she would eat her, too. But Gretel saw what she had in mind, and said: "I do not know how I am to do it; how do I get in?" "Silly goose," said the old woman. "The door is big enough; just look, I can get in myself!" and she crept up and thrust her head into the oven. Then Gretel gave her a push that drove her far into it, and shut the iron door, and fastened the bolt. Oh! then she began to howl quite horribly, but Gretel ran away, and the godless witch was miserably burnt to death.

Gretel, however, ran like lightning to Hänsel, opened his little stable, and cried: "Hänsel, we are saved! The old witch is dead!" Then Hänsel sprang like a bird from its cage when the door is opened. How they did rejoice and embrace each other, and dance about and kiss each other! And as they had no longer any need to fear her, they went into the witch's house, and in every corner there stood chests full of pearls and jewels. "These are far better than pebbles!" said Hänsel, and thrust into his pockets whatever could be got in, and Gretel said: "I, too, will take something home with me," and filled her pinafore full. "But now we must be off," said Hänsel, "that we may get out of the witch's forest."

When they had walked for two hours, they came to a great stretch of water. "We cannot cross," said Hänsel, "I see no footplank, and no bridge." "And there is also no ferry," answered Gretel, "but a white duck is swimming there; if I ask her, she will help us over." Then she cried:

"Little duck, little duck, dost thou see,
Hänsel and Gretel are waiting for thee?
There's never a plank, or bridge in sight,
Take us across on thy back so white."

The duck came to them, and Hänsel seated himself on its back, and told his sister to sit by him. "No," replied Gretel, "that will be too heavy for the little duck; she shall take us across, one after the other." The good little duck did so, and when they were once safely across and had walked for a short time, the forest seemed to be more and more familiar to them, and at length they saw from afar their father's house. Then they began to run, rushed into the parlor, and threw themselves round their father's neck. The man had not known one happy hour since he had left the children in the forest; the woman, however, was dead. Gretel emptied her pinafore until pearls and precious stones ran about the room, and Hänsel threw one handful after another out of his pocket to add to them. Then all anxiety was at an end, and they lived together in perfect happiness. My tale is done, there runs a mouse, whosoever catches it, may make himself a big fur cap out of it.

The Fisherman and His Wife

There was once upon a time a Fisherman who lived with his wife in a pig-stye close by the sea, and every day he went out fishing; and he fished, and he fished. And once he was sitting with his rod, looking at the clear water, and he sat and he sat. Then his line suddenly went down, far down below, and when he drew it up again, he brought out a large Flounder. Then the Flounder said to him: "Hark, you Fisherman, I pray you, let me live, I am no Flounder really, but an enchanted prince. What good will it do you to kill me? I should not be good to eat, put me in the water again, and let me go." "Come," said the Fisherman, "there is no need for so many words about it—a fish that can talk I should certainly let go, anyhow." And with that he put him back again into the clear water, and the Flounder went to the bottom, leaving a long streak of blood behind him. Then the Fisherman got up and went home to his wife in the pig-stye.

"Husband," said the woman, "have you caught nothing to-day?" "No," said the man, "I did catch a Flounder, who said he was an enchanted prince, so I let him go again." "Did you not wish for anything first?" said the woman. "No," said the man; "what should I wish for?" "Ah," said the woman, "it is surely hard to have to live always in this pig-stye which stinks and is so disgusting; you might have wished for a little hut for us. Go back and call him. Tell him we want to have a little hut, he will certainly give us that." "Ah," said the man, "why should I go there again?" "Why," said the woman, "you did catch him, and you let him go again; he is sure to do it. Go at once." The man still did not quite like to go, but did not like to oppose his wife either, and went to the sea.

When he got there the sea was all green and yellow, and no longer so smooth; so he stood and said:

> "Flounder, flounder in the sea,
> Come, I pray thee, here to me;
> For my wife, good Ilsabil,
> Wills not as I'd have her will."

Then the Flounder came swimming to him and said: "Well, what does she want, then?" "Ah," said the man, "I did catch you, and my wife says I really ought to have wished for something. She does not like to live in a pig-stye any longer; she would like to have a hut." "Go, then," said the Flounder, "she has it already."

When the man went home, his wife was no longer in the stye, but instead of it there stood a hut, and she was sitting on a bench before the door. Then she took him by the hand and said to him: "Just come inside. Look, now isn't this a great deal better?" So they went in, and there was a small porch, and a pretty little parlor and bedroom, and a kitchen and pantry, with the best of furniture, and fitted up with the most beautiful things made of tin and brass, whatsoever was wanted. And behind the hut there was a small yard, with hens and ducks, and a little garden with flowers and fruit. "Look," said the wife, "is not that nice!" "Yes," said the husband, "and so it shall remain—now we will live quite contented." "We will think about that," said the wife. With that they ate something and went to bed.

Everything went well for a week or a fortnight, and then the woman said: "Hark you, husband, this hut is far too small for us, and the garden and yard are little; the Flounder might just as well have given us a larger house. I should like to live in a great stone castle; go to the Flounder, and tell him to give us a castle." "Ah, wife," said the man, "the hut is quite good enough; why should we live in a castle?" "What!" said the woman; "just go there, the

Flounder can always do that." "No, wife," said the man, "the Flounder has just given us the hut, I do not like to go back so soon, it might make him angry." "Go," said the woman, "he can do it it quite easily, and will be glad to do it; just you go to him."

The man's heart grew heavy, and he would not go. He said to himself: "It is not right," and yet he went. And when he came to the sea the water was quite purple and dark-blue, and grey and thick, and no longer so green and yellow, but it was still quiet. And he stood there and said:

> "Flounder, flounder in the sea,
> Come, I pray thee, here to me;
> For my wife, good Ilsabil,
> Wills not as I'd have her will."

"Well, what does she want, now?" said the Flounder. "Alas," said the man, half scared, "she wants to live in a great stone castle." "Go to it, then, she is standing before the door," said the Flounder.

Then the man went away, intending to go home, but when he got there, he found a great stone palace, and his wife was just standing on the steps going in, and she took him by the hand and said: "Come in." So he went in with her, and in the castle was a great hall paved with marble, and many servants, who flung wide the doors; and the walls were all bright with beautiful hangings, and in the rooms were chairs and tables of pure gold, and crystal chandeliers hung from the ceiling, and all the rooms and bed-rooms had carpets, and food and wine of the very best were standing on all the tables, so that they nearly broke down beneath it. Behind the house, too, there was a great court-yard, with stables for horses and cows, and the very best of carriages; there was a magnificent large garden, too, with the most beautiful flowers and fruit-trees, and a park quite half a mile long, in which were stags, deer, and hares, and everything that could be desired. "Come," said the woman, "isn't that beautiful?" "Yes, indeed," said the man, "now let it be; and we will live in this beautiful castle and be content." "We will consider about that," said the woman, "and sleep upon it"; thereupon they went to bed.

Next morning the wife awoke first, and it was just daybreak, and from her bed she saw the beautiful country lying before her. Her husband was still stretching himself, so she poked him in the side with her elbow, and said: "Get up, husband, and just peep out of the window. Look you, couldn't we be the King over all that land? Go to the Flounder, we will be the King." "Ah, wife," said the man, "why should we be King? I do not want to be King." "Well," said the wife, "if you won't be King, I will; go to the Flounder, for I will be King." "Ah, wife," said the man, "why do you want to be King? I do not like to say that to him." "Why not?" said the woman; "go to him this instant; I must be King!" So the man went, and was quite unhappy because his wife wished to be King. "It is not right; it is not right," thought he. He did not wish to go, but yet he went.

And when he came to the sea, it was quite dark-grey, and the water heaved up from below, and smelt putrid. Then he went and stood by it, and said:

> "Flounder, flounder in the sea,
> Come, I pray thee, here to me;
> For my wife, good Ilsabil,
> Wills not as I'd have her will."

"Well, what does she want, now?" said the Flounder. "Alas," said the man, "she wants to be King." "Go to her; she is King already."

So the man went, and when he came to the palace, the castle had become much larger, and had a great tower and mangnificent ornaments, and the sentinel was standing before the door, and there were numbers of soldiers with kettle-drums and trumpets. And when he went inside the house, everything was of real marble and gold, with velvet covers and great golden tassels. Then the doors of the hall were opened, and there was the court in all its splendor, and his wife was sitting on a high throne of gold and diamonds, with a great crown of gold on her head, and a sceptre of pure gold and jewels in her hand, and on both sides of her stood her maids-in-waiting in a row, each of them always one head shorter than the last.

Then he went and stood before her, and said: "Ah, wife, and now you are King." "Yes," said the woman, "now I am King." So he stood and looked at her, and when he had looked at her thus for some time, he said: "And now that you are King, let all else be, now we will wish for nothing more." "No, husband," said the woman, quite anxiously, "I find time passes very heavily, I can bear it no longer; go to the Flounder—I am King, but I must be Emperor, too." "Oh, wife, why do you wish to be Emperor?" "Husband," said she, "go to the Flounder. I will be Emperor." "Alas, wife," said the man, "he cannot make you Emperor; I may not say that to the fish. There is only one Emperor in the land. An Emperor the Flounder cannot make you! I assure you he cannot."

"What!" said the woman, "I am the King, and you are nothing but my husband; will you go this moment? go at once! If he can make a king he can make an emperor. I will be Emperor; go instantly." So he was forced to go. As the man went, however, he was troubled in mind, and thought to himself: "It will not end well; it will not end well! Emperor is too shameless! The Flounder will at last be tired out."

With that he reached the sea, and the sea was quite black and thick, and began to boil up from below, so that it threw up bubbles, and such a sharp wind blew over it that it curdled, and the man was afraid. Then he went and stood by it, and said:

> "Flounder, flounder in the sea,
> Come, I pray thee, here to me;
> For my wife, good Ilsabil,
> Wills not as I'd have her will."

"Well, what does she want, now?" said the Flounder. "Alas, Flounder," said he, "my wife wants to be Emperor." "Go to her," said the Flounder; "she is Emperor already."

So the man went, and when he got there the whole palace was made of polished marble with alabaster figures and golden ornaments, and soldiers were marching before the door blowing trumpets, and beating cymbals and drums; and in the house, barons, and counts, and dukes were going about as servants. Then they opened the doors to him, which were of pure gold. And when he entered, there sat his wife on a throne, which was made of one piece of gold, and was quite two miles high; and she wore a great golden crown that was three yards high, and set with diamonds and carbuncles, and in one hand she had the sceptre, and in the other the imperial orb; and on both sides of her stood the yeomen of the guard in two rows, each being smaller than the one before him, from the biggest giant, who was two miles high, to the very smallest dwarf, just as big as my little finger. And before it stood a number of princes and dukes.

Then the man went and stood among them, and said: "Wife, are you Emperor now?" "Yes," said she, "now I am Emperor." Then he stood and looked at her well, and when he had looked at her thus for some time, he said: "Ah, wife, be content, now that you are Emperor." "Husband," said she, "why are you standing there? Now, I am Emperor, but I will be Pope too; go to the Flounder." "Oh, wife," said the man, "what will you not wish for? You cannot be Pope; there is but one in Christendom; he cannot make you Pope." "Husband," said she, "I will be Pope; go immediately, I must be Pope this very day." "No, wife," said the man, "I do not like to say that to him; that would not do, it is too much; the Flounder can't make you Pope." "Husband," said she, "what nonsense! if he can make an emperor he can make a pope. Go to him directly. I am Emperor, and you are nothing but my husband; will you go at once?"

Then he was afraid and went; but he was quite faint, and shivered and shook, and his knees and legs trembled. And a high wind blew over the land, and the clouds flew, and towards evening all grew dark, and the leaves fell from the trees, and the water rose and roared as if it were boiling, and splashed upon the shore; and in the distance he saw ships which were firing guns in their sore need, pitching and tossing on the waves. And yet in the midst of the sky there was still a small patch of blue, though on every side it was as red as in a heavy storm. So, full of despair, he went and stood in much fear and said:

> "Flounder, flounder in the sea,
> Come, I pray thee, here to me;
> For my wife, good Ilsabil,
> Wills not as I'd have her will."

"Well, what does she want, now?" said the Flounder. "Alas," said the man, "she wants to be Pope." "Go to her then," said the Flounder; "she is Pope already."

So he went, and when he got there, he saw what seemed to be a large church surrounded by palaces. He pushed his way through the crowd. Inside, however, everything was lighted up with thousands and thousands of candles, and his wife was clad in gold, and she was sitting on a much higher throne, and had three great golden crowns on, and round about her there was much ecclesiastical splendor; and on both sides of her was a row of candles the largest of which was as tall as the very tallest tower, down to the very smallest kitchen candle, and all the emperors and kings were on their knees before her, kissing her shoe. "Wife," said the man, and looked attentively at her, "are you now Pope?" "Yes," said she, "I am Pope." So he stood and looked at her, and it was just as if he was looking at the bright sun. When he had stood looking at her thus for a short time, he said: "Ah, wife, if you are Pope, do let well alone!" But she looked as stiff as a post, and did not move or show any signs of life. Then said he: "Wife, now that you are Pope, be satisfied, you cannot become anything greater now." "I will consider about that," said the woman. Thereupon they both went to bed, but she was not satisfied, and greediness let her have no sleep, for she was continually thinking what there was left for her to be.

The man slept well and soundly, for he had run about a great deal during the day; but the woman could not fall asleep at all, and flung herself from one side to the other the whole night through, thinking always what more was left for her to be, but unable to call to mind anything else. At length the sun began to rise, and when the woman saw the red of dawn, she sat up in bed and looked at it. And when, through the window, she saw the sun thus rising, she said: "Cannot I, too, order the sun and moon to rise?" "Husband," she said, poking him in the ribs with her elbows, "wake up! go to the Flounder, for I wish to be even as God is." The man was still half asleep, but he was so horrified that he fell out of bed. He thought he must have heard amiss, and rubbed his eyes, and said: "Wife, what are you saying?" "Husband," said she, "if I can't order the sun and moon to rise, and have to look on and see the sun and moon rising, I can't bear it. I shall not know what it is to have another happy hour, unless I can make them rise myself." Then she looked at him so terribly that a shudder ran over him, and said: "Go at once; I wish to be like unto God." "Alas, wife," said the man, falling on his knees before her, "the Flounder cannot do that; he can make an emperor and a pope; I beseech you, go on as you are, and be Pope." Then she fell into a rage, and her hair flew wildly about her head, she tore open her bodice, kicked him with her foot, and screamed: "I can't stand it, I can't stand it any longer! will you go this instant?" Then he put on his trousers and ran away like a madman. But outside a great storm was raging, and blowing so hard that he could scarcely keep his feet; houses and trees toppled over, the mountains trembled, rocks rolled into the sea, the sky was pitch black, and it thundered and lightened,

and the sea came in with black waves as high as church-towers and mountains, and all with crests of white foam at the top. Then he cried, but could not hear his own words:

> "Flounder, flounder in the sea,
> Come, I pray thee, here to me;
> For my wife, good Ilsabil,
> Wills not as I'd have her will."

"Well, what does she want, now?" said the Flounder. "Alas," said he, "she wants to be like unto God." "Go to her, and you will find her back again in the pig-stye." And there they are still living to this day.

The Valiant Little Tailor

One summer's morning a little tailor was sitting on his table by the window; he was in good spirits, and sewed with all his might. Then came a peasant woman down the street crying: "Good jams, cheap! Good jams, cheap!" This rang pleasantly in the tailor's ears; he stretched his delicate head out of the window, and called: "Come up here, dear woman; here you will get rid of your goods." The woman came up the three steps to the tailor with her heavy basket, and he made her unpack all the pots for him. He inspected each one, lifted it up, put his nose to it, and at length said: "The jam seems to me to be good, so weigh me out four ounces, dear woman, and if it is a quarter of a pound that is of no consequence." The woman who had hoped to find a good sale, gave him what he desired, but went away quite angry and grumbling. "Now, this jam shall be blessed by God," cried the little tailor, "and give me health and strength"; so he brought the bread out of the cupboard, cut himself a piece right across the loaf and spread the jam over it. "This won't taste bitter," said he, "but I will just finish the jacket before I take a bite." He laid the bread near him, sewed on, and in his joy, made bigger and bigger stitches. In the meantime the smell of the sweet jam rose to where the flies were sitting in great numbers, and they were attracted and descended on it in hosts. "Hi! who invited you?" said the little tailor, and drove the unbidden guests away. The flies, however, who understood no German, would not be turned away, but came back again in ever-increasing companies. The little tailor at last lost all patience, and drew a piece of cloth from the hole under his worktable, and saying: "Wait, and I will give it to you," struck it mercilessly on them. When he drew it away and counted, there lay before him no fewer than seven, dead and with legs stretched out. "Are you a fellow of that sort?" said he, and could not help admiring his own bravery. "The whole town shall know of this!" And the little tailor hastened to cut himself a girdle, stitched it, and embroidered on it in large letters: "Seven at one stroke!" "What, the town!" he continued, "the whole world shall hear of it!" and his heart wagged with joy like a lamb's tail. The tailor put on the girdle, and resolved to go forth into the world, because he thought his workshop was too small for his valor. Before he went away, he sought about in the house to see if there was anything which he could take with him; however, he found nothing but an old cheese, and that he put in his pocket. In front of the door he observed a bird which had caught himself in the thicket. It had to go into his pocket with the cheese. Now he took to the road boldly, and as he was light and nimble, he felt no fatigue. The road led him up a mountain, and when he had reached the highest point of it, there sat a powerful giant looking peacefully about him. The little tailor went bravely up, spoke to him, and said: "Good day, comrade, so you are sitting there overlooking the wide-spread world! I am just on my way thither, and want to try my luck. Have you any inclination to go with me?" The giant looked contemptuously at the tailor, and said: "You ragamuffin! You miserable creature!"

"Oh, indeed?" answered the little tailor, and unbuttoned his coat, and showed the giant the girdle, "there may you read what kind of a man I am!" The giant read: "Seven at one stroke," and thought that they had been men whom the tailor had killed, and began to feel a little respect for the tiny fellow. Nevertheless, he wished to try him first, and took a stone in his hand and squeezed it together so that water dropped out of it. "Do that likewise," said the giant, "if you have strength." "Is that all?" said the tailor, "that is child's play with us!" and put his hand into his pocket, brought out the soft cheese, and pressed it until the liquid ran out of it. "Faith," said he, "that was a little better, wasn't it?" The giant did not know what to say, and could not believe it of the little man. Then the giant picked up a stone and threw it so high that the eye could scarcely follow it. "Now, little mite of a man, do that likewise." "Well thrown," said the tailor, "but after all the stone came down to earth again; I will throw you one which shall never come back at all," and he put his hand into his pocket, took out the bird, and threw it into the air. The bird, delighted with its liberty, rose, flew away and did not come back. "How does that shot please you, comrade?" asked the tailor. "You can certainly throw," said the giant, "but now we will see if you are able to carry anything properly." He took the little tailor to a mighty oak tree which lay there felled on the ground, and said: "If you are strong enough, help me to carry the tree out of the forest." "Readily," answered the little man; "take you the trunk on your shoulders, and I will raise up the branches and twigs; after all, they are the heaviest." The giant took the trunk on his shoulder, but the tailor seated himself on a branch, and the giant who could not look round, had to carry away the whole tree, and the little tailor into the bargain: he behind, was quite merry and happy, and whistled the song: "Three tailors rode forth from the gate," as if carrying the tree were child's play. The giant, after he had dragged the heavy burden part of the way, could go no further, and cried: "Hark you, I shall have to let the tree fall!" The tailor sprang nimbly down, seized the tree with both arms as if he had been carrying it, and said to the giant: "You are such a great fellow, and yet can not even carry the tree!"

They went on together, and as they passed a cherry-tree, the giant laid hold of the top of the tree where the ripest fruit was hanging, bent it down, gave it into the tailor's hand, and bade him eat. But the little tailor was much too weak to hold the tree, and when the giant let it go, it sprang back again, and the tailor was tossed into the air with it. When he had fallen down again without injury, the giant said: "What is this? Have you not strength enough to hold the weak twig?" "There is no lack of strength," answered the little tailor. "Do you think that could be anything to a man who has struck down seven at one blow? I leapt over the tree because the huntsmen are shooting down there in the thicket. Jump as I did, if you can do it." The giant made the attempt, but could not get over the tree, and remained hanging in the branches, so that in this also the tailor kept the upper hand.

The giant said: "If you are such a valiant fellow, come with me into our cavern and spend the night with us." The little tailor was willing, and followed him. When they went into the cave, other giants were sitting there by the fire, and each of them had a roasted sheep in his hand and was eating it. The little tailor looked around and thought: "It is much more spacious here than in my workshop." The giant showed him a bed, and said he was to lie down in it and sleep. The bed, however, was too big for the little tailor; he did not lie down in it, but crept into a corner. When it was midnight, and the giant thought that the little tailor was lying in a sound sleep, he got up, took a great iron bar, cut through the bed with one blow, and thought he had finished off the grasshopper for good. With the earliest dawn the giants went into the forest, and had quite forgotten the little tailor, when all at once he walked up to them quite merrily and boldly. The giants were terrified, they were afraid that he would strike them all dead, and ran away in a great hurry.

The little tailor went onwards, always following his own pointed nose. After he had walked for a long time, he came to the courtyard of a royal palace, and as he felt weary, he lay down on the grass and fell asleep. Whilst he lay there, the people came and inspected him on all sides, and read on his girdle: "Seven at one stroke." "Ah!" said they, "what does the great warrior here in the midst of peace? He must be a mighty lord." They went and announced him to the King, and gave it as their opinion that if war should break out, this would be a weighty and useful man who ought on no account to be allowed to depart. The counsel pleased the King, and he sent one of his courtiers to the little tailor to offer him military service when he awoke. The ambassador remained standing by the sleeper, waited until he stretched his limbs and opened his eyes, and then conveyed to him this proposal. "For this very reason have I come here," the tailor replied, "I am ready to enter the King's service." He was therefore honorably received, and a special dwelling was assigned him.

The soldiers, however, were set against the little tailor, and wished him a thousand miles away. "What is to be the end of this?" they said among themselves. "If we quarrel with him, and he strikes about him, seven of us will fall at every blow; not one of us can stand against him." They came therefore to a decision, betook themselves in a body to the King, and begged for their dismissal. "We are not prepared," said they, "to stay with a man who kills seven at one stroke." The King was sorry that for the sake of one he should lose all his faithful servants, wished that he had never set eyes on the tailor, and would willingly have been rid of him again. But he did not venture to give him his dismissal, for he dreaded lest he should strike him and all his people dead, and place himself on the royal throne. He thought about it for a long time, and at last found good counsel. He sent to the little tailor and caused him to be informed that as he was such a great warrior, he had one request to make to him. In a forest of his country lived two giants, who caused great mischief with their robbing, murdering, ravaging, and burning, and no one could approach them without putting himself in danger of death. If the tailor conquered and killed these two giants, he would give him his only daughter to wife, and half of his kingdom as a dowry, likewise one hundred horsemen should go with him to assist him. "That would indeed be a fine thing for a man like me!" thought the little tailor. "One is not offered a beautiful princess and half a kingdom every day of one's life!" "Oh, yes," he replied, "I will soon subdue the giants, and do not require the help of the hundred horsemen to do it; he who can hit seven with one blow has no need to be afraid of two."

The little tailor went forth, and the hundred horsemen followed him. When he came to the outskirts of the forest, he said to his followers: "Just stay waiting here, I alone will soon finish off the giants." Then he bounded into the forest and looked about right and left. After a while he perceived both giants. They lay sleeping under a tree, and snored so that the branches waved up and down. The little tailor, not idle, gathered two pocketsful of stones, and with these climbed up the tree. When he was half-way up, he slipped down by a branch, until he sat just above the sleepers, and then let one stone after another fall on the breast of one of the giants. For a long time the giant felt nothing, but at last he awoke, pushed his comrade, and said: "Why are you knocking me?" "You must be dreaming," said the other, "I am not knocking you." They laid themselves down to sleep again, and then the tailor throw a stone down on the second. "What is the meaning of this?" cried the other. "Why are you pelting me?" "I am not pelting you," answered the first, growling. They disputed about it for a time, but as they were weary they let the matter rest, and their eyes closed once more. The little tailor began his game again, picked out the biggest stone, and threw it with all his might on the breast of the first giant. "That is too bad!" cried he, and sprang up like a madman, and pushed his companion against the tree until it shook. The other paid him back in the same coin, and they got into such a rage that they tore up trees and belabored each other so long, that at last they both fell down dead on the ground at the same time. Then the little tailor leapt down. "It is a lucky thing," said he, "that they did not tear up the tree on which I was sitting, or I should have had to spring on to another like a squirrel; but we tailors are nimble." He drew out his sword and gave each of them a couple of thrusts in the breast, and then went out to the horsemen and said: "The work is done; I have finished both of them off, but it was hard

work! They tore up trees in their sore need, and defended themselves with them, but all that is to no purpose when a man like
myself comes, who can kill seven at one blow." "But are you not
wounded?" asked the horsemen. "You need not concern yourself
about that," answered the tailor, "they have not bent one hair of
mine." The horsemen would not believe him, and rode into the
forest; there they found the giants swimming in their blood, and
all round about lay the torn-up trees.

The little tailor demanded of the King the promised reward; he,
however, repented of his promise, and again bethought himself how
he could get rid of the hero. "Before you receive my daughter, and
the half of my kindgom," said he to him, "you must perform one
more heroic deed. In the forest roams a unicorn which does great
harm, and you must catch it first." "I fear one unicorn still less
than two giants. Seven at one blow, is my kind of affair." He took
a rope and an axe with him, went forth into the forest, and again
bade those who were sent with him to wait outside. He had not
long to seek. The unicorn soon came towards him, and rushed directly on the tailor, as if it would gore him with its horn without
more ado. "Softly, softly; it can't be done as quickly as that," said
he, and stood still and waited until the animal was quite close, and
then sprang nimbly behind the tree. The unicorn ran against the
tree with all its strength, and struck its horn so fast in the trunk
that it had not strength enough to draw it out again, and thus it
was caught. "Now, I have got the bird," said the tailor, and came
out from behind the tree and put the rope round its neck, and then
with his axe he hewed the horn out of the tree, and when all was
ready he led the beast away and took it to the King.

The King still would not give him the promised reward, and made
a third demand. Before the wedding the tailor was to catch him a
wild boar that made great havoc in the forest, and the huntsmen
should give him their help. "Willingly," said the tailor, "that is
child's play!" He did not take the huntsmen with him into the forest, and they were well pleased that he did not, for the wild boar
had several times received them in such a manner that they had no
inclination to lie in wait for him. When the boar perceived the tailor, it ran on him with foaming mouth and whetted tusks, and was
about to throw him to the ground, but the hero fled and sprang
into a chapel which was near, and up to the window at once, and

in one bound out again. The boar ran in after him, but the tailor ran round outside and shut the door behind it, and then the raging beast, which was much too heavy and awkward to leap out of the window, was caught. The little tailor called the huntsmen thither that they might see the prisoner with their own eyes. The hero, however, went to the King, who was now, whether he liked it or not, obliged to keep his promise, and gave him his daughter and the half of his kindgom. Had he known that it was no warlike hero, but a little tailor who was standing before him, it would have gone to his heart still more than it did. The wedding was held with great magnificence and small joy, and out of a tailor a king was made.

After some time the young Queen heard her husband say in his dreams at night: "Boy, make me the doublet, and patch the pantaloons, or else I will rap the yard-measure over your ears." Then she discovered in what state of life the young lord had been born, and next morning complained of her wrongs to her father, and begged him to help her to get rid of her husband, who was nothing else but a tailor. The King comforted her and said: "Leave your bedroom door open this night, and my servants shall stand outside, and when he has fallen asleep shall go in, bind him, and take him on board a ship which shall carry him into the wide world." The woman was satisfied with this; but the King's armor-bearer, who had heard all, was friendly with the young lord, and informed him of the whole plot. "I'll put a screw into this business," said the little tailor. At night he went to bed with his wife at the usual time, and when she thought that he had fallen asleep, she got up, opened the door and then lay down again. The little tailor, who was only pretending to be asleep, began to cry out in a clear voice: "Boy, make me the doublet and patch me the pantaloons, or I will rap the yard-measure over your ears. I smote seven at one blow. I killed two giants, I brought away one unicorn, and caught a wild boar, and am I to fear those who are standing outside the room." When these men heard the tailor speaking thus, they were overcome by a great dread, and ran as if the wild huntsman were behind them, and none of them would venture anything further against him. So the little tailor was and remained a king to the end of his life.

Cinderella

The wife of a rich man fell sick, and as she felt that her end was drawing near, she called her only daughter to her bedside and said: "Dear child, be good and pious, and then the good God will always protect you, and I will look down on you from heaven and be near you." Thereupon she closed her eyes and departed. Every day the maiden went out to her mother's grave and wept, and she remained pious and good. When winter came the snow spread a white sheet over the grave, and by the time the spring sun had drawn it off again, the man had taken another wife.

The woman had brought with her into the house two daughters, who were beautiful and fair of face, but vile and black of heart. Now began a bad time for the poor step-child. "Is the stupid goose to sit in the parlor with us?" they said. "He who wants to eat bread must earn it; out with the kitchen-wench." They took her pretty clothes away from her, put an old grey bedgown on her, and gave her wooden shoes. "Just look at the proud princess, how decked out she is!" they cried, and laughed, and led her into the kitchen. There she had to do hard work from morning till night, get up before daybreak, carry water, light fires, cook and wash. Besides this, the sisters did her every imaginable injury—they mocked her and emptied her peas and lentils into the ashes, so that she was forced to sit and pick them out again. In the evening when she had worked till she was weary she had no bed to go to, but had to sleep by the hearth in the cinders. And as on that account she always looked dusty and dirty, they called her Cinderella.

It happened that the father was once going to the fair, and he asked his two step-daughters what he should bring back for them. "Beautiful dresses," said one, "pearls and jewels," said the second. "And you, Cinderella," said he, "what will you have?" "Father, break off for me the first branch which knocks against your hat on your way home." So he bought beautiful dresses, pearls and jewels for his two step-daughters, and on his way home, as he was riding through a green thicket, a hazel twig brushed against him and knocked off his hat. Then he broke off the branch and took it with him. When he reached home he gave his step-daughters the things which they had wished for, and to Cinderella he gave the branch from the hazel-bush. Cinderella thanked him, went to her mother's grave and planted the branch on it, and wept so much that the tears fell down on it and watered it. And it grew and became a handsome tree. Thrice a day Cinderella went and sat beneath it, and wept and prayed, and a little white bird always came on the tree, and if Cinderella expressed a wish, the bird threw down to her what she had wished for.

It happened, however, that the King gave orders for a festival which was to last three days, and to which all the beautiful young girls in the country were invited, in order that his son might choose

himself a bride. When the two step-sisters heard that they too were to appear among the number, they were delighted, called Cinderella and said: "Comb our hair for us, brush our shoes and fasten our buckles, for we are going to the wedding at the King's palace." Cinderella obeyed, but wept, because she too would have liked to go with them to the dance, and begged her step-mother to allow her to do so. "You go, Cinderella!" said she; "covered in dust and dirt as you are, and would go to the festival? You have no clothes and shoes, and yet would dance!" As, however, Cindrella went on asking, the step-mother said at last: "I have emptied a dish of lentils into the ashes for you, if you have picked them out

again in two hours, you shall go with us." The maiden went through
the backdoor into the garden, and called: "You tame pigeons, you
turtledoves, and all you birds beneath the sky, come and help me
to pick

> The good into the pot,
> The bad into the crop."

Then two white pigeons came in by the kitchen-window, and
afterwards the turtle-doves, and at last all the birds beneath the
sky, came whirring and crowding in, and alighted amongst the ashes.
And the pigeons nodded with their heads and began pick, pick,
pick, pick, and the rest began also pick, pick, pick, pick, and gathered all the good grains into the dish. Hardly had one hour passed
before they had finished, and all flew out again. Then the girl took
the dish to her step-mother, and was glad, and believed that now
she would be allowed to go with them to the festival. But the step-
mother said: "No, Cinderella, you have no clothes and you cannot
dance; you would only be laughed at." And as Cinderella wept at
this, the step-mother said: "If you can pick two dishes of lentils
out of the ashes for me in one hour, you shall go with us." And
she thought to herself: "That she most certainly cannot do again."
When the step-mother had emptied the two dishes of lentils amongst
the ashes, the maiden went through the back-door into the garden
and cried: "You tame pigeons, you turtle-doves, and all you birds
beneath the sky, come and help me to pick

> The good into the pot,
> The bad into the crop."

Then two white pigeons came in by the kitchen-window, and
afterwards the turtle-doves, and at length all the birds beneath the
sky, came whirring and crowding in, and alighted amongst the ashes.
And the doves nodded with their heads and began pick, pick, pick,
pick, and the others began also pick, pick, pick, pick, and gathered all the good seeds into the dishes, and before half an hour
was over they had already finished, and all flew out again. Then
the maiden carried the dishes to the step-mother and was de-

lighted, and believed that she might now go with them to the wedding. But the step-mother said: "All this will not help; you cannot go with us, for you have no clothes and cannot dance; we should be ashamed of you!" On this she turned her back on Cinderella, and hurried away with her two proud daughters.

As no one was now at home, Cinderella went to her mother's grave beneath the hazel-tree, and cried:

> "Shiver and quiver, little tree,
> Silver and gold throw down over me."

Then the bird threw a gold and silver dress down to her, and slippers embroidered with silk and silver. She put on the dress with all speed, and went to the wedding. Her step-sisters and the stepmother however did not know her, and thought she must be a foreign princess, for she looked so beautiful in the golden dress. They never once thought of Cinderella, and believed that she was sitting at home in the dirt, picking lentils out of the ashes. The prince approached her, took her by the hand and danced with her. He would dance with no other maiden, and never let loose of her hand, and if anyone else came to invite her, he said: "This is my partner."

She danced till it was evening, and then she wanted to go home. But the King's son said: "I will go with you and bear you company," for he wished to see to whom the beautiful maiden belonged. She escaped from him, however, and sprang into the pigeon-house. The King's son waited until her father came, and then he told him that the unknown maiden had leapt into the pigeon-house. The old man thought: "Can it be Cinderella?" and they had to bring him an axe and a pickaxe that he might hew the pigeon-house to pieces, but no one was inside it. And when they got home Cinderella lay in her dirty clothes among the ashes, and a dim little oil-lamp was burning on the mantle-piece, for Cinderella had jumped quickly down from the back of the pigeon-house and had run to the little hazel-tree, and there she had taken off her beautiful clothes and laid them on the grave, and the bird had taken them away again, and then she had seated herself in the kitchen amongst the ashes in her grey gown.

Next day when the festival began afresh, and her parents and the step-sisters had gone once more, Cinderella went to the hazel-tree and said:

> "Shiver and quiver, my little tree,
> Silver and gold throw down over me."

Then the bird threw down a much more beautiful dress than on the preceding day. And when Cinderella appeared at the wedding in this dress, everyone was astonished at her beauty. The King's son had waited until she came, and instantly took her by the hand and danced with no one but her. When others came and invited her, he said: "This is my partner." When evening came she wished to leave, and the King's son followed her and wanted to see into which house she went. But she sprang away from him, and into the garden behind the house. Therein stood a beautiful tall tree on which hung the most magnificent pears. She clambered so nimbly between the branches like a squirrel that the King's son did not know where she was gone. He waited until her father came, and said to him: "The unknown maiden has escaped from me, and I believe she has climbed up the pear-tree." The father thought: "Can it be Cinderella?" and had an axe brought and cut the tree down, but no one was on it. And when they got into the kitchen, Cinderella lay there among the ashes, as usual, for she had jumped down on the other side of the tree, had taken the beautiful dress to the bird on the little hazel-tree, and put on her grey gown.

On the third day, when the parents and sisters had gone away, Cinderella went once more to her mother's grave and said to the little tree:

> "Shiver and quiver, my little tree,
> Silver and gold throw down over me."

And now the bird threw down to her a dress which was more splendid and magnificent than any she had yet had, and the slippers were golden. And when she went to the festival in the dress, no one know how to speak for astonishment. The King's son danced with her only, and if anyone invited her to dance, he said: "This is my partner."

When evening came, Cinderella wished to leave, and the King's son was anxious to go with her, but she escaped from him so quickly that he could not follow her. The King's son, however, had employed a ruse, and had caused the whole staircase to be smeared with pitch, and there, when she ran down, had the maiden's left slipper remained stuck. The King's son picked it up, and it was small and dainty, and all golden. Next morning, he went with it to the father, and said to him: "No one shall be my wife but she whose foot this golden slipper fits." Then were the two sisters glad, for they had pretty feet. The eldest went with the shoe into her room and wanted to try it on, and her mother stood by. But she could not get her big toe into it, and the shoe was too small for her. Then her mother gave her a knife and said: "Cut the toe off; when you are Queen you will have no more need to go on foot." The maiden cut the toe off, forced the foot into the shoe, swallowed the pain, and went out to the King's son. Then he took her on his horse as his bride and rode away with her. They were obliged, however, to pass the grave, and there, on the hazel-tree, sat the two pigeons and cried:

> "Turn and peep, turn and peep,
> There's blood within the shoe,
> The shoe it is too small for her,
> The true bride waits for you."

Then he looked at her foot and saw how the blood was trickling from it. He turned his horse round and took the false bride home again, and said she was not the true one, and that the other sister was to put the shoe on. Then this one went into her chamber and got her toes safely into the shoe, but her heel was too large. So her mother gave her a knife and said: "Cut a bit off your heel; when you are Queen you will have no more need to go on foot." The maiden cut a bit off her heel, forced her foot into the shoe, swallowed the pain, and went out to the King's son. He took her on his horse as his bride, and rode away with her, but when they passed by the hazel-tree, the two little pigeons sat on it and cried:

"Turn and peep, turn and peep,
There's blood within the shoe,
The shoe it is too small for her,
The true bride waits for you."

He looked down at her foot and saw how the blood was running out of her shoe, and how it had stained her white stocking quite red. Then he turned his horse and took the false bride home again. "This also is not the right one," said he, "have you no other daughter?" "No," said the man, "there is still a little stunted kitchen-wench which my late wife left behind her, but she cannot possibly be the bride." The King's son said he was to send her up to him; but the mother answered: "Oh no, she is much too dirty, she cannot show herself!" But he absolutely insisted on it, and Cinderella had to be called. She first washed her hands and face clean, and then went and bowed down before the King's son, who gave her the golden shoe. Then she seated herself on a stool, drew her foot out of the heavy wooden shoe, and put it into the slipper, which fitted like a glove. And when she rose up and the King's son looked at her face he recognized the beautiful maiden who had danced with him and cried: "That is the true bride!" The step-mother and the two sisters were horrified and became pale with rage; he, however, took Cinderella on his horse and rode away with her. As they passed by the hazel-tree, the two white doves cried:

"Turn and peep, turn and peep,
No blood is in the shoe,
The shoe is not too small for her,
The true bride rides with you,"

and when they had cried that, the two came flying down and placed themselves on Cinderella's shoulders, one on the right, the other on the left, and remained sitting there.

When the wedding with the King's son was to be celebrated, the two false sisters came and hoped to gain favor with Cinderella and share her good fortune. When the betrothed couple went to church, the elder was at the right side and the younger at the left, and the pigeons pecked out one eye from each of them. Afterwards as they came back, the elder was at the left, and the younger at the right, and then the pigeons pecked out the other eye from each. And thus, for their wickedness and falsehood, they were punished with blindness all their days.

Mother Holle

There was once a widow who had two daughters—one of whom was pretty and industrious, whilst the other was ugly and idle. But she was much fonder of the ugly and idle one, because she was her own daughter; and the other, who was a step-daughter, was obliged to do all the work, and be the Cinderella of the house. Every day the poor girl had to sit by a well on the high road, and spin and spin till her fingers bled.

Now it happened that one day the shuttle was marked with her blood, so she dipped it in the well, to wash the mark off; but it dropped out of her hand and fell to the bottom. She began to weep and ran to her step-mother and told her of the mishap. But she scolded her sharply, and was so merciless as to say: "Since you have let the shuttle fall in, you must fetch it out again."

So the girl went back to the well, and did not know what to do; and in the sorrow of her heart she jumped into the well to get the shuttle. She lost her senses; and when she awoke and came to herself again, she was in a lovely meadow where the sun was shining and many thousands of flowers were growing. Across this meadow she went, and at last came to a baker's oven full of bread, and the bread cried out: "Oh, take me out! take me out! or I shall burn; I have been baked a long time!" So she went up to it, and took out all the loaves one after another with the bread-shovel. After that she went on till she came to a tree covered with apples, which called out to her: "Oh, shake me! shake me! we apples are all ripe!" So she shook the tree till the apples fell like rain, and went on shaking till they were all down, and when she had gathered them into a heap, she went on her way.

At last she came to a little house, out of which an old woman peeped; but she had such large teeth that the girl was frightened, and was about to run away. But the old woman called out to her:

"What are you afraid of, dear child? Stay with me; if you will do all the work in the house properly, you shall be the better for it. Only you must take care to make my bed well, and to shake it thoroughly till the feathers fly—for then there is snow on the earth. I am Mother Holle."

As the old woman spoke so kindly to her, the girl took courage and agreed to enter her service. She attended to everything to the satisfaction of her mistress, and always shook her bed so vigorously that the feathers flew about like snowflakes. So she had a pleasant life with her; never an angry word; and to eat she had boiled or roast meat every day.

She stayed some time with Mother Holle, before she became sad. At first she did not know what was the matter with her, but found at length that it was home-sickness: although she was many thousand times better off here than at home, still she had a longing to be there. At last she said to the old woman: "I have a longing for home; and however well off I am down here, I cannot stay any longer; I must go up again to my own people." Mother Holle said: "I am pleased that you long for your home again, and as you have served me so truly, I myself will take you up again." Thereupon she took her by the hand, and led her to a large door. The door was opened, and just as the maiden was standing beneath the doorway, a heavy shower of golden rain fell, and all the gold clung to her, so that she was completely covered over with it.

"You shall have that because you have been so industrious," said Mother Holle; and at the same time she gave her back the shuttle which she had let fall into the well. Thereupon the door closed, and the maiden found herself up above upon the earth, not far from her mother's house.

And as she went into the yard the cock was sitting on the well, and cried:

> "Cock-a-doodle-doo!
> Your golden girl's come back to you!"

So she went in to her mother, and as she arrived thus covered with gold, she was well received, both by her and her sister.

The girl told all that had happened to her; and as soon as the mother heard how she had come by so much wealth, she was very anxious to obtain the same good luck for the ugly and lazy daughter. She had to seat herself by the well and spin; and in order that her shuttle might be stained with blood, she stuck her hand into a thorn bush and pricked her finger. Then she threw her shuttle into the well, and jumped in after it.

She came, like the other, to the beautiful meadow and walked along the very same path. When she got to the oven the bread again cried: "Oh, take me out! take me out! or I shall burn; I have been baked a long time!" But the lazy thing answered: "As if I had any wish to make myself dirty!" and on she went. Soon she came to the apple-tree, which cried: "Oh, shake me! shake me! we apples are all ripe!" But she answered: "I like that! one of you might fall on my head," and so went on. When she came to Mother Holle's house she was not afraid, for she had already heard of her big teeth, and she hired herself out to her immediately.

The first day she forced herself to work diligently, and obeyed Mother Holle when she told her to do anything, for she was thinking of all the gold that she would give her. But on the second day she began to be lazy, and on the third day still more so, and then she would not get up in the morning at all. Neither did she make Mother Holle's bed as she ought, nor did she shake it so as to make the feathers fly up. Mother Holle was soon tired of this, and gave her notice to leave. The lazy girl was willing enough to go, and thought that now the golden rain would come. Mother Holle led her also to the great door; but while she was standing beneath it, instead of the gold a big kettleful of pitch was emptied over her. "That is the reward for your service," said Mother Holle, and shut the door.

So the lazy girl went home; but she was quite covered with pitch, and the cock on the well, as soon as he saw her, cried out:

> "Cock-a-doodle-doo!
> Your dirty girl's come back to you!"

But the pitch clung fast to her, and could not be got off as long as she lived.

The Seven Ravens

There was once a man who had seven sons, and still he had no daughter, however much he wished for one. At length his wife again gave him hope of a child, and when it came into the world it was a girl. His joy was great, but the child was sickly and small, and had to be privately baptized on account of its weakness. The father sent one of the boys in haste to the spring to fetch water for the baptism. The other six went with him, and as each of them wanted to be first to fill it, the jug fell into the well. There they stood and did not know what to do, and none of them dared to go home. As they still did not return, the father grew impatient, and said: "They have certainly forgotten it while playing some game, the wicked boys!" He became afraid that the girl would have to die without being baptized, and in his anger cried: "I wish the boys were all turned into ravens." Hardly was the word spoken before he heard a whirring of wings over his head, looked up and saw seven coal-black ravens flying away.

The parents could not withdraw the curse, and however sad they were at the loss of their seven sons, they still to some extent comforted themselves with their dear little daughter, who soon grew strong and every day became more beautiful. For a long time she did not know that she had had brothers, for her parents were careful not to mention them before her, but one day she accidentally heard some people saying of herself, that the girl was certainly beautiful, but that in reality she was to blame for the misfortune which had befallen her seven brothers. Then she was much troubled, and went to her father and mother and asked if it was true that she had had brothers, and what had become of them. The parents now dared keep the secret no longer, but said that what had befallen her brothers was the will of Heaven, and that her birth had only been the innocent cause. But the maiden took it to heart daily, and thought she must save her brothers. She had no rest or peace until she set out secretly, and went forth into the wide world to search for her brothers and set them free, let it cost what it might. She took nothing with her but a little ring belonging to her parents as a keepsake, a loaf of bread against hunger, a little pitcher of water against thirst, and a little chair as a provision against weariness.

And now she went continually onwards, far, far, to the very end of the world. Then she came to the sun, but it was too hot and terrible, and devoured little children. Hastily she ran away, and ran to the moon, but it was far too cold, and also awful and malicious, and when it saw the child, it said: "I smell, I smell the flesh of men." At this she ran swiftly away, and came to the stars, which were kind and good to her, and each of them sat on its own particular little chair. But the morning star arose, and gave her the drumstick of a chicken, and said: "If you have not that drumstick you can not open the Glass mountain, and in the Glass mountain are your brothers."

The maiden took the drumstick, wrapped it carefully in a cloth, and went onwards again until she came to the Glass mountain. The door was shut, and she thought she would take out the drumstick; but when she undid the cloth, it was empty, and she had lost the good star's present. What was she now to do? She wished to rescue her brothers, and had no key to the Glass mountain. The good sister took a knife, cut off one of her little fingers, put it in the door, and succeeded in opening it. When she had gone inside, a little dwarf came to meet her, who said: "My child, what are you looking for?" "I am looking for my brothers, the seven ravens," she replied. The dwarf said: "The lord ravens are not at home, but if you will wait here until they come, step in." Thereupon the little dwarf carried the ravens' dinner in, on seven little plates, and in seven little glasses, and the little sister ate a morsel from each plate, and from each little glass she took a sip, but in the last little glass she dropped the ring which she had brought away with her.

Suddenly she heard a whirring of wings and a rushing through the air, and then the little dwarf said: "Now the lord ravens are flying home." Then they came, and wanted to eat and drink, and looked for their little plates and glasses. Then said one after the other: "Who has eaten something from my plate? Who has drunk out of my little glass? It was a human mouth." And when the seventh came to the bottom of the glass, the ring rolled against his mouth. Then he looked at it, and saw that it was a ring belonging to his father and mother, and said: "God grant that our sister may be here, and then we shall be free." When the maiden, who was standing behind the door watching, heard that wish, she came forth, and on this all the ravens were restored to their human form again. And they embraced and kissed each other, and went joyfully home.

Little Red-Cap

Once upon a time there was a dear little girl who was loved by everyone who looked at her, but most of all by her grandmother, and there was nothing that she would not have given to the child. Once she gave her a little cap of red velvet, which suited her so well that she would never wear anything else; so she was always called 'Little Red-Cap.'

One day her mother said to her: "Come, Little Red-Cap, here is a piece of cake and a bottle of wine; take them to your grandmother, she is ill and weak, and they will do her good. Set out before it gets hot, and when you are going, walk briskly but do not run, and do not stray from the path, or you may fall and break the bottle, and then your grandmother will get nothing; and when you go into her room, don't forget to say, 'Good-morning,' and don't peep into every corner before you do it."

"I will take great care," said Little Red-Cap to her mother, and gave her her promise.

The grandmother lived out in the wood, half a league from the village, and just as Little Red-Cap entered the wood, a wolf met her. Red-Cap did not know what a wicked creature he was, and was not at all afraid of him.

"Good-day, Little Red-Cap," said he.

"Thank you kindly, wolf."

"Whither away so early, Little Red-Cap?"

"To my grandmother's."

"What have you got in your apron?"

"Cake and wine; yesterday was baking-day, so poor sick grandmother is to have something good, to make her stronger."

"Where does your grandmother live, Little Red-Cap?"

"A good quarter of a league farther on in the wood; her house stands under the three large oak-trees, the nut-trees are just below; you surely must know it," replied Little Red-Cap.

The wolf thought to himself: "What a tender young creature! what a nice plump mouthful—she will be better to eat than the old woman. I must act craftily, so as to catch both." So he walked for a short time by the side of Little Red-Cap, and then he said: "See, Little Red-Cap, how pretty the flowers are about here—why do you not look round? I believe, too, that you do not hear how sweetly the little birds are singing; you walk gravely along as if you were going to school, while everything else out here in the wood is merry."

Little Red-Cap raised her eyes, and when she saw the sunbeams dancing here and there through the trees, and pretty flowers growing everywhere, she thought: "Suppose I take grandmother a fresh nosegay; that would please her too. It is so early in the day that I shall still get there in good time"; and so she ran from the path into the wood to look for flowers. And whenever she had picked one, she fancied that she saw a still prettier one farther on, and ran after it, and so got deeper and deeper into the wood.

Meanwhile the wolf ran straight to the grandmother's house and knocked at the door.

"Who is there?"

"Little Red-Cap," replied the wolf. "She is bringing cake and wine; open the door."

"Lift the latch," called out the grandmother, "I am too weak, and cannot get up."

The wolf lifted the latch, the door sprang open, and without saying a word he went straight to the grandmother's bed, and devoured her. Then he put on her clothes, dressed himself in her cap, laid himself in bed and drew the curtains.

Little Red-Cap, however, had been running about picking flowers, and when she had gathered so many that she could carry no more, she remembered her grandmother, and set out on her way again.

She was surprised to find the cottage-door standing open, and when she went into the room, she had such a strange feeling that she said to herself: "Oh dear! how uneasy I feel to-day, and at other times I like being with grandmother so much." She called out: "Good morning," but received no answer; so she went to the bed and drew back the curtains. There lay her grandmother with her cap pulled far over her face, and looking very strange.

"Oh! grandmother," she said, "what big ears you have!"

"The better to hear you with, my child," was the reply.

"But, grandmother, what big eyes you have!" she said.

"The better to see you with, my dear."

"But, grandmother, what large hands you have!"

"The better to hug you with."

"Oh! but, grandmother, what a terrible big mouth you have!"

"The better to eat you with!"

And scarcely had the wolf said this, than with one bound he was out of bed and swallowed up Red-Cap.

When the wolf had appeased his appetite, he lay down again in the bed, fell asleep and began to snore very loud. The huntsman was just passing the house, and thought to himself: "How the old woman is snoring! I must just see if she wants anything." So he went into the room, and when he came to the bed, he saw that the wolf was lying in it. "Do I find you here, you old sinner!" said he. "I have long sought you!" Then just as he was going to fire at him, it occurred to him that the wolf might have devoured the grandmother, and that she might still be saved, so he did not fire, but took a pair of scissors, and began to cut open the stomach of the sleeping wolf. When he had made two snips, he saw the little Red-Cap shining, and then he made two snips more, and the little girl sprang out, crying: "Ah, how frightened I have been! How dark it was inside the wolf"; and after that the aged grandmother came out alive also, but scarcely able to breathe. Red-Cap, however, quickly fetched great stones with which they filled the wolf's belly, and when he awoke, he wanted to run away, but the stones were so heavy that he collapsed at once, and fell dead.

Then all three were delighted. The huntsman drew off the wolf's skin and went home with it; the grandmother ate the cake and drank the wine which Red-Cap had brought, and revived, but Red-Cap thought to herself: "As long as I live, I will never by myself leave the path, to run into the wood, when my mother has forbidden me to do so."

It is also related that once when Red-Cap was again taking cakes to the old grandmother, another wolf spoke to her, and tried to entice her from the path. Red-Cap, however, was on her guard, and went straight forward on her way, and told her grandmother that she had met the wolf, and that he had said "good-morning" to her, but with such a wicked look in his eyes, that if they had not been on the public road she was certain he would have eaten her up. "Well," said the grandmother, "we will shut the door, that he may not come in." Soon afterwards the wolf knocked, and cried:

"Open the door, grandmother, I am little Red-Cap, and am bringing you some cakes." But they did not speak, or open the door, so the greybeard stole twice or thrice round the house, and at last jumped on the roof, intending to wait until Red-Cap went home in the evening, and then to steal after her and devour her in the darkness. But the grandmother saw what was in his thoughts. In front of the house was a great stone trough, so she said to the child: "Take the pail, Red-Cap; I made some sausages yesterday, so carry the water in which I boiled them to the trough." Red-Cap carried until the great trough was quite full. Then the smell of the sausages reached the wolf, and he sniffed and peeped down, and at last stretched out his neck so far that he could no longer keep his footing and began to slip, and slipped down from the roof straight into the great trough, and was drowned. But Red-Cap went joyously home, and no one ever did anything to harm her again.

The Bremen Town-Musicians

A certain man had a donkey, which had carried the corn-sacks to the mill untiringly for many a long year; but his strength was going, and he was growing more and more unfit for work. Then his master began to consider how he might best save his keep; but the donkey, seeing that no good wind was blowing, ran away and set out on the road to Bremen. "There," he thought, "I can surely be town-musician." When he had walked some distance, he found a hound lying on the road, gasping like one who had run till he was tired. "What are you gasping so for, you big fellow?" asked the donkey.

"Ah," replied the hound, "As I am old, and daily grow weaker, and no longer can hunt, my master wanted to kill me, so I took to flight; but now how am I to earn my bread?"

"I tell you what," said the donkey, "I am going to Bremen, and shall be town-musician there; go with me and engage yourself also as a musician. I will play the lute, and you shall beat the kettle-drum."

The hound agreed, and on they went.

Before long they came to a cat, sitting on the path, with a face like three rainy days! "Now then, old shaver, what has gone askew with you?" asked the donkey.

"Who can be merry when his neck is in danger?" answered the cat. "Because I am now getting old, and my teeth are worn to stumps, and I prefer to sit by the fire and spin, rather than hunt about after mice, my mistress wanted to drown me, so I ran away. But now good advice is scarce. Where am I to go?"

"Go with us to Bremen. You understand night-music, so you can be a town-musician."

The cat thought well of it, and went with them. After this the three fugitives came to a farm-yard, where the cock was sitting upon the gate, crowing with all his might. "Your crowing is piercing my ears," said the donkey. "What is the matter?"

"I have been foretelling fine weather, because it is the day on which Our Lady washes the Christ-child's little shirts, and wants to dry them," said the cock; "but guests are coming for Sunday, so the housewife has no pity, and has told the cook that she intends to eat me in the soup to-morrow, and this evening I am to have my head cut off. Now I am crowing at the top of my lungs while still I can."

"Ah, but red-comb," said the donkey, "you had better come away with us. We are going to Bremen; you can find something better than death everywhere: you have a good voice, and if we make music together it must have some quality!"

The cock agreed to this plan, and all four went on together. They could not reach the city of Bremen in one day, however, and in the evening they came to a forest where they meant to pass the night. The donkey and the hound laid themselves down under a large tree, the cat and the cock settled themselves in the branches; but the cock flew right to the top, where he was most safe. Before he went to sleep he looked round on all four sides, and thought he saw in the distance a little spark burning; so he called out to his companions that there must be a house not far off, for he saw a light. The donkey said: "If so, we had better get up and go on, for the shelter here is bad." The hound thought too that a few bones with some meat on them would do him good!

So they made their way to the place where the light was, and soon saw it shine brighter and grow larger, until they came to a well-lighted robbers' house. The donkey, as the biggest, went to the window and looked in.

"What do you see, my grey-horse?" asked the cock. "What do I see?" answered the donkey; "a table covered with good things to eat and drink, and robbers sitting at it enjoying themselves." "That would be the sort of thing for us," said the cock. "Yes, yes; ah, if only we were there!" said the donkey.

Then the animals took counsel together how they should manage to drive away the robbers, and at last they thought of a plan. The donkey was to place himself with his fore-feet upon the window-ledge, the hound was to jump on the donkey's back, the cat was to climb upon the dog, and lastly the cock was to fly up and perch upon the head of the cat.

When this was done, at a given signal, they began to perform their music together: the donkey brayed, the hound barked, the cat mewed, and the cock crowed; then they burst through the window into the room, shattering the glass! At this horrible din, the robbers sprang up, thinking no otherwise than that a ghost had come in, and fled in a great fright out into the forest. The four companions now sat down at the table, well content with what was left, and ate as if they were going to fast for a month.

As soon as the four minstrels had done, they put out the light, and each sought for himself a sleeping-place according to his nature and to what suited him. The donkey laid himself down upon some straw in the yard, the hound behind the door, the cat upon the hearth near the warm ashes, and the cock perched himself upon a beam of the roof; and being tired from their long walk, they soon went to sleep.

When it was past midnight, and the robbers saw from afar that the light was no longer burning in their house, and all appeared quiet, the captain said: "We ought not to have let ourselves be frightened out of our wits"; and ordered one of them to go and examine the house.

The messenger finding all still, went into the kitchen to light a candle, and, taking the glistening fiery eyes of the cat for live coals, he held a lucifer-match to them to light it. But the cat did not understand the joke, and flew in his face, spitting and scratching. He was dreadfully frightened, and ran to the back-door, but the dog, who lay there, sprang up and bit his leg; and as he ran across the yard by the dunghill, the donkey gave him a smart kick with its hind foot. The cock, too, who had been awakened by the noise, and had become lively, cried down from the beam: "Cock-a-doodle-doo!"

Then the robber ran back as fast as he could to his captain, and said: "Ah, there is a horrible witch sitting in the house, who spat on me and scratched my face with her long claws; and by the door stands a man with a knife, who stabbed me in the leg; and in the yard there lies a black monster, who beat me with a wooden club; and above, upon the roof, sits the judge, who called out, 'Bring the rogue here to me!' so I got away as well as I could."

After this the robbers never again dared enter the house; but it suited the four musicians of Bremen so well that they did not care to leave it any more. And the mouth of him who last told this story is still warm.

The Girl Without Hands

A certain miller had little by little fallen into poverty, and had nothing left but his mill and a large apple-tree behind it. Once when he had gone into the forest to fetch wood, an old man stepped up to him whom he had never seen before, and said: "Why do you plague yourself with cutting wood, I will make you rich, if you will promise me what is standing behind your mill." "What can that be but my apple-tree?" thought the miller, and said: "Yes," and gave a written promise to the stranger. He, however, laughed mockingly and said: "When three years have passed, I will come and carry away what belongs to me," and then he went. When the miller got home, his wife came to meet him and said: "Tell me, miller, from whence comes this sudden wealth into our house? All at once every box and chest was filled; no one brought it in, and I know not how it happened." He answered: "It comes from a stranger who met me in the forest, and promised me great treasure. I, in return, have promised him what stands behind the mill; we can very well give him the big apple-tree for it." "Ah, husband," said the terrified wife, "that must have been the Devil! He did not mean the apple-tree, but our daughter, who was standing behind the mill sweeping the yard."

The miller's daughter was a beautiful, pious girl, and lived through the three years in the fear of God and without sin. When therefore the time was over, and the day came when the Evil One was to fetch her, she washed herself clean, and made a circle round herself with chalk. The Devil appeared quite early, but he could not come near to her. Angrily, he said to the miller: "Take all water away from her, that she may no longer be able to wash herself, for otherwise I have no power over her." The miller was afraid, and did so. The next morning the Devil came again, but she had wept on her hands, and they were quite clean. Again he could not get near her, and furiously said to the miller: "Cut her hands off, or else I have no power over her." The miller was shocked and answered: "How could I cut off my own child's hands?" Then the Evil One threatened him and said: "If you do not do it you are mine, and I will take you yourself." The father became alarmed, and promised to obey him. So he went to the girl and said: "My child, if I do not cut off both your hands, the Devil will carry me away, and in my terror I have promised to do it. Help me in my need, and forgive me the harm I do you." She replied: "Dear father, do with me what you will, I am your child." Thereupon she laid down both her hands, and let them be cut off. The Devil came for the third time, but she had wept so long and so much on the stumps, that after all they were quite clean. Then he had to give in, and had lost all right over her.

The miller said to her: "I have by means of you received such great wealth that I will keep you most handsomely as long as you live." But she replied: "Here I cannot stay, I will go forth, compassionate people will give me as much as I require." Thereupon she caused her maimed arms to be bound to her back, and by sunrise she set out on her way, and walked the whole day until night fell. Then she came to a royal garden, and by the shimmering of the moon she saw that trees covered with beautiful fruits grew in it, but she could not enter, for it was surrounded by water. And as she had walked the whole day and not eaten one mouthful, and hunger tormented her, she thought: "Ah, if I were but inside, that I might eat of the fruit, else must I die of hunger!" Then she knelt down, called on the Lord God, and prayed. And suddenly an angel came down to her and made a dam in the water, so that the moat became dry and she could walk through it. And now she went into the garden and the angel went with her. She saw a tree covered with beautiful pears, but they were all counted. Then she went to them, and to still her hunger, ate one with her mouth from the tree, but no more. The gardener was watching; but as the angel was standing by, he was afraid and thought the maiden was a spirit, and was silent; he did not dare to cry out or to speak to the spirit. When she had eaten the pear, she was satisfied, and went and concealed herself among the bushes. The King to whom the garden belonged came down to it the next morning, and counting his pears, saw that one was missing, and asked the gardener what had become of it, as it was not lying beneath the tree, but was gone. Then answered the gardener: "Last night, a spirit came in, who had no hands, and ate off one of the pears with its mouth." The King said: "How did the spirit get over the water, and where did it go after it had eaten the pear?" The gardener answered: "Someone came in a snow-white garment from heaven who made a dam, and kept back the water, that the spirit might walk through the moat. And as it must have been an angel, I was afraid, and asked no questions, and did not cry out. When the spirit had eaten the pear, it went back again." The King said: "If it be as you say, I will watch with you to-night."

When it grew dark the King came into the garden and brought a priest with him, who was to speak to the spirit. All three seated themselves beneath the tree and watched. At midnight the maiden came creeping out of the thicket, went to the tree, and again ate one pear off it with her mouth, and beside her stood the angel in white garments. Then the priest went out to them and said: "Do you come from heaven or from earth? Are you a spirit, or a human being?" She replied: "I am no spirit, but an unhappy mortal deserted by all but God." The King said: "If you are forsaken by all the world, yet will I not forsake you." He took her with him into his royal palace, and as she was so beautiful and good, he loved her with all his heart, had silver hands made for her, and took her to wife.

After a year the King had to go on a journey, so he commended his young Queen to the care of his mother and said: "If she is brought to child-bed take care of her, nurse her well, and tell me of it at once in a letter." Then she gave birth to a fine boy. So the old mother made haste to write and announce the joyful news to him. But the messenger rested by a brook on the way, and as he was fatigued by the great distance, he fell asleep. Then came the Devil, who was always seeking to injure the good Queen, and exchanged the letter for another, in which was written that the Queen had brought a monster into the world. When the King read the letter he was shocked and much troubled, but he wrote in answer that they were to take great care of the Queen and nurse her well until his arrival. The messenger went back with the letter, but rested at the same place and again fell asleep. Then came the Devil once more, and put a different letter in his pocket, in which it was written that they were to put the Queen and her child to death. The old mother was terribly shocked when she received the letter, and could not believe it. She wrote back again to the King, but received no other answer, because each time the Devil substituted a false letter, and in the last letter it was also written that she was to preserve the Queen's tongue and eyes as a token that she had obeyed.

But the old mother wept to think such innocent blood was to be shed, and had a hind brought by night and cut out her tongue and eyes, and kept them. Then said she to the Queen: "I cannot have you killed as the King commands, but here you may stay no longer. Go forth into the wide world with your child, and never come here again." The poor woman tied her child on her back, and went away with eyes full of tears. She came into a great wild forest, and then she fell on her knees and prayed to God, and the angel of the Lord appeared to her and led her to a little house on which was a sign with the words: "Here all dwell free." A snow-white maiden came out of the little house and said: "Welcome, Lady Queen," and conducted her inside. Then she unbound the little boy from her back, and held him to her breast that he might feed, and laid him in a beautifully-made little bed. Then said the poor woman: "From whence do you know that I was a queen?" The white maiden answered: "I am an angel sent by God, to watch over you and your child." The Queen stayed seven years in the little house, and was well cared for, and by God's grace, because of her piety, her hands which had been cut off grew once more.

At last the King came home again from his journey, and his first wish was to see his wife and the child. Then his aged mother began to weep and said: "You wicked man, why did you write to me that I was to take those two innocent lives?" and she showed him the two letters which the Evil One had forged, and then continued: "I did as you bade me," and she showed the tokens, the tongue and eyes. Then the King began to weep for his poor wife and his little son so much more bitterly than she was doing, that the aged mother had compassion on him and said: "Be at peace, she still lives; I secretly caused a hind to be killed, and took these tokens from it; but I bound the child to your wife's back and bade her go forth into the wide world, and made her promise never to come back here again, because you were so angry with her." Then spoke the King: "I will go as far as the sky is blue, and will neither eat nor drink until I have found again my dear wife and my child, if in the meantime they have not been killed, or died of hunger."

Thereupon the King traveled about for seven long years, and sought her in every cleft of the rocks and in every cave, but he found her not, and thought she had died of want. During the whole of this time he neither ate nor drank, but God supported him. At length he came into a great forest, and found therein the little house whose sign was, "Here all dwell free." Then forth came the white maiden, took him by the hand, led him in, and said: "Welcome, Lord King," and asked him from whence he came. He answered: "Soon shall I have traveled about for the space of seven years, and I seek my wife and her child, but cannot find them." The angel offered him meat and drink, but he did not take anything, and only wished to rest a little. Then he lay down to sleep, and laid a handkerchief over his face.

Thereupon the angel went into the chamber where the Queen sat with her son, whom she usually called "Sorrowful," and said to her: "Go out with your child, your husband has come." So she went to the place where he lay, and the handkerchief fell from his face. Then said she: "Sorrowful, pick up your father's handkerchief, and cover his face again." The child picked it up, and put it over his face again. The King in his sleep heard what passed, and had pleasure in letting the handkerchief fall once more. But the child grew impatient, and said: "Dear mother, how can I cover my father's face when I have no father in this world? I have learnt to say the prayer, 'Our Father, who art in Heaven,' you have told me that my father was in Heaven, and was the good God, and how can I know a wild man like this? He is not my father." When the King heard that, he got up, and asked who they were. Then said she: "I am your wife, and this is your son, Sorrowful." And he saw her living hands, and said: "My wife had silver hands." She answered: "The good God has caused my natural hands to grow again"; and the angel went into the inner room, and brought the silver hands, and showed them to him. Hereupon he knew for a certainty that it was his dear wife and his dear child, and he kissed them, and was glad, and said: "A heavy stone has fallen from off my heart." Then the angel of God ate with them once again, and after that they went home to the King's aged mother. There were great rejoicings everywhere, and the King and Queen were married again, and lived contentedly to their happy end.

Clever Elsie

There was once a man who had a daughter who was called Clever Elsie. And when she had grown up her father said: "We will get her married." "Yes," said the mother, "if only someone would come who would have her." At length there came a man from afar by the name of Hans who wooed her, but he stipulated that Clever Elsie should be really smart. "Oh," said the father, "she has plenty of good sense"; and the mother said: "Oh, she can see the wind coming up the street, and hear the flies coughing." "Well," said Hans, "if she is not really smart, I won't have her." When they were sitting at dinner and had eaten, the mother said: "Elsie, go into the cellar and fetch some beer." Then Clever Elsie took the pitcher from the wall, went into the cellar, and tapped the lid briskly as she went, so that the time might not appear long. When she was below she fetched herself a chair, and set it before the barrel so that she had no need to stoop, and did not hurt her back or do herself any unexpected injury. Then she placed the can before her, and turned the tap, and while the beer was running she would not let her eyes be idle, but looked up at the wall, and after much peering here and there, saw a pick-axe exactly above her, which the masons had accidentally left there.

Then Clever Elsie began to weep and said: "If I get Hans, and we have a child, and he grows big, and we send him into the cellar here to draw beer, then the pick-axe might fall on his head and kill him." Then she sat and wept and screamed with all the strength of her body, over the misfortune which lay before her. Those up-

stairs waited for the drink, but Clever Elsie still did not come. Then
the woman said to the servant: "Just go down into the cellar and
see where Elsie is." The maid went and found her sitting in front
of the barrel, screaming loudly. "Elsie, why do you weep?" asked
the maid. "Ah," she answered, "have I not reason to weep? If I
get Hans, and we have a child, and he grows big, and has to draw
beer here, the pick-axe will perhaps fall on his head, and kill him."
Then said the maid: "What a clever Elsie we have!" and sat down
beside her and began loudly to weep over the misfortune. After a
while, as the maid did not come back, and those upstairs were
thirsty for the beer, the man said to the boy: "Just go down into
the cellar and see where Elsie and the girl are." The boy went down,
and there sat Clever Elsie and the girl both weeping together. Then
he asked: "Why are you weeping?" "Ah," said Elsie, "have I not
reason to weep? If I get Hans, and we have a child, and he grows
big, and has to draw beer here, the pick-axe will fall on his head
and kill him." Then said the boy: "What a clever Elsie we have!"
and sat down by her, and likewise began to howl loudly. Upstairs
they waited for the boy, but as he still did not return, the man said
to the woman: "Just go down into the cellar and see where Elsie
is!" The woman went down, and found all three in the midst of
their lamentations, and inquired what was the cause; then Elsie told
her also that her future child was to be killed by the pick-axe, when
it grew big and had to draw beer, and the pick-axe fell down. Then
said the mother likewise: "What a clever Elsie we have!" and sat
down and wept with them. The man upstairs waited a short time,
but as his wife did not come back and his thirst grew ever greater,
he said: "I must go into the cellar myself and see where Elsie is."
But when he got into the cellar, and they were all sitting together
crying, and he heard the reason, and that Elsie's child was the cause,
and that Elsie might perhaps bring one into the world some day,
and that he might be killed by the pick-axe, if he should happen
to be sitting beneath it, drawing beer just at the very time when it
fell down, he cried: "Oh, what a clever Elsie!" and sat down, and
likewise wept with them. The bridegroom stayed upstairs alone for
a long time; then as no one would come back he thought: "They
must be waiting for me below: I too must go there and see what
they are about." When he got down, the five of them were sitting
screaming and lamenting quite piteously, each out-doing the other.

"What misfortune has happened then?" asked he. "Ah, dear Hans," said Elsie, "if we marry each other and have a child, and he is big, and we perhaps send him here to draw something to drink, then the pick-axe which has been left up there might dash his brains out if it were to fall down, so have we not reason to weep?" "Come," said Hans, "more understanding than that is not needed for my household, as you are such a clever Elsie, I will have you," and he seized her hand, took her upstairs with him, and married her.

After Hans had had her some time, he said: "Wife, I am going out to work and earn some money for us; go into the field and cut the corn that we may have some bread." "Yes, dear Hans, I will do that." After Hans had gone away, she cooked herself some good broth and took it into the field with her. When she came to the field she said to herself: "What shall I do; shall I cut first, or shall I eat first? Oh, I will eat first." Then she drank her cup of broth, and when she was fully satisfied, she once more said: "What shall I do? Shall I cut first, or shall I sleep first? I will sleep first." Then she lay down among the corn and fell asleep. Hans had been at home for a long time, but Elsie did not come; then said he: "What a clever Elsie I have; she is so industrious that she does not even come home to eat." But when evening came and she still stayed away, Hans went out to see what she had cut, but nothing was cut, and she was lying among the corn asleep. Then Hans hastened home and brought a fowler's net with little bells and hung it round about her, and she still went on sleeping. Then he ran home, shut the house-door, and sat down in his chair and worked. At length, when it was quite dark, Clever Elsie awoke and when she got up there was a jingling all round about her, and the bells rang at each step which she took. Then she was alarmed, and became uncertain whether she really was Clever Elsie or not, and said: "Is it I, or is it not I?" But she knew not what answer to make to this, and stood for a time in doubt; at length she thought: "I will go home and ask if it be I, or if it be not I, they will be sure to know." She ran to the door of her own house, but it was shut; then she knocked at the window and cried: "Hans, is Elsie within?" "Yes," answered Hans, "she is within." Hereupon she was terrified, and said: "Ah, heavens! Then it is not I," and went to another door; but when the people heard the jingling of the bells they would not open it, and she could get in nowhere. Then she ran out of the village, and no one has seen her since.

The Wishing-Table, the Gold-Ass, and the Cudgel in the Sack

There was once upon a time a tailor who had three sons, and only one goat. But as the goat supported all of them with her milk, she was obliged to have good food, and to be taken every day to pasture. The sons did this, in turn. Once the eldest took her to the churchyard, where the finest herbs were to be found, and let her eat and run about there. At night when it was time to go home he asked: "Goat, have you had enough?" The goat answered:

> "I have eaten so much,
> Not a leaf more I'll touch, meh! meh!"

"Come home, then," said the youth, and took hold of the cord round her neck, led her into the stable and tied her up securely. "Well," said the old tailor, "has the goat had as much food as she ought?" "Oh," answered the son, "she has eaten so much, not a leaf more she'll touch." But the father wished to satisfy himself, and went down to the stable, stroked the dear animal and asked: "Goat, are you satisfied?" The goat answered:

> "How should I be satisfied?
> Among the ditches I leapt about,
> Found no leaf, so went without, meh! meh!"

"What do I hear?" cried the tailor, and ran upstairs and said to the youth: "Hi, you liar; you said the goat had had enough, and have let her hunger!" and in his anger he took the yard-measure from the wall, and drove him out with blows.

Next day it was the turn of the second son, who sought a place in the fence of the garden, where nothing but good herbs grew, and the goat gobbled them all up. At night when he wanted to go home, he asked: "Goat, are you satisfied?" The goat answered:

> "I have eaten so much,
> Not a leaf more I'll touch, meh! meh!"

"Come home, then," said the youth, and led her home, and tied her up in the stable. "Well," said the old tailor, "has the goat had as much food as she ought?" "Oh," answered the son, "she has eaten so much, not a leaf more she'll touch." The tailor would not rely on this, but went down to the stable and said: "Goat, have you had enough?" The goat answered:

> "How should I be satisfied?
> Among the ditches I leapt about,
> Found no leaf, so went without, meh! meh!"

"The godless wretch!" cried the tailor, "to let such a good animal hunger," and he ran up and drove the youth out of doors with the yard-measure.

Now came the turn of the third son, who wanted to do his duty well, and sought out some bushes with the finest leaves, and let the goat devour them. In the evening when he wanted to go home, he asked: "Goat, have you had enough?" The goat answered:

> "I have eaten so much,
> Not a leaf more I'll touch, meh! meh!"

"Come home, then," said the youth, and led her into the stable, and tied her up. "Well," said the old tailor, "has the goat had her full share of food?" "She has eaten so much, not a leaf more she'll touch." The tailor was distrustful, went down and asked: "Goat, have you had enough?" The wicked beast answered:

> "How should I be satisfied?
> Among the ditches I leapt about,
> Found no leaf, so went without, meh! meh!"

"Oh, the brood of liars!" cried the tailor, "each as wicked and forgetful of his duty as the other! You shall no longer make a fool of me," and, quite beside himself with anger, he ran upstairs and belabored the poor young fellow so vigorously with the yard-measure that he sprang out of the house.

The old tailor was now alone with his goat. Next morning he went down into the stable, stroked the goat and said: "Come, my dear little animal, I myself will take you to feed." He took her by the rope and conducted her to green hedges, and amongst milfoil, and whatever else goats like to eat. "There you may for once eat to your heart's content," said he to her, and let her browse till evening. Then he asked: "Goat, are you satisfied?" she replied:

"I have eaten so much,
Not a leaf more I'll touch, meh! meh!"

"Come home, then," said the tailor, and led her into the stable, and tied her fast. When he was going away, he turned round again and said: "Well, are you satisfied for once?" But the goat behaved no better to him, and cried:

"How should I be satisfied?
Among the ditches I leapt about,
Found no leaf, so went without, meh! meh!"

When the tailor heard that, he was shocked, and saw clearly that he had driven away his three sons without cause. "Wait, you ungrateful creature," cried he, "it is not enough to drive you forth, I will brand you so that you will no more dare to show yourself amongst honest tailors." In great haste he ran upstairs, fetched his razor, lathered the goat's head, and shaved her as clean as the palm of his hand. And as the yard-measure would have been too good for her, he brought the horsewhip, and gave her such cuts with it that she bounded away with tremendous leaps.

When the tailor was thus left quite alone in his house he fell into great grief, and would gladly have had his sons back again, but no one knew whither they were gone. The eldest had apprenticed himself to a joiner, and learnt industriously and untiringly, and when the time came for him to go traveling, his master presented him with a little table which was not particularly beautiful, and was made of common wood, but which had one good property; if anyone set it out, and said: "Little table, spread yourself," the good little table was at once covered with a clean little cloth, and a plate was there, and a knife and fork beside it, and dishes with boiled meats and roasted meats, as many as there was room for, and a great glass of red wine shone so that it made the heart glad. The young journeyman thought: "With this you have enough for your whole life," and went joyously about the world and never troubled himself at all whether an inn was good or bad, or if anything was to be found in it or not. When it suited him he did not enter an inn at all, but either on the plain, in a wood, a meadow, or wherever he fancied, he took his little table off his back, set it down before him, and said: "Spread yourself," and then everything appeared that his heart desired. At length he took it into his head to go back to his father, whose anger would now be appeased, and who would now willingly receive him with his magic table. It came to pass that on his way home, he came one evening to an inn which was filled with guests. They bade him welcome, and invited him to sit and eat with them, for otherwise he would have difficulty in getting anything. "No," answered the joiner, "I will not take the few morsels out of your mouths; rather than that, you shall be my guests." They laughed, and thought he was jesting with them; he but placed his wooden table in the middle of the room, and said, "Little table, spread yourself." Instantly it was covered with food, so good that the host could never have procured it, and the smell of it ascended pleasantly to the nostrils of the guests. "Fall to, dear friends," said the joiner; and the guests when they saw that he meant it, did not need to be asked twice, but drew near, pulled out their knives and attacked it valiantly. And what surprised them the most was that when a dish became empty, a full one instantly took its place of its own accord. The innkeeper stood in one corner and watched the affair; he did not at all know what to say, but thought: "You could easily find a use for such a cook as that in your household." The joiner and his comrades made merry until late into the night; at length they lay down to sleep, and the young apprentice also went to bed, and set his magic table against the wall. The host's thoughts, however, let him have no rest; it occurred to him that there was a little old table in his lumber-room, which looked just like the apprentice's, and he brought it out, and carefully exchanged it for the wishing table. Next morning, the joiner paid for his bed, took up his table, never thinking that he had got a false one, and went his way. At midday he reached his father, who received him with great joy. "Well, my dear son, what have you learnt?" said he to him. "Father, I have become a joiner."

"A good trade," replied the old man; "but what have you brought back with you from your apprenticeship?" "Father, the best thing which I have brought back with me is this little table." The tailor inspected it on all sides and said: "You did not make a masterpiece when you made that; it is a bad old table." "But it is a table which furnishes itself," replied the son. "When I set it out, and tell it to spread itself, the most beautiful dishes stand on it, and a wine also, which gladdens the heart. Just invite all our relations and friends, they shall refresh and enjoy themselves for once, for the table will give them all they require." When the company was assembled, he put his table in the middle of the room and said: "Little table, spread yourself," but the little table did not bestir itself, and remained just as bare as any other table which does not understand language. Then the poor apprentice became aware that his table had been changed, and was ashamed at having to stand there like a liar. The relations, however, mocked him, and were forced to go home without having eaten or drunk. The father brought out his patches again, and went on tailoring, but the son went to a master in the craft.

The second son had gone to a miller and had apprenticed himself to him. When his years were over, the master said: "As you have conducted yourself so well, I give you an ass of a peculiar kind, which neither draws a cart nor carries a sack." "What good is he, then?" asked the young apprentice. "He spews forth gold," answered the miller. "If you set him on a cloth and say 'Bricklebrit,' the good animal will spew forth gold pieces for you from back and front." "That is a fine thing," said the apprentice, and thanked the master, and went out into the world. When he had need of gold, he had only to say "Bricklebrit" to his ass, and it rained gold pieces, and he had nothing to do but pick them off the ground. Wheresoever he went, the best of everything was good enough for him, and the dearer the better, for he had always a full purse. When he had looked about the world for some time, he thought: "You must seek out your father. If you go to him with the gold-ass he will forget his anger, and receive you well." It came to pass that he came to the same inn in which his brother's table had been exchanged. He led his ass by the bridle, and the host was about to take the animal from him and tie him up, but the young apprentice said: "Don't trouble yourself, I will take my grey horse into the stable, and tie him up myself too, for I must know where he stands." This struck the host as odd, and he thought that a man who was forced to look after his ass himself, could not have much to spend; but when the stranger put his hand in his pocket and brought out two gold pieces, and said he was to provide something good for him, the host opened his eyes wide, and ran and sought out the best he could muster. After dinner the guest asked what he owed. The host did not see why he should not double the reckoning, and said the apprentice must give two more gold pieces. He felt in his pocket, but his gold was just at an end. "Wait an instant, sir host," said he, "I will go and fetch some money"; but he took the table-cloth with him. The host could not imagine what this could mean, and being curious, stole after him, and as the guest bolted the stable door, he peeped through a hole left by a knot in the wood. The stranger spread out the cloth under the animal and cried: "Bricklebrit," and immediately the beast began to let gold pieces fall from back and front, so that it fairly rained down money on the ground. "Eh, my word," said the host, "ducats are quickly coined there! A purse like that is not to be sniffed at!" The guest paid his score, and went to bed, but in the night the host stole down into the stable, led away the master of the mint, and tied up another ass in his place.

Early next morning the apprentice traveled away with his ass, and thought that he had his gold-ass. At mid-day he reached his father, who rejoiced to see him again, and gladly took him in. "What have you made of yourself, my son?" asked the old man. "A miller, dear father," he answered. "What have you brought back with you from your travels?" "Nothing else but an ass." "There are asses enough here," said the father, "I would rather have had a a good goat." "Yes," replied the son, "but it is no common ass, but a gold-ass. When I say 'Bricklebrit,' the good beast spews forth a whole sheetful of gold pieces. Just summon all our relations hither, and

I will make them rich folks." "That suits me well," said the tailor, "for then I shall have no need to torment myself any longer with the needle," and ran out himself and called the relations together. As soon as they were assembled, the miller bade them make way, spread out his cloth, and brought the ass into the room. "Now watch," said he, and cried: "Bricklebrit," but what fell were not gold pieces, and it was clear that the animal knew nothing of the art, for every ass does not attain such perfection. Then the poor miller pulled a long face, saw that he was betrayed, and begged pardon of the relatives, who went home as poor as they came. There was no help for it, the old man had to betake him to his needle once more, and the youth hired himself to a miller.

The third brother had apprenticed himself to a turner, and as that is skilled labor, he was the longest in learning. His brothers, however, told him in a letter how badly things had gone with them, and how the innkeeper had cheated them of their beautiful wishing-gifts on the last evening before they reached home. When the turner had served his time, and had to set out on his travels, as he had conducted himself so well, his master presented him with a sack and said: "There is a cudgel in it." "I can put on the sack," said he, "and it may be of good service to me, but why should the cudgel be in it? It only makes it heavy." "I will tell you why," replied the master; "if anyone has done anything to injure you, do but say 'Out of the sack, Cudgel!' and the cudgel will leap forth among the people, and play such a dance on their backs that they will not be able to stir or move for a week, and it will not leave off until you say, 'Into the sack, Cudgel!' " The apprentice thanked him, put the sack on his back, and when anyone came too near him, and wished to attack him, he said: "Out of the sack, Cudgel!" and instantly the cudgel sprang out, and dusted the coat or jacket of one after the other on their backs, and never stopped until it had stripped it off them, and it was done so quickly, that before anyone was aware, it was already his own turn. In the evening the young turner reached the inn where his brothers had been cheated. He laid his sack on the table before him, and began to talk of all the wonderful things which he had seen in the world. "Yes," said he, "people may easily find a table which will spread itself, a gold-ass, and things of that kind—extremely good things which I by no means despise—but these are nothing in comparison with the treasure which I have won for myself, and am carrying about with me in my sack there." The innkeeper pricked up his ears. "What in the world can that be?" thought he; "the sack must be filled with nothing but jewels; I ought to get them cheap too, for all good things go in threes." When it was time for sleep, the guest stretched himself on the bench, and laid his sack beneath him for a pillow. When the innkeeper thought his guest was lying in a sound sleep, he went to him and pushed and pulled quite gently and carefully at the sack to see if he could possibly draw it away and lay another in its place. The turner, however, had been waiting for this for a long time, and now just as the innkeeper was about to give a hearty tug, he cried: "Out of the sack, Cudgel!" Instantly the little cudgel came forth, and fell on the innkeeper, and gave him a sound thrashing.

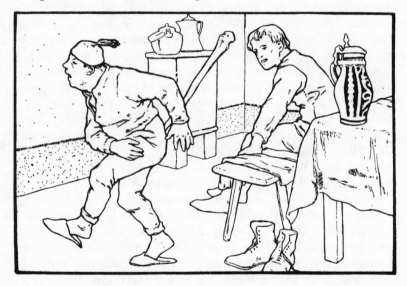

The host cried for mercy; but the louder he cried, the harder the cudgel beat the time on his back, until at length he fell to the ground exhausted. Then the turner said: "If you do not give back the table which spreads itself, and the gold-ass, the dance shall begin afresh." "Oh, no," cried the host, quite humbly, "I will gladly produce everything, only make the accursed kobold creep back into the sack." Then said the apprentice: "I will let mercy take the place of justice, but beware of getting into mischief again!" So he cried: "Into the sack, Cudgel!" and let him have rest.

Next morning the turner went home to his father with the wishing-table, and the gold-ass. The tailor rejoiced when he saw him once more, and asked him likewise what he had learned in foreign parts. "Dear father," said he, "I have become a turner." "A skilled trade," said the father. "What have you brought back with you from your travels?"

"A precious thing, dear father," replied the son, "a cudgel in the sack."

"What!" cried the father, "a cudgel! That's certainly worth your trouble! From every tree you can cut yourself one." "But not one like this, dear father. If I say 'Out of the sack, Cudgel!' the cudgel springs out and leads anyone ill-disposed toward me a weary dance, and never stops until he lies on the ground and prays for fair weather. Look you, with this cudgel have I rescued the wishing-table and the gold-ass which the thievish innkeeper took away from my brothers. Now let them both be sent for, and invite all our kinsmen. I will give them to eat and to drink, and will fill their pockets with gold into the bargain." The old tailor had not much confidence; nevertheless he summoned the relatives together. Then the turner spread a cloth in the room and led in the gold-ass, and said to his brother: "Now, dear brother, speak to him." The miller said: "Bricklebrit," and instantly the gold pieces rained down on the cloth like a thunder-shower, and the ass did not stop until every one of them had so much that he could carry no more. (I can see by your face that you also would have liked to be there.)

Then the turner brought the little table, and said: "Now, dear brother, speak to it." And scarcely had the carpenter said: "Table, spread yourself," than it was spread and amply covered with the most exquisite dishes. Then such a meal took place as the good tailor had never yet known in his house, and the whole party of kinsmen stayed together till far in the night, and were all merry and glad. The tailor locked away needle and thread, yard-measure and goose, in a closet, and lived with his three sons in joy and splendor.

What, however, happened to the goat who was to blame for the tailor driving out his three sons? That I will tell you. She was ashamed that she had a bald head, and ran to a fox's hole and crept into it. When the fox came home, he was met by two great eyes shining out of the darkness, and was terrified and ran away. A bear met him, and as the fox looked quite disturbed, he said: "What is the matter with you, brother Fox, why do you look like that?" "Ah," answered Redskin, "a fierce beast is in my cave and stared at me with its fiery eyes." "We will soon drive him out," said the bear, and went with him to the cave and looked in, but when he saw the fiery eyes, fear seized on him likewise; he would have nothing to do with the furious beast, and took to his heels. The bee met him, and as she saw that he was ill at ease, she said: "Bear, you are really pulling a very pitiful face; what has become of all your gaiety?" "It is all very well for you to talk," replied the bear, "a furious beast with staring eyes is in Redskin's house, and we can't drive him out." The bee said: "Bear, I pity you, I am a poor weak creature whom you would not turn aside to look at, but still, I believe, I can help you." She flew into the fox's cave, lighted on the goat's smoothly-shorn head, and stung her so violently, that she sprang up, crying "Meh, meh," and ran forth into the world as if mad, and to this hour no one knows where she has gone.

Thumbling, or Tom Thumb

There was once a poor peasant who sat in the evening by the hearth and poked the fire, and his wife sat and spun. Then said he: "How sad it is that we have no children! With us all is so quiet, and in other houses it is noisy and lively."

"Yes," replied the wife, and sighed, "even if we had only one, and it were quite small, and only as big as a thumb, I should be quite satisfied, and we would still love it with all our hearts." Now it so happened that the woman fell ill, and after seven months, gave birth to a child, that was perfect in all its limbs, but no longer than a thumb. Then said they: "It is as we wished it to be, and it shall be our dear child"; and because of its size, they called it Thumbling. Though they did not let it want for food, the child did not grow taller, but remained as it had been at the first. Nevertheless it looked sensibly out of its eyes, and soon showed itself to be a wise and nimble creature, for everything it did turned out well.

One day the peasant was getting ready to go into the forest to cut wood, when he said as if to himself: "How I wish that there was someone who would bring the cart to me!" "Oh, father," cried Thumbling, "I will soon bring the cart, rely on that; it shall be in the forest at the appointed time." The man smiled and said: "How can that be done, you are far too small to lead the horse by the reins?" "That's of no consequence, father, if my mother will only harness it, I will sit in the horse's ear, and call out to him how he is to go." "Well," answered the man, "for once we will try it."

When the time came, the mother harnessed the horse, and placed Thumbling in its ear, and then the little creature cried "Gee up, gee up!"

Then it went quite properly as if with its master, and the cart went the right way into the forest. It so happened that just as he was turning a corner, and the little one was crying "Gee up," two strange men came towards him. "My word!" said one of them. "What is this? There is a cart coming, and a driver is calling to the horse, and still he is not to be seen!" "That can't be right," said the other, "we will follow the cart and see where it stops." The cart, however, drove right into the forest, and exactly to the place where the wood had been cut. When Thumbling saw his father, he cried to him: "Do you see, father, here I am with the cart; now take me down." The father got hold of the horse with his left hand, and with the right took his little son out of the ear. Thumbling sat down quite merrily on a straw, but when the two strange men saw him, they did not know what to say for astonishment. Then one of them took the other aside and said: "Listen, the little fellow would make our fortune if we exhibited him in a large town, for money. We will buy him." They went to the peasant and said: "Sell us the little man. He shall be well treated with us." "No," replied the father, "he is the apple of my eye, and all the money in the world cannot buy him from me." Thumbling, however, when he heard of the bargain, had crept up the folds of his father's coat, placed himself on his shoulder, and whispered in his ear: "Father, do give me away, I will soon come back again." Then the father parted with him to the two men for a handsome sum of money. "Where will you sit?" they said to him. "Oh, just set me on the rim of your hat, and then I can walk backwards and forwards and look at the country, and still not fall down." They did as he wished, and when Thumbling had taken leave of his father, they went away with him. They walked until it was dusk, and then the little fellow said: "Do take me down, it is necessary." "Just stay up there," said the man on whose hat he sat, "it makes no difference to me. The birds sometimes let things fall on me." "No," said Thumbling, "I know what's manners; take me quickly down." The man took his hat off, and put the little fellow on the ground by the wayside, and he leapt and crept about a little between the sods, and then he suddenly slipped into a mousehole which he had sought out. "Good evening, gentlemen, just go home without me," he cried to them, and mocked them. They ran thither and stuck their sticks into the mouse-hole, but it was all in vain. Thumbling crept still farther in, and as it soon became quite dark, they were forced to go home with their vexation and their empty purses.

When Thumbling saw that they were done, he crept back out of the subterranean passage. "It is so dangerous to walk on the ground in the dark," said he; "how easily a neck or a leg is broken!" Fortunately he stumbled against an empty snail-shell. "Thank God!" said he. "In that I can pass the night in safety," and got into it. Not long afterwards, when he was just going to sleep, he heard two men go by, and one of them was saying: "How shall we set about getting hold of the rich pastor's silver and gold?" "I could tell you that," cried Thumbling, interrupting them. "What was that?" said one of the thieves in a fright, "I heard someone speaking." They stood still listening, and Thumbling spoke again, and said: "Take me with you, and I'll help you."

"But where are you?" "Just look on the ground, and observe from whence my voice comes," he replied. There the thieves at length found him, and lifted him up. "You little imp, how will you help us?" they said. "Listen," said he, "I will creep into the pastor's room through the iron bars, and will reach out to you whatever you want to have." "Come then," they said, "and we will see what you can do." When they got to the pastor's house, Thumbling crept into the room, but instantly cried out with all his might: "Do you want to have everything that is here?" The thieves were alarmed, and said: "But do speak softly, so as not to waken anyone!" Thumbling, however, behaved as if he had not understood this, and cried again: "What do you want? Do you want to have everything that is here?" The cook, who slept in the next room, heard this and sat up in bed, and listened. The thieves, however, had in their fright run some distance away, but at last they took courage, and thought: "The little rascal wants to mock us." They came back and whispered to him: "Come, be serious, and reach something out to us." Then Thumbling again cried as loudly as he could: "I really will give you everything, just put your hands in." The maid who was listening, heard this quite distinctly, and jumped out of bed and rushed to the door. The thieves took flight, and ran as if the Wild Huntsman were behind them, but as the maid could not see anything, she went to strike a light. When she came to the place with it, Thumbling, unperceived, betook himself to the granary, and the maid, after she had examined every corner and found nothing, lay down in her bed again, and believed that, after all, she had only been dreaming with open eyes and ears.

Thumbling had climbed up among the hay and found a beautiful place to sleep in; there he intended to rest until day, and then go home again to his parents. But there were other things in store for him. Truly, there is much worry and affliction in this world! When day dawned, the maid arose from her bed to feed the cows. Her first walk was into the barn, where she laid hold of an armful of hay, and precisely that very one in which Poor Thumbling was lying asleep. He, however, was sleeping so soundly that he was aware of nothing, and did not awake until he was in the mouth of the cow, who had picked him up with the hay. "Ah, heavens!" cried he, "how have I got into the fulling mill?" but he soon discovered where he was. Then he had to take care not to let himself go between the teeth and be dismembered, but he was subsequently forced to slip down into the stomach with the hay. "In this little room the windows are forgotten," said he, "and no sun shines in, neither will a candle be brought." His quarters were especially unpleasing to him, and the worst was that more and more hay was always coming in by the door, and the space grew less and less. Then, at length in his anguish, he cried as loud as he could: "Bring me no more fodder, bring me no more fodder." The maid was just milking the cow, and when she heard someone speaking, and saw no one, and perceived that it was the same voice that she had heard in the night, she was so terrified that she slipped off her stool, and spilt the milk. She ran in the greatest haste to her master, and said: "Oh, heavens, pastor, the cow has been speaking!" "You are mad," replied the pastor; but he went himself to the byre to see what was there. Hardly, however, had he set his foot inside when Thumbling again cried: "Bring me no more fodder, bring me no more fodder." Then the pastor himself was alarmed, and thought that an evil spirit had gone into the cow, and ordered her to be killed. She was killed, but the stomach, in which Thumbling was, was thrown on the dunghill. Thumbling had great difficulty in working his way out; however, he succeeded so far as to get some room, but, just as he was going to thrust his head out, a new misfortune occurred. A hungry wolf ran thither, and swallowed the whole stomach at one gulp. Thumbling did not lose courage. "Perhaps," thought he, "the wolf will listen to what I have got to say," and he called to him from out of his belly: "Dear wolf, I know of a magnificent feast for you."

"Where is it to be had?" said the wolf.

"In such and such a house; you must creep into it through the kitchen-sink, and will find cakes, and bacon, and sausages, and as much of them as you can eat," and he described to him exactly his father's house. The wolf did not require to be told this twice. He squeezed himself in at night through the sink, and ate to his heart's content in the larder. When he had eaten his fill, he wanted to go out again, but he had become so big that he could not go out by the same way. Thumbling had reckoned on this, and now began to make a violent noise in the wolf's body, and raged and screamed as loudly as he could. "Will you be quiet," said the wolf, "you will waken up the people!" "What do I care!" replied the little fellow, "you have eaten your fill, and I will make merry likewise," and began once more to scream with all his strength. At last his father and mother were aroused by it, and ran to the room and looked in through the opening in the door. When they saw that a wolf was inside, they ran away, and the husband fetched his axe, and the wife the scythe. "Stay behind," said the man, when they entered the room. "When I have given him a blow, if he is not killed by it, you must cut him down and hew his body to pieces." Then Thumbling heard his parents' voices, and cried: "Dear father, I am here; I am in the wolf's body." Said the father, full of joy: "Thank God, our dear child has found us again," and bade the woman take away her scythe, that Thumbling might not be hurt with it. After that he raised his arm, and struck the wolf such a blow on his head that he fell down dead, and then they got knives and scissors and cut his body open, and drew the little fellow forth. "Ah," said the father, "what sorrow we have gone through for your sake." "Yes, father, I have gone about the world a great deal. Thank heaven, I breathe fresh air again!" "Where have you been, then?" "Ah, father, I have been in a mouse's hole, in a cow's belly, and then in a wolf's paunch; now I will stay with you." "And we will not sell you again, no, not for all the riches in the world," said his parents, and they embraced and kissed their dear Thumbling. They gave him to eat and to drink, and had some new clothes made for him, for his own had been spoiled on his journey.

The Elves

FIRST STORY

A shoemaker, by no fault of his own, had become so poor that at last he had nothing left but leather for one pair of shoes. So in the evening, he cut out the shoes which he wished to begin to make the next morning, and as he had a good conscience, he lay down quietly in his bed, commended himself to God, and fell asleep. In the morning, after he had said his prayers, and was just going to sit down to work, the two shoes stood quite finished on his table. He was astounded, and knew not what to think. He took the shoes in his hands to observe them closer, and they were so neatly made, and with not one bad stitch in them, that it was just as if they were intended as a masterpiece. Before long, a buyer came in, and as the shoes pleased him so well, he paid more for them than was customary, and, with the money, the shoemaker was able to purchase leather for two pairs of shoes. He cut them out at night, and next morning was about to set to work with fresh courage; but he had no need to do so, for, when he got up, they were already made, and buyers also were not wanting, who gave him money enough to buy leather for four pairs of shoes. Again the following morning he found the four pairs made; and so it went on constantly, what he cut out in the evening was finished by the morning, so that he soon had his honest independence again, and at last became a wealthy man.

Now it befell that one evening not long before Christmas, when the man had been cutting out, he said to his wife, before going to bed: "What think you if we were to stay up to-night to see who it is that lends us this helping hand?" The woman liked the idea, and lighted a candle, and then they hid themselves in a corner of the room, behind some clothes which were hanging up there, and watched. When it was midnight, two pretty little naked men came, sat down by the shoemaker's table, took all the work which was cut out before them and began to stitch, and sew, and hammer so skilfully and so quickly with their little fingers that the shoemaker could not avert his eyes for astonishment. They did not stop until all was done, and stood finished on the table, and then they ran quickly away.

Next morning the woman said: "The little men have made us rich, and we really must show that we are grateful for it. They run about so, and have nothing on, and must be cold. I'll tell you what I'll do: I will make them little shirts, and coats, and vests, and trousers, and knit both of them a pair of stockings, and you make them two little pairs of shoes." The man said: "I shall be very glad to do it"; and one night, when everything was ready, they laid their presents all together on the table instead of the cut-out work, and then concealed themselves to see how the little men would behave. At midnight they came bounding in, and wanted to get to work at once, but as they did not find any leather cut out, but only the pretty little articles of clothing, they were at first astonished, and then they showed intense delight. They dressed themselves with the greatest rapidity, put on the beautiful clothes, and sang:

> "Now we are boys so fine to see,
> Why should we longer cobblers be?"

Then they danced and skipped and leapt over chairs and benches. At last they danced out of doors. From that time forth they came no more, but as long as the shoemaker lived all went well with him, and all his efforts prospered.

SECOND STORY

There was once a poor servant-girl, who was industrious and cleanly, and swept the house every day, and emptied her sweepings on the green heap in front of the door. One morning when she was just going back to her work, she found a letter on this heap, and as she could not read, she put her broom in the corner, and took the letter to her employers, and behold it was an invitation from the elves, who asked the girl to hold a child for them at its christening. The girl did not know what to do, but at length, after much persuasion, and as they told her that it was not right to refuse an invitation of this kind, she consented. Then three elves came and conducted her to a hollow mountain, where the little folks lived. Everything there was small, but more elegant and beautiful than can be described. The baby's mother lay in a bed of black ebony ornamented with pearls, the covers were embroidered with gold, the cradle was of ivory, the bath-tub of gold. The girl stood as godmother, and then wanted to go home again, but the little elves urgently entreated her to stay three days with them. So she stayed, and passed the time in pleasure and gaiety, and the little folks did all they could to make her happy. At last she set out on her way home. But first they filled her pockets quite full of money, and then they led her out of the mountain again. When she got home, she wanted to begin her work, and took the broom, which was still standing in the corner, in her hand and began to sweep. Then some strangers came out of the house, who asked her who she was, and what business she had there. And she had not, as she thought, been three days with the little men in the mountains, but seven years, and in the meantime her former masters had died.

THIRD STORY

A certain mother had her child taken out of its cradle by the elves, and a changeling with a large head and staring eyes, which would do nothing but eat and drink, lay in its place. In her trouble she went to her neighbor, and asked her advice. The neighbor said that she was to carry the changeling into the kitchen, set it down on the hearth, light a fire, and boil some water in two egg-shells, which would make the changeling laugh, and if he laughed, all would be over with him. The woman did everything that her neighbor bade her. When she put the egg-shells with water on the fire, goggle-eyes said: "I am as old now as the Wester Forest, but never yet have I seen anyone boil anything in an egg-shell!" And he began to laugh at it. Whilst he was laughing, suddenly came a host of little elves, who brought the right child, set it down on the hearth, and took the changeling away with them.

Herr Korbes

There were once a cock and a hen who wanted to take a journey together. So the cock built a beautiful carriage, which had four red wheels, and harnessed four mice to it. The hen seated herself in it with the cock, and they drove away together. Not long afterwards they met a cat who said: "Where are you going?" The cock replied: "'We are going to the house of Herr Korbes." "Take me with you," said the cat. The cock answered: "Most willingly, get up behind, lest you fall off in front. Take great care not to dirty my little red wheels. And you little wheels, roll on, and you little mice pipe out, as we go forth on our way to the house of Herr Korbes."

After this came a millstone, then an egg, then a duck, then a pin, and at last a needle, who all seated themselves in the carriage, and drove with them. When they reached the house of Herr Korbes, however, Herr Korbes was not there. The mice drew the carriage into the barn, the hen flew with the cock upon a perch. The cat sat down by the hearth, the duck on the well-pole. The egg rolled itself into a towel, the pin stuck itself into the chair-cushion, the needle jumped on to the bed in the middle of the pillow, and the millstone laid itself over the door. Then Herr Korbes came home, went to the hearth, and was about to light the fire, when the cat threw a quantity of ashes in his face. He ran into the kitchen in a great hurry to wash it off, and the duck splashed some water in his face. He wanted to dry it with the towel, but the egg rolled up against him, broke, and glued up his eyes. He wanted to rest, and sat down in the chair, and then the pin pricked him. He fell in a passion, and threw himself on his bed, but as soon as he laid his head on the pillow, the needle pricked him, so that he screamed aloud, and was just going to run out into the wide world in his rage, but when he came to the house-door, the millstone fell down and struck him dead. Herr Korbes must have been a very wicked man!

Godfather Death

A poor man had twelve children and was forced to work night and day to give them even bread. When therefore the thirteenth came into the world, he knew not what to do in his trouble, but ran out into the great highway, and resolved to ask the first person whom he met to be godfather. The first to meet him was the good Lord who already knew what filled his heart, and said to him: "Poor man, I pity you. I will hold your child at its christening, and will take charge of it and make it happy on earth." The man said: "Who are you?" "I am God." "Then I do not desire to have you for a

godfather," said the man; "you give to the rich, and leave the poor
to hunger." Thus spoke the man, for he did not know how wisely
God apportions riches and poverty. He turned therefore away from
the Lord, and went farther. Then the Devil came to him and said:
"What do you seek? If you will take me as a godfather for your
child, I will give him gold in plenty and all the joys of the world
as well." The man asked: "Who are you?" "I am the Devil." "Then
I do not desire to have you for godfather," said the man; "you
deceive men and lead them astray." He went onwards, and then
came Death striding up to him with withered legs, and said: "Take
me as godfather." The man asked: "Who are you?" "I am Death,
and I make all equal." Then said the man, "You are the right one,
you take the rich as well as the poor, without distinction; you shall
be godfather." Death answered: "I will make your child rich and
famous, for he who has me for a friend can lack nothing." The
man said: "Next Sunday is the christening; be there at the right
time." Death appeared as he had promised, and stood godfather
quite in the usual way.

When the boy had grown up, his godfather one day appeared
and bade him go with him. He led him forth into a forest, and
showed him a herb which grew there, and said: "Now you shall
receive your godfather's present. I make you a celebrated physician. When you are called to a patient, I will always appear to you.
If I stand by the head of the sick man, you may say with confidence that you will make him well again, and if you give him of
this herb he will recover; but if I stand by the patient's feet, he is
mine, and you must say that all remedies are in vain, and that no
physician in the world could save him. But beware of using the
herb against my will, or it might fare ill with you."

It was not long before the youth was the most famous physician
in the whole world. "He had only to look at the patient and he
knew his condition at once, whether he would recover, or must
needs die." So they said of him, and from far and wide people came
to him, sent for him when they had anyone ill, and gave him so
much money that he soon became a rich man. Now it so befell
that the King became ill, and the physician was summoned, and
was to say if recovery were possible. But when he came to the bed,
Death was standing by the feet of the sick man, and the herb did
not grow which could save him. "If I could but cheat Death for

once," thought the physician, "he is sure to take it ill if I do but, as I am his godson, he will shut one eye; I will risk it." He therefore took up the sick man, and laid him the other way, so that now Death was standing by his head. Then he gave the King some of the herb, and he recovered and grew healthy again. But Death came to the physician, looking very black and angry, threatened him with his finger, and said: "You have betrayed me; this time I will pardon it, as you are my godson; but if you venture it again, it will cost you your neck, for I will take you yourself away with me."

Soon afterwards the King's daughter fell into a severe illness. She was his only child, and he wept day and night, so that he began to lose the sight of his eyes, and he caused it to be made known that whosoever rescued her from death should be her husband and inherit the crown. When the physician came to the sick girl's bed, he saw Death by her feet. He ought to have remembered the warning given by his godfather, but he was so infatuated by the great beauty of the King's daughter, and the happiness of becoming her husband, that he flung all thought to the winds. He did not see that Death was casting angry glances on him, that he was raising his hand in the air, and threatening him with his withered fist. He raised up the sick girl, and placed her head where her feet had lain. Then he gave her some of the herb, and instantly her cheeks flushed red, and life stirred afresh in her.

When Death saw that for a second time his own property had been misused, he walked up to the physician with long strides, and said: "All is over with you, and now the lot falls on you," and seized him so firmly with his ice-cold hand, that he could not resist, and led him into a cave below the earth. There he saw how thousands and thousands of candles were burning in countless rows, some large, some medium-sized, others small. Every instant some were extinguished, and others again burnt up, so that the flames seemed to leap hither and thither in perpetual change. "See," said Death, "these are the lights of men's lives. The large ones belong to children, the medium-sized ones to married people in their prime, the little ones belong to old people; but children and young folks likewise have often only a tiny candle." "Show me the light of my life," said the physician, and he thought that it would be still very tall. Death pointed to a little end which was just threatening to go out, and said: "Behold, it is there." "Ah, dear godfather," said the horrified physician, "light a new one for me, do it for love of me, that I may enjoy my life, be King, and the husband of the King's beautiful daughter." "I cannot," answered Death, "one must go out before a new one is lighted." "Then place the old one on a new one, that will go on burning at once when the old one has come to an end," pleaded the physician. Death behaved as if he were going to fulfill his wish, and took hold of a tall new candle; but as he desired to revenge himself, he purposely made a mistake in fixing it, and the little piece fell down and was extinguished. Immediately the physician fell on the ground, and now he himself was in the hands of Death.

The Six Swans

Once upon a time, a certain King was hunting in a great forest, and he chased a wild beast so eagerly that none of his attendants could follow him. When evening drew near he stopped and looked around him, and then he saw that he had lost his way. He sought a way out, but could find none. Then he perceived an aged woman with a head which nodded perpetually, who came towards him, but she was a witch. "Good woman," said he to her, "can you not show me the way through the forest?" "Oh, yes, Lord King," she answered, "that I certainly can, but on one condition, and if you do not fulfil that, you will never get out of the forest, and will die of hunger in it."

"What kind of condition is it?" asked the King.

"I have a daughter," said the old woman, "who is as beautiful as anyone in the world, and well deserves to be your consort, and if you will make her your Queen, I will show you the way out of the forest." In the anguish of his heart the King consented, and the old woman led him to her little hut, where her daughter was sitting by the fire. She received the King as if she had been expecting him, and he saw that she was very beautiful, but still she did not please him, and he could not look at her without secret horror. After he had taken the maiden up on his horse, the old woman showed him the way, and the King reached his royal palace again, where the wedding was celebrated.

The King had already been married once, and had by his first wife, seven children, six boys and a girl, whom he loved better than anything else in the world. As he now feared that the step-mother might not treat them well, and even do them some injury, he took them to a lonely castle which stood in the midst of a forest. It lay so concealed, and the way was so difficult to find, that he himself would not have found it, if a wise woman had not given him a ball of yarn with wonderful properties. When he threw it down before him, it unrolled itself and showed him his path. The King, however, went so frequently away to his dear children that the Queen observed his absence; she was curious and wanted to know what he did when he was quite alone in the forest. She gave a great deal of money to his servants, and they betrayed the secret to her, and told her likewise of the ball which alone could point out the way. And now she knew no rest until she had learnt where the King kept the ball of yarn, and then she made little shirts of white silk, and as she had learnt the art of witchcraft from her mother, she sewed a charm inside them. And once when the King had ridden forth to hunt, she took the little shirts and went into the forest, and the ball showed her the way. The children, who saw from a distance that someone was approaching, thought that their dear father was coming to them, and full of joy, ran to meet him. Then she threw one of the little shirts over each of them, and no sooner had the shirts touched their bodies than they were changed into swans, and flew away over the forest. The Queen went home quite delighted, and thought she had got rid of her step-children, but the girl had not run out with her brothers, and the Queen knew nothing about her. Next day the King went to visit his children, but he found no one but the little girl. "Where are your brothers?" asked the King. "Alas, dear father," she answered, "they have gone away and left me alone!" and she told him that she had seen from her little window how her brothers had flown away over the forest in the shape of swans, and she showed him the feathers, which they had let fall in the courtyard, and which she had picked up. The King mourned, but he did not think that the Queen had done this wicked deed, and as he feared that the girl would also be stolen away from him, he wanted to take her away with him. But she

was afraid of her step-mother, and entreated the King to let her stay just this one night more in the forest castle.

The poor girl thought: "I can no longer stay here. I will go and seek my brothers." And when night came, she ran away, and went straight into the forest. She walked the whole night long, and next day also without stopping, until she could go no farther for weariness. Then she saw a forest-hut, and went into it, and found a room with six litle beds, but she did not venture to get into one of them, but crept under one, and lay down on the hard ground, intending to pass the night there. Just before sunset, however, she heard a rustling, and saw six swans come flying in at the window. They alighted on the ground and blew at each other, and blew all the feathers off, and their swans' skins stripped off like a shirt. Then the maiden looked at them and recognized her brothers, was glad and crept forth from beneath the bed. The brothers were not less delighted to see their little sister, but their joy was of short duration. "Here you cannot abide," they said to her. "This is a shelter for robbers; if they come home and find you, they will kill you." "But can you not protect me?" asked the little sister. "No," they replied, "only for one quarter of an hour each evening can we lay aside our swans' skins and have during that time our human form, after that, we are once more turned into swans." The little sister wept and said: "Can you not be set free?" "Alas, no," they answered, "the conditions are too hard! For six years you may neither speak nor laugh, and in that time you must sew together six little shirts of starwort for us. And if one single word falls from your lips, all your work will be lost." And when the brothers had said this, the quarter of an hour was over, and they flew out of the window again as swans.

The maiden, however, firmly resolved to deliver her brothers, even if it should cost her her life. She left the hut, went into the midst of the forest, seated herself on a tree, and there passed the night. Next morning she went out and gathered starwort and began to sew. She could not speak to anyone, and she had no inclination to laugh; she sat there and looked at nothing but her work. When she had already spent a long time there it came to pass that the King of the country was hunting in the forest, and his huntsmen came to the tree on which the maiden was sitting. They called to her and said: "Who are you?" But she made no answer. "Come down to us," said they. "We will not do you any harm." She only shook her head. As they pressed her further with questions she threw her golden necklace down to them, and thought to content them thus. They, however, did not cease, and then she threw her girdle down to them, and as this also was to no purpose, her garters, and by degrees everything that she had on that she could do without until she had nothing left but her shift. The huntsmen, however, did not let themselves be turned aside by that, but climbed the tree and fetched the maiden down and led her before the King. The King asked: "Who are you? What are you doing on the tree?" But she did not answer. He put the question in every language that he knew, but she remained as mute as a fish. As she was so beautiful, the King's heart was touched, and he was smitten with a great love for her. He put his mantle on her, took her before him on his horse, and carried her to his castle. Then he caused her to be dressed in rich garments, and she shone in her beauty like bright daylight, but no word could be drawn from her. He placed her by his side at table, and her modest bearing and courtesy pleased him so much that he said: "She is the one whom I wish to marry, and no other woman in the world." And after some days he united himself to her.

The King, however, had a wicked mother who was dissatisfied with this marriage and spoke ill of the young Queen. "Who knows," said she, "from whence the creature who can't speak, comes? She is not worthy of a king!" After a year had passed, when the Queen brought her first child into the world, the old woman took it away from her, and smeared her mouth with blood as she slept. Then she went to the King and accused the Queen of being a man-eater. The King would not believe it, and would not suffer anyone to do her any injury. She, however, sat continually sewing at the shirts, and cared for nothing else. The next time, when she again bore a beautiful boy, the false mother-in-law used the same treachery, but the King could not bring himself to give credit to her words. He said: "She is too pious and good to do anything of that kind; if she were not dumb, and could defend herself, her innocence would come to light." But when the old woman stole away the newly-born child for the third time, and accused the Queen, who did not utter one word of defence, the King could do no otherwise than deliver her over to justice, and she was sentenced to suffer death by fire.

When the day came for the sentence to be carried out, it was the last day of the six years during which she was not to speak or laugh, and she had delivered her dear brothers from the power of the enchantment. The six shirts were ready, only the left sleeve of the sixth was wanting. When, therefore, she was led to the stake, she laid the shirts on her arm, and when she stood on high and the fire was just going to be lighted, she looked around and six swans came flying through the air towards her. Then she saw that her deliverance was near, and her heart leapt with joy. The swans swept towards her and sank down so that she could throw the shirts over them, and as they were touched by them, their swans' skins fell off, and her brothers stood in their own bodily form before her, and were vigorous and handsome. The youngest only lacked his left arm, and had in the place of it a swan's wing on his shoulder. They embraced and kissed each other, and the Queen went to the King, who was greatly moved, and she began to speak and said: "Dearest husband, now I may speak and declare to you that I am innocent, and false accused." And she told him of the treachery of the old woman who had taken away her three children and hidden them. Then to the great joy of the King they were brought thither, and as a punishment, the wicked mother-in-law was bound to the stake, and burnt to ashes. But the King and the Queen with her six brothers lived many years in happiness and peace.

Little Briar-Rose

A long time ago there were a King and Queen who said every day: "Ah, if only we had a child!" but they never had one. But it happened that once when the Queen was bathing, a frog crept out of the water on to the land, and said to her: "Your wish shall be fulfilled; before a year has gone by, you shall have a daughter."

What the frog had said came true, and the Queen had a little girl who was so pretty that the King could not contain himself for joy, and ordered a great feast. He invited not only his kindred, friends and acquaintances, but also the Wise Women, in order that they might be kind and well-disposed towards the child. There were thirteen of them in his kingdom, but, as he had only twelve golden plates for them to eat out of, one of them had to be left at home.

The feast was held with all manner of splendor, and when it came to an end the Wise Women bestowed their magic gifts upon the baby: one gave virtue, another beauty, a third riches, and so on with everything in the world that one can wish for.

When eleven of them had made their promises, suddenly the thirteenth came in. She wished to avenge herself for not having been invited, and without greeting, or even looking at anyone, she cried with a loud voice: "The King's daughter shall in her fifteenth year prick herself with a spindle, and fall down dead." And, without saying a word more, she turned round and left the room.

They were all shocked; but the twelfth, whose good wish still remained unspoken, came forward, and as she could not undo the evil sentence, but only soften it, she said: "It shall not be death, but a deep sleep of a hundred years, into which the princess shall fall."

The King, who would fain keep his dear child from the misfortune, gave orders that every spindle in the whole kingdom should be burnt. Meanwhile the gifts of the Wise Women were plenteously fulfilled on the young girl, for she was so beautiful, modest, good-natured, and wise, that everyone who saw her was bound to love her.

It happened that on the very day when she was fifteen years old, the King and Queen were not at home, and the maiden was left in the palace quite alone. So she went round into all sorts of places, looked into rooms and bed-chambers just as she liked, and at last came to an old tower. She climbed up the narrow winding-staircase, and reached a little door. A rusty key was in the lock, and when she turned it the door sprang open, and there in a little room sat an old woman with a spindle, busily spinning her flax.

"Good day, old mother," said the King's daughter; "what are you doing there?" "I am spinning," said the old woman, and nodded her head. "What sort of thing is that, the rattles round so merrily?" said the girl, and she took the spindle and wanted to spin too. But scarcely had she touched the spindle when the magic decree was fulfilled, and she pricked her finger with it.

And, in the very moment when she felt the prick, she fell down upon the bed that stood there, and lay in a deep sleep. And this sleep extended over the whole palace; the King and Queen who had just come home, and had entered the great hall, began to go to sleep, and the whole of the court with them. The horses, too, went to sleep in the stable, the dogs in the yard, the pigeons upon

the roof, the flies on the wall; even the fire that was flaming on the hearth became quiet and slept, the roast meat left off frizzling, and the cook, who was just going to pull the hair of the scullery boy, because he had forgotten something, let him go, and went to sleep. And the wind fell, and on the trees before the castle not a leaf moved again.

But round about the castle there began to grow a hedge of thorns, which every year became higher, and at last grew close up round the castle and all over it, so that there was nothing of it to be seen, not even the flag upon the roof. But the story of the beautiful sleeping "Briar-rose," for so the princess was named, went about the country, so that from time to time Kings' sons came and tried to get through the thorny hedge into the castle.

But they found it impossible, for the thorns held fast together, as if they had hands, and the youths were caught in them, could not get loose again, and died a miserable death.

After long, long years a King's son came again to that country, and heard an old man talking about the thorn-hedge, and that a castle was said to stand behind it in which a wonderfully beautiful princess, named Briar-rose, had been asleep for a hundred years; and that the King and Queen and the whole court were asleep likewise. He had heard, too, from his grandfather, that many kings' sons had already come, and had tried to get through the thorny hedge, but they had remained sticking fast in it, and had died a pitiful death. Then the youth said: "I am not afraid, I will go and see the beautiful Briar-rose." The good old man might dissuade him as he would, he did not listen to his words.

But by this time the hundred years had just passed, and the day had come when Briar-rose was to awake again. When the King's son came near to the thorn-hedge, it was nothing but large and beautiful flowers, which parted from each other of their own accord, and let him pass unhurt, then they closed again behind him like a hedge. In the castle yard he saw the horses and the spotted hounds lying asleep; on the roof sat the pigeons with their heads under their wings. And when he entered the house, the flies were asleep upon the wall, the cook in the kitchen was still holding out his hand to seize the boy, and the maid was sitting by the black hen which she was going to pluck.

He went on farther, and in the great hall he saw the whole of the court lying asleep, and up by the throne lay the King and Queen.

Then he went on still farther, and all was so quiet that a breath could be heard, and at last he came to the tower, and opened the door into the little room where Briar-rose was sleeping. There she lay, so beautiful that he could not turn his eyes away; and he stooped down and gave her a kiss. But as soon as he kissed her,

Briar-rose opened her eyes and awoke, and looked at him quite sweetly.

Then they went down together, and the King awoke, and the Queen, and the whole court, and looked at each other in great astonishment. And the horses in the courtyard stood up and shook themselves; the hounds jumped up and wagged their tails; the pigeons upon the roof pulled out their heads from under their wings, looked round, and flew into the open country; the flies on the wall crept again; the fire in the kitchen burned up and flickered and cooked the meat; the joint began to turn and sizzle again, and the cook gave the boy such a box on the ear that he screamed, and the maid finished plucking the fowl.

And then the marriage of the King's son with Briar-rose was celebrated with all splendor, and they lived contented to the end of their days.

King Thrushbeard

A king had a daughter who was beautiful beyond all measure, but so proud and haughty withal that no suitor was good enough for her. She sent away one after the other, and ridiculed them as well.

Once the King made a great feast and invited thereto, from far and near, all the young men likely to marry. They were all marshalled in a row according to their rank and standing; first came the kings, then the grand-dukes, then the princes, the earls, the barons, and the gentry. Then the King's daughter was led through the ranks, but to each one she had some objection to make; one was too fat, "The wine-barrel," she said. Another was too tall, "Long and thin has little in." The third was too short, "Short and thick is never quick." The fourth was too pale, "As pale as death." The fifth too red, "A fighting-cock." The sixth was not straight enough, "A green log dried behind the stove."

So she had something to say against each one, but she made herself especially merry over a good king who stood quite high up in the row, and whose chin had grown a little crooked. "Look," she cried and laughed, "he has a chin like a thrush's beak!" and from that time he got the name of King Thrushbeard.

But the old King, when he saw that his daughter did nothing but mock the people, and despised all the suitors who were gathered there, was very angry, and swore that she should have for her husband the very first beggar that came to his doors.

A few days afterwards a fiddler came and sang beneath the windows, trying to earn a few pennies. When the King heard him he said: "Let him come up." So the fiddler came in, in his dirty, ragged clothes, and sang before the King and his daughter, and when he had ended he asked for a trifling gift. The King said: "Your song has pleased me so well that I will give you my daughter there, to wife."

The King's daughter shuddered, but the King said: "I have taken an oath to give you to the very first beggar-man, and I will keep it." All she could say was in vain; the priest was brought, and she had to let herself be wedded to the fiddler on the spot. When that was done the King said: "Now it is not proper for you, a beggar-woman, to stay any longer in my palace, you may just go away with your husband."

The beggar-man led her out by the hand, and she was obliged to walk away on foot with him. When they came to a large forest she asked: "To whom does that beautiful forest belong?" "It belongs to King Thrushbeard; if you had taken him, it would have been yours." "Ah, unhappy girl that I am, if I had but taken King Thrushbeard!"

Afterwards they came to a meadow, and she asked again: "To whom does this beautiful green meadow belong?" "It belongs to King Thrushbeard; if you had taken him, it would have been yours." "Ah, unhappy girl that I am, if I had but taken King Thrushbeard!"

Then they came to a large town, and she asked again: "To whom does this fine large town belong?" "It belongs to King Thrushbeard; if you had taken him, it would have been yours." "Ah, unhappy girl that I am, if I had but taken King Thrushbeard!"

"It does not please me," said the fiddler, "to hear you always wishing for another husband; am I not good enough for you?" At last they came to a very little hut, and she said: "Oh, goodness! what a small house; to whom does this miserable, tiny hovel belong?" The fiddler answered: "That is my house and yours, where we shall live together."

She had to stoop in order to go in at the low door. "Where are the servants?" said the King's daughter. "What servants?" answered the beggar-man; "you must yourself do what you wish to have done. Just make a fire at once, and set on water to cook my supper, I am quite tired." But the King's daughter knew nothing about lighting fires or cooking, and the beggar-man had to lend a hand himself to get anything fairly done. When they had finished their scanty meal they went to bed; but he forced her to get up quite early in the morning in order to look after the house.

For a few days they lived in this way as well as might be, and came to the end of all their provisions. Then the man said: "Wife, we cannot go on any longer eating and drinking here and earning nothing. You must make baskets." He went out, cut some willows, and brought them home. Then she began to make baskets, but the tough willows wounded her delicate hands.

"I see that this will not do," said the man; "you had better spin, perhaps you can do that better." She sat down and tried to spin, but the hard thread soon cut her soft fingers so that the blood ran down. "See," said the man, "you are fit for no sort of work; I have made a bad bargain with you. Now I will try to make a business with pots and earthenware; you must sit in the market-place and sell the ware." "Alas," thought she, "if any of the people from my father's kingdom come to the market and see me sitting there, selling, how they will mock me!" But it was of no use, she had to yield unless she chose to die of hunger.

For the first time she succeeded well, for the people were glad to buy the woman's wares because she was good-looking, and they paid her what she asked; many even gave her the money and left the pots with her as well. So they lived on what she had earned as long as it lasted, then the husband bought a lot of new crockery. With this she sat down at the corner of the market-place, and set it out round about her ready for sale. But suddenly there came a drunken hussar galloping along, and he rode right amongst the pots so that they were all broken into a thousand bits. She began to weep, and did not know what to do for fear. "Alas! what will happen to me?" cried she; "what will my husband say to this?"

She ran home and told him of the misfortune. "Who would seat herself at a corner of the market-place with crockery?" said the man; "leave off crying, I see very well that you cannot do any ordinary work, so I have been to our King's palace and have asked whether they cannot find a place for a kitchen-maid, and they have promised me to take you; in that way you will get your food for nothing."

The King's daughter was now a kitchen-maid, and had to be at the cook's beck and call, and do the dirtiest work. In both her pockets she fastened a little jar, in which she took home her share of the leavings, and upon this they lived.

It happened that the wedding of the King's eldest son was to be celebrated, so the poor woman went up and placed herself by the door of the hall to look on. When all the candles were lit, and people, each more beautiful than the other, entered, and all was full of pomp and splendor, she thought of her lot with a sad heart, and cursed the pride and haughtiness which had humbled her and brought her to so great poverty.

The smell of the delicious dishes which were being taken in and out reached her, and now and then the servants threw her a few morsels of them: these she put in her jars to take home.

All at once the King's son entered, clothed in velvet and silk, with gold chains about his neck. And when he saw the beautiful woman standing by the door he seized her by the hand, and would have danced with her; but she refused and shrank with fear, for she saw that it was King Thrushbeard, her suitor whom she had driven away with scorn. Her struggles were of no avail, he drew her into the hall; but the string by which her pockets were hung broke, the pots fell down, the soup ran out, and the scraps were scattered all about. And when the people saw it, there arose general laughter and derision, and she was so ashamed that she would rather have been a thousand fathoms below the ground. She sprang to the door and would have run away, but on the stairs a man caught her and brought her back; and when she looked at him it was King Thrushbeard again. He said to her kindly: "Do not be afraid, I and the fiddler who has been living with you in that wretched hovel are one. For love of you I disguised myself so; and I also was the hussar who rode through your crockery. This was all done to humble your proud spirit, and to punish you for the insolence with which you mocked me."

Then she wept bitterly and said: "I have done great wrong, and am not worthy to be your wife." But he said: "Be comforted, the evil days are past; now we will celebrate our wedding." Then the maids-in-waiting came and put on her the most splendid clothing, and her father and his whole court came and wished her happiness in her marriage with King Thrushbeard, and the joy now began in earnest. I wish you and I had been there too.

Little Snow-White

Once upon a time in the middle of winter, when the flakes of snow were falling like feathers from the sky, a Queen sat at a window sewing, and the frame of the window was made of black ebony. And whilst she was sewing and looking out of the window at the snow, she pricked her finger with the needle, and three drops of blood fell upon the snow. And the red looked pretty upon the white snow, and she thought to herself: "Would that I had a child as white as snow, as red as blood, and as black as the wood of the window-frame."

Soon after that she had a little daughter, who was as white as snow, and as red as blood, and her hair was as black as ebony; and she was therefore called Little Snow-white. And when the child was born, the Queen died.

After a year had passed the King took to himself another wife. She was a beautiful woman, but proud and haughty, and she could not bear that anyone else should surpass her in beauty. She had a wonderful looking-glass, and when she stood in front of it and looked at herself in it, and said:

"Looking-glass, Looking-glass, on the wall,
Who in this land is the fairest of all?"

the looking-glass answered:

"Thou, O Queen, art the fairest of all!"

Then she was satisfied, for she knew that the looking-glass spoke the truth.

But Snow-white was growing up, and grew more and more beautiful; and when she was seven years old she was as beautiful as the day, and more beautiful than the Queen herself. And once when the Queen asked her looking-glass:

"Looking-glass, Looking-glass, on the wall,
Who in this land is the fairest of all?

it answered:

"Thou art fairer than all who are here, Lady Queen.
But more beautiful still is Snow-white, as I ween."

Then the Queen was shocked, and turned yellow and green with envy. From that hour, whenever she looked at Snow-white, her heart heaved in her breast, she hated the girl so much.

And envy and pride grew higher and higher in her heart like a weed, so that she had no peace day or night. She called a huntsman, and said: "Take the child away into the forest; I will no longer have her in my sight. Kill her, and bring me back her lung and liver as a token." The huntsman obeyed, and took her away; but when he had drawn his knife, and was about to pierce Snow-white's innocent heart, she began to weep, and said: "Ah, dear huntsman, leave me my life! I will run away into the wild forest, and never come home again."

And as she was so beautiful the huntsman had pity on her and said: "Run away, then, you poor child." "The wild beasts will soon have devoured you," thought he, and yet it seemed as if a stone had been rolled from his heart since it was no longer needful for him to kill her. And as a young boar just then came running by he stabbed it, and cut out its lung and liver and took them to the Queen as proof that the child was dead. The cook had to salt them, and the wicked Queen ate them, and thought she had eaten the lung and liver of Snow-white.

But now the poor child was all alone in the great forest, and so terrified that she looked at all the leaves on the trees, and did not know what to do. Then she began to run, and ran over sharp stones and through thorns, and the wild beasts ran past her, but did her no harm.

She ran as long as her feet would go until it was almost evening; then she saw a little cottage and went into it to rest herself. Everything in the cottage was small, but neater and cleaner than can be told. There was a table on which was a white cover, and seven little plates, and on each plate a little spoon; moreover, there were seven little knives and forks, and seven little mugs. Against the wall stood seven little beds side by side, and covered with snow-white counterpanes.

Little Snow-white was so hungry and thirsty that she ate some vegetables and bread from each plate and drank a drop of wine out of each mug, for she did not wish to take all from one only. Then, as she was so tired, she laid herself down on one of the little beds, but none of them suited her; one was too long, another too short, but at last she found that the seventh one was right, and so she remained in it, said a prayer and went to sleep.

When it was quite dark the owners of the cottage came back; they were seven dwarfs who dug and delved in the mountains for ore. They lit their seven candles, and as it was now light within the cottage they saw that someone had been there, for everything was not in the same order in which they had left it.

The first said: "Who has been sitting on my chair?"
The second: "Who has been eating off my plate?"
The third: "Who has been taking some of my bread?"
The fourth: "Who has been eating my vegetables?"
The fifth: "Who has been using my fork?"
The sixth: "Who has been cutting with my knife?"
The seventh: "Who has been drinking out of my mug?"

Then the first looked round and saw that there was a little hollow on his bed, and he said: "Who has been getting into my bed?" The others came up and each called out: "Somebody has been lying in my bed too." But the seventh when he looked at his bed saw little Snow-white, who was lying asleep therein. And he called the others, who came running up, and they cried out with astonishment, and brought their seven little candles and let the light fall on little Snow-white. "Oh, heavens! oh, heavens!" cried they, "what a lovely child!" and they were so glad that they did not wake her up, but let her sleep on in the bed. And the seventh dwarf slept with his companions, one hour with each, and so passed the night.

When it was morning little Snow-white awoke, and was frightened when she saw the seven dwarfs. But they were friendly and asked her what her name was. "My name is Snow-white," she answered. "How have you come to our house?" said the dwarfs. Then she told them that her step-mother had wished to have her killed, but that the huntsman had spared her life, and that she had run for the whole day, until at last she had found their dwelling. The dwarfs said: "If you will take care of our house, cook, make the beds, wash, sew, and knit, and if you will keep everything neat and clean, you can stay with us and you shall want for nothing." "Yes," said Snow-white, "with all my heart," and she stayed with them. She kept the house in order for them; in the mornings they went to the mountains and looked for copper and gold, in the evenings they came back, and then their supper had to be ready. The girl was alone the whole day, so the good dwarfs warned her and said: "Beware of your step-mother, she will soon know that you are here; be sure to let no one come in."

But the Queen, believing that she had eaten Snow-white's lung and liver, could not but think that she was again the first and most beautiful of all; and she went to her looking-glass and said:

> "Looking-glass, Looking-glass, on the wall,
> Who in this land is the fairest of all?"

and the glass answered:

> "Oh, Queen, thou art fairest of all I see,
> But over the hills, where the seven dwarfs dwell,
> Snow-white is still alive and well,
> And none is so fair as she."

Then she was astounded, for she knew that the looking-glass never spoke falsely, and she knew that the huntsman had betrayed her, and that little Snow-white was still alive.

And so she thought and thought again how she might kill her, for so long as she was not the fairest in the whole land, envy let her have no rest. And when she had at last thought of something to do, she painted her face, and dressed herself like an old pedlar-woman, and no one could have known her. In this disguise she went over the seven mountains to the seven dwarfs, and knocked at the door and cried: "Pretty things to sell, very cheap, very cheap." Little Snow-white looked out of the window and called out: "Good-day, my good woman, what have you to sell?" "Good things, pretty things," she answered; "stay-laces of all colors," and she pulled out one which was woven of bright-colored silk. "I may let the worthy old woman in," thought Snow-white, and she unbolted the door and bought the pretty laces. "Child," said the old woman, "what a fright you look; come, I will lace you properly for once." Snow-white had no suspicion, but stood before her, and let herself be laced with the new laces. But the old woman laced so quickly and laced so tightly that Snow-white lost her breath and fell down as if dead. "Now I am the most beautiful," said the Queen to herself, and ran away.

Not long afterwards, in the evening, the seven dwarfs came home, but how shocked they were when they saw their dear little Snow-white lying on the ground, and that she neither stirred nor moved, and seemed to be dead. They lifted her up, and, as they saw that she was laced too tightly, they cut the laces; then she began to breathe a little, and after a while came to life again. When the dwarfs heard what had happened they said: "The old pedlar-woman was no one else than the wicked Queen; take care and let no one come in when we are not with you."

But the wicked woman when she had reached home went in front of the glass and asked:

> "Looking-glass, Looking-glass, on the wall,
> Who in this land is the fairest of all?"

and it answered as before:

> "Oh, Queen, thou art fairest of all I see,
> But over the hills, where the seven dwarfs dwell,
> Snow-white is still alive and well,
> And none is so fair as she."

When she heard that, all her blood rushed to her heart with fear, for she saw plainly that little Snow-white was again alive. "But now," she said, "I will think of something that shall really put an end to you," and by the help of witchcraft, which she understood, she made a poisonous comb. Then she disguised herself and took the shape of another old woman. So she went over the seven mountains to the seven dwarfs, knocked at the door, and cried: "Good things to sell, cheap, cheap!" Little Snow-white looked out and said: "Go away; I cannot let anyone come in." "I suppose you can look," said the old woman, and pulled the poisonous comb out and held it up. It pleased the girl so well that she let herself be beguiled, and opened the door. When they had made a bargain the old woman said: "Now I will comb you properly for once." Poor little Snow-white had no suspicion, and let the old woman do as she pleased, but hardly had she put the comb in her hair than the poison in it took effect, and the girl fell down senseless. "You paragon of beauty," said the wicked woman, "you are done for now," and she went away.

But fortunately it was almost evening, and it wasn't long before the seven dwarfs came home. When they saw Snow-white lying as if dead upon the ground they at once suspected the step-mother, and they looked and found the poisoned comb. Scarcely had they taken it out when Snow-white came to herself, and told them what had happened. Then they warned her once more to be upon her guard and to open the door to no one.

The Queen, at home, went in front of the glass and said:

> "Looking-glass, Looking-glass, on the wall,
> Who in this land is the fairest of all?"

then it answered as before:

> "Oh, Queen, thou art fairest of all I see,
> But over the hills, where the seven dwarfs dwell,
> Snow-white is still alive and well,
> And none is so fair as she."

When she heard the glass speak thus she trembled and shook with rage. "Snow-white shall die," she cried, "even if it costs me my life!"

Thereupon she went into a quite secret, lonely room, where no one ever came, and there she made a very poisonous apple. Outside it looked pretty, white with a red cheek, so that everyone who saw it longed for it; but whoever ate a piece of it must surely die.

When the apple was ready she painted her face, and dressed herself up as a farmer's wife, and so she went over the seven mountains to the seven dwarfs. She knocked at the door. Snow-white put her head out of the window and said: "I cannot let any-one in; the seven dwarfs have forbidden me." "It is all the same to me," answered the woman, "I shall soon get rid of my apples. There, I will give you one."

"No," said Snow-white, "I dare not take anything." "Are you afraid of poison?" said the old woman; "look, I will cut the apple in two pieces; you eat the red cheek, and I will eat the white." The apple was so cunningly made that only the red cheek was poisoned. Snow-white longed for the fine apple, and when she saw that the woman ate part of it she could resist no longer, and stretched out her hand and took the poisonous half. But hardly had she a bit of it in her mouth than she fell down dead. Then the Queen looked at her with a dreadful look, and laughed aloud and said: "White as snow, red as blood, black as ebony-wood! this time the dwarfs cannot wake you up again."

And when she asked of the looking-glass at home:

"Looking-glass, Looking-glass, on the wall,
Who in this land is the fairest of all?"

it answered at last:

"Oh, Queen, in this land thou art fairest of all."

Then her envious heart had rest, so far as an envious heart can have rest.

The dwarfs, when they came home in the evening, found Snow-white lying upon the ground; she breathed no longer and was dead. They lifted her up, looked to see whether they could find anything poisonous, unlaced her, combed her hair, washed her with water and wine, but it was all of no use; the poor child was dead, and remained dead. They laid her upon a bier, and all seven of them sat round it and wept for her, and wept three days long.

Then they were going to bury her, but she still looked as if she were living, and still had her pretty red cheeks. They said: "We could not bury her in the dark ground," and they had a transparent coffin of glass made, so that she could be seen from all sides, and they laid her in it, and wrote her name upon it in golden letters, and that she was a king's daughter. Then they put the coffin out upon the mountain, and one of them always stayed by it and watched it. And birds came too, and wept for Snow-white; first an owl, then a raven, and last a dove.

And now Snow-white lay a long, long time in the coffin, and she did not change, but looked as if she were asleep; for she was as white as snow, as red as blood, and her hair was as black as ebony.

It happened, however, that a king's son came into the forest, and went to the dwarfs' house to spend the night. He saw the coffin on the mountain, and the beautiful Snow-white within it, and read what was written upon it in golden letters. Then he said to the dwarfs: "Let me have the coffin, I will give you whatever you want for it." But the dwarfs answered: "We will not part with it for all the gold in the world." Then he said: "Let me have it as a gift, for

I cannot live without seeing Snow-white. I will honor and prize her as my dearest possession." As he spoke in this way the good dwarfs took pity upon him, and gave him the coffin.

And now the King's son had it carried away by his servants on their shoulders. And it happened that they stumbled over a tree-stump, and with the shock the poisonous piece of apple which Snow-white had bitten off came out of her throat. And before long she opened her eyes, lifted up the lid of the coffin, sat up, and was once more alive. "Oh, heavens, where am I?" she cried. The King's son, full of joy, said: "You are with me," and told her what had happened, and said: "I love you more than everything in the world; come with me to my father's palace, you shall be my wife."

And Snow-white was willing, and went with him, and their wedding was held with great show and splendor. But Snow-white's wicked step-mother was also bidden to the feast. When she had arrayed herself in beautiful clothes she went before the Looking-glass, and said:

"Looking-glass, Looking-glass, on the wall,
Who in this land is the fairest of all?"

the glass answered:

"Oh, Queen, of all here the fairest art thou,
But the young Queen is fairer by far as I trow."

Then the wicked woman uttered a curse, and was so wretched, so utterly wretched, that she knew not what to do. At first she would not go to the wedding at all, but she had no peace, and had to go to see the young Queen. And when she went in she recognized Snow-white; and she stood still with rage and fear, and could not stir. But iron slippers had already been put upon the fire, and they were brought in with tongs, and set before her. Then she was forced to put on the red-hot shoes, and dance until she dropped down dead.

The Knapsack, the Hat, and the Horn

There were once three brothers who had fallen deeper and deeper into poverty, and at last their need was so great that they had to endure hunger, and had nothing to eat or drink. Then said they: "It cannot go on like this, we had better go into the world and seek our fortune." They therefore set out, and had already walked over many a long road and many a blade of grass, but had not yet met with good luck. One day they arrived in a great forest, and in the midst of it was a hill, and when they came nearer they saw that the hill was all silver. Then spoke the eldest: "Now I have found the good luck I wished for, and I desire nothing more." He took as much of the silver as he could possibly carry, and then turned back and went home again. But the two others said: "We want something more from good luck than mere silver," and did not touch it, but went onwards. After they had walked for two days longer without stopping, they came to a hill which was all gold. The second brother stopped, took thought with himself, and was undecided. "What shall I do?" said he; "shall I take for myself so much of this gold, that I have sufficient for all the rest of my life, or shall I go farther?" At length he made a decision, and putting as much into his pockets as would go in, said farewell to his brother, and went home. But the third said: "Silver and gold do not move me, I will not renounce my chance of fortune, perhaps something better still will be given me." He journeyed onwards, and when he had walked for three days, he came to a forest which was still larger than the one before, and never would come to an end, and as he found nothing to eat or to drink, he was all but exhausted. Then he climbed up a high tree to find out if up there he could see the end of the forest, but so far as his eye could peer he saw nothing but the top of trees. Then he began to descend the tree again, but hunger tormented him, and he thought to himself: "If I could but eat my fill once more!" When he got down he saw with astonishment a table beneath the tree richly spread with food, the steam of which rose up to meet him. "This time," said he, "my wish has been fulfilled at the right moment." And without inquiring who had brought the food, or who had cooked it, he approached the table, and ate with enjoyment until he had appeased his hunger. When he was done, he thought: "It would after all be a pity if the pretty little table-cloth were to be spoilt in the forest here," and folded it up tidily and put it in his pocket. Then he went onwards, and in the evening, when hunger once more returned to him, he wanted to make a trial of his little cloth, and spread it out and said: "I wish you to be covered with good cheer again," and scarcely had the wish crossed his lips than as many dishes with the most exquisite food on them stood on the table as there was room for. "Now I perceive," said he, "in what kitchen my cooking is done. You shall be dearer to me than the mountains of silver and gold." For he saw plainly that it was a wishing-cloth. The cloth, however, was still not enough to enable him to sit down quietly at home; he preferred to wander about the world and pursue his fortune further.

One night he met, in a lonely wood, a dusty, black charcoal-burner, who was burning charcoal there, and had some potatoes by the fire, on which he was going to make a meal. "Good evening, blackbird!" said the youth. "How do you get on in your solitude?"

"One day is like another," replied the charcoal-burner, "and every night potatoes! Have you a mind to have some, and will you be my guest?" "Many thanks," replied the traveler, "I won't rob you of your supper; you did not reckon on a visitor, but if you will put up with what I have, you shall have an invitation."

"Who is to prepare it for you?" said the charcoal-burner. "I see that you have nothing with you, and there is no one within a two hours' walk who could give you anything." "And yet there shall be a meal," answered the youth, "and better than any you have ever tasted." Thereupon he brought his cloth out of his knapsack, spread it on the ground, and said: "Little cloth, cover yourself," and instantly boiled meat and baked meat stood there, and as hot as if it had just come out of the kitchen. The charcoal-burner stared with wide-open eyes, but did not require much pressing; he fell to, and thrust larger and larger mouthfuls into his black mouth. When they had eaten everything, the charcoal-burner smiled contentedly, and said: "Listen, your table-cloth has my approval; it would be a fine thing for me in this forest, where no one ever cooks me anything good. I will propose an exchange to you; there in the corner hangs a soldier's knapsack, which is certainly old and shabby, but in it lie concealed wonderful powers; but, as I no longer use it, I will give it to you for the table-cloth."

"I must first know what these wonderful powers are," answered the youth.

"That will I tell you," replied the charcoal-burner; "every time you tap it with your hand, a corporal comes with six men armed from head to foot, and they do whatsoever you command them." "So far as I am concerned," said the youth, "if nothing else can be done, we will exchange," and he gave the charcoal-burner the cloth, took the knapsack from the hook, put it on, and bade farewell. When he had walked a while, he wished to make a trial of the magical powers of his knapsack and tapped it. Immediately the seven warriors stepped up to him, and the corporal said: "What does my lord and ruler wish for?"

"March with all speed to the charcoal-burner, and demand my wishing-cloth back." They faced to the left, and it was not long before they brought what he required, and had taken it from the charcoal-burner without asking many questions. The young man bade them retire, went onwards, and hoped fortune would shine yet more brightly on him. By sunset he came to another charcoal-burner, who was making his supper ready by the fire. "If you will eat some potatoes with salt, but with no dripping, come and sit down with me," said the sooty fellow.

"No," he replied, "this time you shall be my guest," and he spread out his cloth, which was instantly covered with the most beautiful dishes. They ate and drank together, and enjoyed themselves heartily. After the meal was over, the charcoal-burner said: "Up there on that shelf lies a little old worn-out hat which has strange properties: the moment someone puts it on, and turns it round on his head, the cannons go off as if twelve were fired all together, and they demolish everything so that no one can withstand them. The hat is of no use to me, and I will willingly give it for your table-cloth."

"That suits me very well," he answered, took the hat, put it on, and left his table-cloth behind him. But hardly had he walked away than he tapped on his knapsack, and his soldiers had to fetch the cloth back again. "One thing comes on the top of another," thought he, "and I feel as if my luck had not yet come to an end." Neither had his thoughts deceived him. After he had walked on for the whole of one day, he came to a third charcoal-burner, who like the previous ones, invited him to potatoes without dripping. But he let him also dine with him from his wishing-cloth, and the charcoal-burner liked it so well, that at last he offered him a horn for it, which had very different properties from those of the hat. The moment someone blew it all the walls and fortifications fell down, and all towns and villages became ruins. For this he immediately gave the charcoal-burner the cloth, but he afterwards sent his soldiers to demand it back again, so that at length he had the knapsack, hat and horn, all three. "Now," said he, "I am a made man, and it is time for me to go home and see how my brothers are getting on."

When he reached home, his brothers had built themselves a handsome house with their silver and gold, and were living in clover. He went to see them, but as he came in a ragged coat, with his shabby hat on his head, and his old knapsack on his back, they would not acknowledge him as their brother. They mocked and said: "You give out that you are our brother who despised silver and gold, and craved for something still better for himself. Such a person arrives in his carriage in full splendor like a mighty king, not like a beggar," and they drove him out of doors. Then he fell into a rage, and tapped his knapsack until a hundred and fifty men stood before him armed from head to foot. He commanded them to surround his brothers' house, and two of them were to take hazelsticks with them, and beat the two insolent men until they knew who he was. A violent disturbance broke out, people ran together, and wanted to lend the two sons help in their need, but against the soldiers they could do nothing. News of this at length came to the King, who was very angry, and ordered a captain to march out with his troop, and drive this disturber of the peace out of the town; but the man with the knapsack soon got a greater body of men together, who repulsed the captain and his men, so that they were forced to retire with bloody noses. The King said: "This vagabond is not brought to order yet," and next day sent a still larger troop against him, but they could do even less. The youth set still more men against them, and in order to be done the sooner, he turned his hat twice round on his head, and heavy guns began to play, and the king's men were beaten and put to flight. "And now," said he, "I will not make peace until the King gives me his daughter to wife, and I govern the whole kingdom in his name." He caused this to be announced to the King, and the latter said to his daughter: "Necessity is a hard nut to crack—what else is there for me to do but what he desires? If I want peace and to keep the crown on my head, I must give you away."

So the wedding was celebrated, but the King's daughter was vexed that her husband should be a common man, who wore a shabby hat, and put on an old knapsack. She longed to get rid of him, and night and day studied how she could accomplish this. Then she thought to herself: "Is it possible that his wonderful powers lie in the knapsack?" and she feigned affection and caressed him, and when his heart was softened, she said: "If you would but lay aside that horrid knapsack, it makes you look so ugly, that I can't help being ashamed of you." "Dear child," said he, "this knapsack is my greatest treasure; as long as I have it, there is no power on earth that I am afraid of." And he revealed to her the wonderful virtue with which it was endowed. Then she threw herself in his arms as if she were going to kiss him, but cleverly took the knapsack off his shoulders, and ran away with it. As soon as she was alone she tapped it, and commanded the warriors to seize their former master, and take him out of the royal palace. They obeyed, and the false wife sent still more men after him, who were to drive him quite out of the country. Then he would have been ruined if he had not had the little hat. And hardly were his hands free before he turned it twice. Immediately the cannon began to thunder, and demolished everything, and the King's daughter herself was forced to come and beg for mercy. As she entreated in such moving terms, and promised to better her ways, he allowed himself to be persuaded and granted her peace. She behaved in a friendly manner to him, and acted as if she loved him very much, and after some time managed so to befool him, that he confided to her that even if someone got the knapsack into his power, he could do nothing against him so long as the old hat was still his. When she knew the secret, she waited until he was asleep, and then she took the hat away from him, and had it thrown out into the street. But the horn still remained to him, and in great anger he blew it with all his strength. Instantly all walls, fortifications, towns, and villages, toppled down, and crushed the King and his daughter to death. And had he not put down the horn and had blown just a little longer, everything would have been in ruins, and not one stone would have been left standing on another. Then no one opposed him any longer, and he made himself King of the whole country.

Rumpelstiltskin

Once there was a miller who was poor, but who had a beautiful daughter. Now it happened that he had to go and speak to the King, and in order to make himself appear important he said to him: "I have a daughter who can spin straw into gold." The King said to the miller: "That is an art which pleases me well; if your daughter is as clever as you say, bring her to-morrow to my palace, and I will put her to the test."

And when the girl was brought to him he took her into a room which was quite full of straw, gave her a spinning-wheel and a reel, and said: "Now set to work, and if by to-morrow morning early you have not spun this straw into gold during the night, you must die." Thereupon he himself locked up the room, and left her in it alone. So there sat the poor miller's daughter, and for the life of her could not tell what to do; she had no idea how straw could be spun into gold, and she grew more and more frightened, until at last she began to weep.

But all at once the door opened, and in came a little man who said: "Good evening, Mistress Miller; why are you crying so?" "Alas!" answered the girl, "I have to spin straw into gold, and I do not know how to do it." "What will you give me," said the manikin, "if I do it for you?" "My necklace," said the girl. The little man took the necklace, seated himself in front of the wheel, and whirr, whirr, whirr, three turns, and the reel was full; then he put another on, and whirr, whirr, whirr, three times round, and the second was full too. And so it went on until the morning, when all the straw was spun, and all the reels were full of gold. By daybreak the King was already there, and when he saw the gold he was astonished and delighted, but his heart became only more greedy. He had the miller's daughter taken into another room full of straw, which was much larger, and commanded her to spin that also in one night if she valued her life. The girl knew not how to help herself, and was crying, when the door opened again, and the little man appeared, and said: "What will you give me if I spin that straw into gold for you?" "The ring on my finger," answered the girl. The little man took the ring, again began to turn the wheel, and by morning had spun all the straw into glittering gold.

The King rejoiced beyond measure at the sight, but still he had not gold enough; and he had the miller's daughter taken into a still larger room full of straw, and said: "You must spin this, too, in the course of this night; and if you succeed, you shall be my wife." "Even if she be a miller's daughter," thought he, "I could not find a richer wife in the whole world."

When the girl was alone the manikin came again for the third time, and said: "What will you give me if I spin the straw for you this time also?" "I have nothing left that I could give," answered the girl. "Then promise me, if you should become Queen, to give me your first child." "Who knows whether that will ever happen?" thought the miller's daughter; and, not knowing how else to help herself in this strait, she promised the manikin what he wanted, and for that he once more spun the straw into gold.

And when the King came in the morning, and found all as he had wished, he took her in marriage, and the pretty miller's daughter became a Queen.

A year after, she brought a beautiful child into the world, and she never gave a thought to the manikin. But suddenly he appeared in her room one day and said: "Now give me what you promised." The Queen was horror-struck, and offered the manikin all the riches of the kingdom if he would leave her the child. But the manikin said: "No, something alive is dearer to me than all the treasures in the world." Then the Queen began to lament and cry, so that the manikin pitied her. "I will give you three days' time," said he; "if by that time you find out my name, then shall you keep your child."

So the Queen thought the whole night of all the names that she had ever heard, and she sent a messenger over the country to inquire, far and wide, for any other names that there might be. When the manikin came the next day, she began with Caspar, Melchior, Balthazar, and said all the names she knew, one after another; but to every one the little man said: "That is not my name." On the second day she had inquiries made in the neighborhood as to the names of the people there, and she repeated to the manikin the most uncommon and curious. "Perhaps your name is Shortribs, or Sheepshanks, or Laceleg?" but he always answered: "That is not my name."

On the third day the messenger came back again, and said: "I have not been able to find a single new name, but as I came to a high mountain at the end of the forest, where the fox and the hare bid each other good night, there I saw a little house, and before the house a fire was burning, and round about the fire quite a ridiculous little man was jumping: he hopped upon one leg, and shouted:

" 'To-day I bake, to-morrow brew,
   The next I'll have the young Queen's child.
Ha! glad am I that no one knew
   That Rumpelstiltskin I am styled.' "

You may imagine how glad the Queen was when she heard the name! And when soon afterwards the little man came in, and asked: "Now, Mistress Queen, what is my name?" at first she said, "Is your name Conrad?" "No." "Is your name Harry?" "No."

"Perhaps your name is Rumpelstiltskin?"

"The devil has told you that! the devil has told you that!" cried the little man, and in his anger he plunged his right foot so deep into the earth that his whole leg went in; and then in rage he pulled at his left leg so hard with both hands that he tore himself in two.

Frederick and Catherine

There was once upon a time a man who was called Frederick and a woman called Catherine, who had married each other and lived together as young married folks. One day Frederick said: "I will now go and plough, Catherine; when I come back, there must be some roast meat on the table for hunger, and a fresh draught for thirst." "Just go, Frederick," answered Kate, "just go, I will have all ready for you." So when dinner-time drew near she got a sausage out of the chimney, put it in the frying-pan, put some butter to it, and set it on the fire. The sausage began to fry and to hiss. Catherine stood beside it and held the handle of the pan, and had her own thoughts as she was doing it. Then it occurred to her: "While the sausage is getting done you could go into the cellar and draw beer." So she set the frying pan safely on the fire, took a can, and went down into the cellar to draw beer. The beer ran into the can and Kate watched it, and then she thought: "Oh, dear! The dog upstairs is not fastened up, it might get the sausage out of the pan. Lucky I thought of it." And in a trice she was up the cellar-steps again, but the Spitz had the sausage in its mouth already, and trailed it away on the ground. But Catherine, who was not idle, set out after it, and chased it a long way into the field; the dog, however, was swifter than Catherine and did not let the sausage go, but skipped over the furrows with it. "What's gone is gone!" said Kate, and turned round, and as she had run till she was weary, she walked quietly and comfortably, and cooled herself. During this time the beer was still running out of the cask, for Kate had not turned the tap. And when the can was full and there was no other place for it, it ran into the cellar and did not stop until the whole cask was empty. As soon as Kate was on the steps she saw the accident. "Good gracious!" she cried. "What shall I do now to stop Frederick finding out?" She thought for a while, and at last she remembered that up in the garret was still standing a sack of the finest wheat flour from the last fair, and she would fetch that down and strew it over the beer. "Yes," said she, "he who saves a thing when he ought, has it afterwards when he needs it," and she climbed up to the garret and carried the sack below, and threw it straight down on the can of beer, which she knocked over, and Frederick's draught swam also in the cellar. "It is all right," said Kate, "where the one is the other ought to be also," and she strewed the meal over the whole cellar. When it was done she was heartily delighted with her work, and said: "How clean and wholesome it does look here!" At midday home came Frederick: "Now, wife, what have you ready for me?" "Ah, Freddy," she answered, "I was frying a sausage for you, but whilst I was drawing the beer to drink with it, the dog took it away out of the pan, and whilst I was running after the dog, all the beer ran out, and whilst I was drying up the beer with the flour, I knocked over the can as well, but be easy, the cellar is quite dry again." Said Frederick: "Kate, Kate, you should not have done that! to let the sausage be carried off and the beer run out of the cask, and throw out all our flour into the bargain!" "Well, Frederick, I did not know that; you should have told me." The man thought: "If this is the kind of wife I have, I had better take more care of things." Now he had saved up a good number of talers which he changed into gold, and said to Catherine: "Look, these are yellow counters for playing games; I will put them in a pot and bury them in the stable under the cow's manger, but mind you keep away from them, or it will be the worse for you." Said she: "Oh, no, Frederick, I certainly will not go near them." And when Frederick was gone some pedlars came into the village who had cheap earthen bowls and pots, and asked the young woman if there was nothing she wanted to bargain with them for. "Oh, dear people," said Catherine, "I have no money and can buy nothing, but if you have any use for yellow counters I will buy of you." "Yellow counters, why not? But just let us see them." "Then go into the stable and dig under the cow's manger, and you will find the yellow counters. I am not allowed to go there." The rogues went thither, dug and found pure gold. Then they laid hold of it, ran away, and left their pots and bowls behind in the house. Catherine thought she must use her new things, and as she had no lack in the kitchen already without these, she knocked the bottom out of every pot, and set them all as ornaments on the paling which went round about the house. When Frederick came and saw the new decorations, he said: "Catherine, what have you been about?" "I have bought them, Frederick, for the counters which were under the cow's manger. I did not go there myself, the pedlars had to dig them out for themselves." "Ah, wife," said Frederick, "what have you done? Those were not counters, but pure gold, and all our wealth; you should not have done that." "Indeed, Frederick," said she, "I did not know that, you should have forewarned me."

Catherine stood for a while and wondered; then she said: "Listen, Frederick, we will soon get the gold back again, we will run after the thieves." "Come, then," said Frederick, "we will try it; but take with you some butter and cheese that we may have something to eat on the way." "Yes, Frederick, I will take them." They set out, and as Frederick was the better walker, Catherine followed him. "It is to my advantage," thought she, "when we turn back I shall be a little way in advance." Then she same to a hill where there were deep ruts on both sides of the road. "There one can see," said Catherine, "how they have torn and skinned and galled the poor earth, it will never be whole again as long as it lives," and in her heart's compassion she took her butter and smeared the ruts right and left, that they might not be so hurt by the wheels, and as she was thus bending down in her charity, one of the cheeses rolled out of her pocket down the hill. Said Catherine: "I have made my way once up here, I will not go down again; another may run and fetch it back." So she took another cheese and rolled it down. But the cheeses did not come back, so she let a third run down, thinking: "Perhaps they are waiting for company, and do not like to walk alone." As all three stayed away she said: "I do not know what that can mean, but it may perhaps be that the third has not found the way, and has gone wrong, I will just send the fourth to call it." But the fourth did no better than the third. Then Catherine was angry, and threw down the fifth and sixth as well, and these were her last. She remained standing for some time watching for their coming, but when they still did not come, she said: "Oh, you are good folks to send in search of death, you stay a fine long time away! Do you think I will wait any longer for you? I shall go my way, you may run after me; you have younger legs than I." Catherine went on and found Frederick, who was standing waiting for her because he wanted something to eat. "Now just let us have what you have brought with you," said he. She gave him the dry bread. "Where have you the butter and the cheeses?" asked the man. "Ah, Freddy," said Catherine, "I smeared the cart-ruts with the butter and the cheeses will come soon; one ran away from me, so I sent the others after to call it." Said Frederick: "You should not have done that, Catherine, to smear the butter on the road, and let the cheeses run down the hill!" "Really, Frederick, you should have told me."

Then they ate the dry bread together, and Frederick said: "Catherine, did you make the house safe when you came away?" "No, Frederick, you should have told me to do it before." "Then go home again, and make the house safe before we go any farther, and bring with you something else to eat. I will wait here for you." Catherine went back and thought: "Frederick wants something more to eat, he does not like butter and cheese, so I will take with me a handkerchief full of dried pears and a pitcher of vinegar for him to drink." Then she bolted the upper half of the door fast, but unhinged the lower door, and took it on her back, believing that when she had placed the door in security the house must be well taken care of. Catherine took her time on the way, and thought: "Frederick will rest himself so much the longer." When she had once more reached him she said: "Here is the house-door for you, Frederick, and now you can take care of the house yourself." "Oh, heavens," said he, "what a wise wife I have! She takes the under-door off the hinges that everything may run in, and bolts the upper one. It is now too late to go back home again, but since you have brought the door here, you shall just carry it farther." "I will carry the door, Frederick, but the dried pears and the vinegar-jug will be too heavy for me; I will hang them on the door so that it may carry them."

And now they went into the forest, and sought the rogues, but did not find them. At length as it grew dark they climbed into a tree and resolved to spend the night there. Scarcely, however, had they sat down at the top of it than the rascals came thither who carry away with them what does not want to go, and find things before they are lost. They sat down under the very tree in which

Frederick and Catherine were sitting, lighted a fire, and were about to share their booty. Frederick got down on the other side and collected some stones together. Then he climbed up again with them, and wished to throw them at the thieves and kill them. The stones, however, did not hit them, and the knaves cried: "It will soon be morning, the wind is shaking down the fir-cones." Catherine still had the door on her back, and as it pressed so heavily on her, she thought it was the fault of the dried pears, and said: "Frederick, I must throw the pears down." "No, Catherine, now now," he replied, "they might betray us." "Oh, but, Frederick, I must! They weigh me down far too much." "Do it, then, and be hanged!" Then the dried pears rolled down between the branches, and the rascals below said: "Those are birds' droppings."

A short time afterwards, as the door was still heavy, Catherine said: "Ah, Frederick, I must pour out the vinegar." "No, Catherine, you must not, it might betray us." "Ah, but, Frederick, I must, it weighs me down far too much." "Then do it and be hanged!" So she emptied out the vinegar, and it spattered over the robbers. They said amongst themselves: "The dew is already falling." At length Catherine thought: "Can it really be the door which weighs me down so?" and said: "Frederick, I must throw the door down." "No, not now, Catherine, it might betray us." "Oh, but, Frederick, I must. It weighs me down far too much." "Oh, no, Catherine, do hold it fast." "Ah, Frederick, I am letting it fall!" "Let it go, then, in the devil's name." Then it fell down with a violent clatter, and the rascals below cried: "The devil is coming down the tree!" and they ran away and left everything behind them. Early next morning, when the two came down they found all their gold again, and carried it home.

When they were once more at home, Frederick said: "And now, Catherine, you, too, must be industrious and work." "Yes, Frederick, I will soon do that, I will go into the field and cut corn." When Catherine got into the field, she said to herself: "Shall I eat before I cut, or shall I sleep before I cut? Oh, I will eat first." Then Catherine ate and eating made her sleepy, and she began to cut, and half in a dream cut all her clothes to pieces, her apron, her gown, and her shift. When Catherine woke again after a long sleep she was standing there half-naked, and said to herself: "Is it I, or

is it not I? Alas, it is not I." In the meantime night came, and
Catherine ran into the village, knocked at her husband's window,
and cried: "Frederick."

"What is the matter?" "I should very much like to know if
Catherine is in?""Yes, yes," replied Frederick, "she must be in and
asleep."

Said she, "That's all right, then I am certainly at home already,"
and ran away.

Outside Catherine found some vagabonds who were going to
steal. Then she went to them and said: "I will help you to steal."
The rascals thought that she knew what opportunities the place
offered, and were willing. Catherine went in front of the houses,
and cried: "Good folks, have you anything? We want to steal."
The thieves thought to themselves: "That's a fine way of doing
things," and wished themselves once more rid of Catherine. Then
they said to her: "Outside the village the pastor has some turnips
in the field. Go there and pull up some turnips for us." Catherine
went to the ground, and began to pull them up, but was so lazy
that she never stood up straight. Then a man came by, saw her,
and stood still and thought that it was the devil who was thus

rooting amongst the turnips. He ran away into the village to the pastor, and said: "Mr. Pastor, the devil is in your turnip-ground, rooting up turnips." "Ah, heavens," answered the pastor, "I have a lame foot, I cannot go out and drive him away." Said the man: "Then I will carry you on my back," and he carried him out on his back. And when they came to the ground, Catherine arose and stood up her full height. "Ah, the devil!" cried the pastor, and both hurried away, and in his great fright the pastor could run better with his lame foot than the man who had carried him on his back could do on his sound legs.

The Three Feathers

There was once upon a time a King who had three sons, of whom two were clever and wise, but the third did not speak much, and was simple, and was called the Simpleton. When the King had become old and weak, and was thinking of his end, he did not know which of his sons should inherit the kingdom after him. Then he said to them: "Go forth, and he who brings me the most beautiful carpet shall be King after my death." And that there should be no dispute amongst them, he took them outside his castle, blew three feathers in the air, and said: "You shall go as they fly." One feather flew to the east, the other to the west, but the third flew straight up and did not fly far, but soon fell to the ground. And now one brother went to the right, and the other to the left, and they mocked Simpleton, who was forced to stay where the third feather had fallen. He sat down and was sad. Then all at once he saw that there was a trap-door close by the feather. He raised it up, found some steps, and went down them. Then he came to another door, knocked at it, and heard somebody inside calling:

> "Little green waiting-maid,
> Waiting-maid with the limping leg,
> Little dog of the limping leg,
> Hop hither and thither,
> And quickly see who is without."

The door opened, and he saw a great, fat toad sitting, and round about her a crowd of little toads. The fat toad asked what he wanted. He answered: "I should like to have the prettiest and finest carpet in the world." Then she called a young one and said:

> "Little green waiting-maid,
> Waiting-maid with the limping leg,
> Little dog of the limping leg,
> Hop hither and thither,
> And bring me the great box."

The young toad brought the box, and the fat toad opened it, and gave Simpleton a carpet out of it, so beautiful and so fine, that on the earth above, none could have been woven like it. Then he thanked her, and climbed out again. The two others, however, had looked on their youngest brother as so stupid that they believed he would find and bring nothing at all. "Why should we give ourselves a great deal of trouble searching?" said they, and got some coarse handkerchiefs from the first shepherds' wives whom they met, and carried them home to the King. At the same time Simpleton also came back, and brought his beautiful carpet, and when the King saw it he was astonished, and said: "If justice be done, the kingdom belongs to the youngest." But the two others let their father have no peace, and said that it was impossible that Simpleton, who in everything lacked understanding, should be King, and entreated him to make a new agreement with them. Then the father said: "He who brings me the most beautiful ring shall inherit the kingdom," and led the three brothers out, and blew into the air three feathers, which they were to follow. Those of the two eldest again went east and west, and Simpleton's feather flew straight up, and fell down near the door into the earth. Then he went down again to the fat toad, and told her that he wanted the most beautiful ring. She at once ordered her big box to be brought, and gave him a ring out of it, which sparkled with jewels, and was so beautiful that no goldsmith on earth would have been able to make it. The two eldest laughed at Simpleton for going to seek a golden ring. They gave themselves no trouble, but knocked the nails out of an old carriage-ring, and took it to the King; but when Simpleton produced his golden ring, his father again said: "The kingdom belongs to him." The two eldest did not cease from tormenting the King until he made a third condition, and declared that the one who brought the most beautiful woman home, should have the kingdom. He again blew the three feathers into the air, and they flew as before.

Then Simpleton without more ado went down to the fat toad, and said: "I am to take home the most beautiful woman!" "Oh," answered the toad, "the most beautiful woman! She is not at hand at the moment, but still you shall have her." She gave him a yellow turnip which had been hollowed out, to which six mice were harnessed. Then Simpleton said quite mournfully: "What am I to do with that?" The toad answered: "Just put one of my little toads into it." Then he seized one at random out of the circle, and put her into the yellow coach, but hardly was she seated inside it than she turned into a wonderfully beautiful maiden, and the turnip into a coach, and the six mice into horses. So he kissed her, and drove off quickly with the horses, and took her to the King. His brothers, who returned later, had not even taken the trouble of looking for beautiful girls, but had brought with them the first peasant women they chanced to meet. When the king saw them he said: "After my death the kingdom belongs to my youngest son." But the two eldest deafened the King's ears afresh with their clamor: "We cannot consent to Simpleton's being King," and demanded that the one whose wife could leap through a ring which hung in the center of the hall should have the preference. They thought: "The peasant women can do that easily; they are strong enough, but the delicate maiden will jump herself to death." The aged King agreed likewise to this. Then the two peasant women jumped, and jumped through the ring, but were so clumsy that they fell, and their coarse arms and legs broke in two. And then the pretty maiden whom Simpleton had brought with him, sprang, and sprang through as lightly as a deer, and all opposition had to cease. So he received the crown, and has ruled wisely for quite some time.

The Golden Goose

There was a man who had three sons, the youngest of whom was called Dummling, (Simpleton) and was despised, mocked, and sneered at on every occasion.

It happened that the eldest wanted to go into the forest to hew wood, and before he went his mother gave him a beautiful sweet cake and a bottle of wine in order that he might not suffer from hunger or thirst.

When he entered the forest he met a little grey-haired old man who bade him good-day, and said: "Do give me a piece of cake out of your pocket, and let me have a draught of your wine; I am so hungry and thirsty." But the clever son answered: "If I give you my cake and wine, I shall have none for myself; be off with you," and he left the little man standing there and went on.

But when he began to hew down a tree, it was not long before he made a false stroke, and the axe cut him in the arm, so that he had to go home and have it bound up. And this was the little grey man's doing.

After this the second son went into the forest, and his mother gave him, like the eldest, a cake and a bottle of wine. The little old grey man met him likewise, and asked him for a piece of cake and a drink of wine. But the second son, too, said sensibly enough: "What I give you will be taken away from myself; be off!" and he left the little man standing there and went on. His punishment, however, was not delayed; when he had made a few blows at the tree he struck himself in the leg, so that he had to be carried home.

Then Dummling said: "Father, do let me go and cut wood." The father answered: "Your brothers have hurt themselves with it, leave it alone, you do not understand anything about it." But Dummling begged so long that at last he said: "Just go then, you will have to learn by hurting yourself." His mother gave him a cake made with water and baked in the cinders, and with it a bottle of sour beer.

When he came to the forest the little old grey man met him likewise, and greeting him, said: "Give me a piece of your cake and a drink out of your bottle; I am so hungry and thirsty." Dummling answered: "I have only cinder-cake and sour beer; if that pleases you, we will sit down and eat." So they sat down, and when Dummling pulled out his cinder-cake, it was a fine sweet cake, and the sour beer had become good wine. So they ate and drank, and after that the little man said: "Since you have a good heart, and are willing to divide what you have, I will give you good luck. There stands an old tree, cut it down, and you will find something at the roots." Then the little man took leave of him.

Dummling went and cut down the tree, and when it fell there was a goose sitting in the roots with feathers of pure gold. He lifted her up, and taking her with him, went to an inn where he thought he would stay the night. Now the host had three daughters, who saw the goose and were curious to know what such a wonderful bird might be, and would have liked to have one of its golden feathers.

The eldest thought : "I shall soon find an opportunity of pulling out a feather," and as soon as Dummling had gone out she seized the goose by the wing, but her finger and hand remained stuck fast to it.

The second came soon afterwards, thinking only of how she might get a feather for herself, but she had scarcely touched her sister than she was held fast.

At last the third also came with the like intent, and the others screamed out: "Keep away; for goodness' sake keep away!" But she did not understand why she was to keep away. "The others are there," she thought, "I may as well be there too," and ran to them; but as soon as she had touched her sister, she remained stuck fast to her. So they had to spend the night with the goose.

The next morning Dummling took the goose under his arm and set out, without troubling himself about the three girls who were hanging on to it. They were obliged to run after him continually, now left, now right, wherever his legs took him.

In the middle of the fields the parson met them, and when he saw the procession he said: "For shame, you good-for-nothing girls, why are you running across the fields after this young man? Is that seemly?" At the same time he seized the youngest by the hand in order to pull her away, but as soon as he touched her he likewise stuck fast, and was himself obliged to run behind.

Before long the sexton came by and saw his master, the parson, running behind three girls. He was astonished at this and called out: "Hi! your reverence, whither away so quickly? Do not forget that we have a christening to-day!" and running after him he took him by the sleeve, but was also held fast to it.

Whilst the five were trotting thus one behind the other, two laborers came with their hoes from the fields; the parson called out to them and begged that they would set him and the sexton free. But they had scarcely touched the sexton when they were held fast, and now there were seven of them running behind Dummling and the goose.

Soon afterwards he came to a city, where a king ruled who had a daughter who was so serious that no one could make her laugh. So he had put forth a decree that whosoever should be able to make her laugh should marry her. When Dummling heard this, he went with his goose and all her train before the King's daughter, and as soon as she saw the seven people running on and on, one behind the other, she began to laugh quite loudly, and as if she would never stop. Thereupon Dummling asked to have her for his wife; but the King did not like the son-in-law, and made all manner of excuses and said he must first produce a man who could drink a cellarful of wine. Dummling thought of the little grey man, who could certainly help him; so he went into the forest, and in the same place where he had felled the tree, he saw a man sitting, who had a very sorrowful face. Dummling asked him what he was taking to heart so sorely, and he answered: "I have such a great thirst and cannot quench it; cold water I cannot stand, a barrel of wine I have just emptied, but that to me is like a drop on a hot stone!"

"There, I can help you," said Dummling, "just come with me and you shall be satisfied."

He led him into the king's cellar, and the man bent over the huge barrels, and drank and drank till his loins hurt, and before the day was out he had emptied all the barrels. Then Dummling asked once more for his bride, but the king was vexed that such an ugly fellow, whom everyone called Dummling, should take away his daughter, and he made a new condition; he must first find a man who could eat a whole mountain of bread. Dummling did not think long, but went straight into the forest, where in the same place there sat a man who was tying up his body with a strap, and making an awful face, and saying: "I have eaten a whole ovenful of rolls, but what good is that when one has such a hunger as I? My stomach remains empty, and I must tie myself up if I am not to die of hunger."

At this Dummling was glad, and said: "Get up and come with me; you shall eat your fill." He led him to the King's palace, where all the flour in the whole Kingdom was collected, and from it he had a huge mountain of bread baked. The man from the forest stood before it, began to eat, and by the end of one day the whole mountain had vanished. Then Dummling for the third time asked for his bride; but the King again sought a way out, and ordered a ship which could sail on land and on water. "As soon as you come sailing back in it," said he, "you shall have my daughter for your wife."

Dummling went straight into the forest, and there sat the little grey man to whom he had given his cake. When he heard what Dummling wanted, he said: "Since you have given me food and drink, I will give you the ship; and I do all this because you once were kind to me." Then he gave him the ship which could sail on land and water, and when the king saw that, he could no no longer prevent him from having his daughter. The wedding was celebrated, and after the King's death, Dummling inherited his Kingdom and lived for a long time contentedly with his wife.

Allerleirauh *

There was once upon a time a King who had a wife with golden hair, and she was so beautiful that her equal was not to be found on earth. It came to pass that she lay ill, and as she felt that she must soon die, she called the King and said: "If you wish to marry again after my death, take no one who is not quite as beautiful as I am, and who has not just such golden hair as I have: this you must promise me." And after the King had promised her this she closed her eyes and died.

For a long time the King could not be comforted, and had no thought of taking another wife. At length his councillors said: "This cannot go on. The King must marry again, that we may have a Queen." And now messengers were sent about far and wide, to seek a bride who equalled the late Queen in beauty. In the whole world, however, none was to be found, and even if one had been found, still there would have been no one who had such golden hair. So the messengers came home exactly as they had set out.

Now the King had a daughter, who was just as beautiful as her dead mother, and had the same golden hair. When she was grown up the King looked at her one day, and saw that in every respect she was like his late wife, and suddenly felt a violent love for her. Then he spoke to his councillors: "I will marry my daughter, for she is the counterpart of my late wife, otherwise I can find no bride who resembles her." When the councillors heard that, they were shocked, and said: "God has forbidden a father to marry his daughter. No good can come from such a crime, and the kingdom will be involved in the ruin."

The daughter was still more shocked when she became aware of her father's resolution, but hoped to turn him from his design. Then she said to him: "Before I fulfil your wish, I must have three dresses, one as golden as the sun, one as silvery as the moon, and one as bright as the stars; besides this, I wish for a mantle of a thousand different kinds of fur and peltry joined together, and one of every kind of animal in your kingdom must give a piece of his skin for it." For she thought: "To get that will be quite impossible, and

* Of many different kinds of fur.

thus I shall divert my father from his wicked intentions." The King, however, did not give it up, and the cleverest maidens in his kingdom had to weave the three dresses, one as golden as the sun, one as silvery as the moon, and one as bright as the stars, and his huntsmen had to catch one of every kind of animal in the whole of his kingdom, and take from it a piece of its skin, and out of these was made a mantle of a thousand different kinds of fur. At length, when all was ready, the King caused the mantle to be brought, spread it out before her, and said: "The wedding shall be tomorrow."

When, therefore, the King's daughter saw that there was no longer any hope of turning her father's heart, she resolved to run away. In the night whilst everyone was asleep, she got up, and took three different things from her treasures, a golden ring, a golden spinning-wheel, and a golden reel. The three dresses of the sun, moon, and stars she placed into a nutshell, put on her mantle of all kinds of fur, and blackened her face and hands with soot. Then she commended herself to God, and went away, and walked the whole night until she reached a great forest. And as she was tired, she got into a hollow tree, and fell asleep.

The sun rose, and she slept on, and she was still sleeping when it was full day. Then it so happened that the King to whom this forest belonged, was hunting in it. When his dogs came to the tree, they sniffed, and ran barking around about it. The King said to the huntsmen: "Just see what kind of wild beast has hidden itself in there." The huntsmen obeyed his order, and when they came back they said: "A wondrous beast is lying in the hollow tree; we have never before seen one like. Its skin is fur of a thousand different kinds, but it is lying asleep." Said the King: "See if you can catch it alive, and then fasten it to the carriage, and we will take it with us." When the huntsmen laid hold of the maiden, she awoke full of terror, and cried to them: "I am a poor child, deserted by father and mother; have pity on me, and take me with you." Then said they: "Allerleirauh, you will be useful in the kitchen, come with us, and you can sweep up the ashes." So they put her in the carriage, and took her home to the royal palace. There they pointed out to her a closet under the stairs, where no daylight entered, and said: "Hairy animal, there you can live and sleep." Then she was sent into the kitchen, and there she carried wood and water, swept the hearth, plucked the fowls, picked the vegetables, raked the ashes, and did all the dirty work.

Allerleirauh lived there for a long time in great wretchedness. Alas, fair princess, what is to become of you now! It happened, however, that one day a feast was held in the palace, and she said to the cook: "May I go upstairs for a while, and look on? I will place myself outside the door." The cook answered: "Yes, go, but you must be back here in half-an-hour to sweep the hearth." Then she took her oil-lamp, went into her den, put off her dress of fur, and washed the soot off her face and hands, so that her full beauty once more came to light. And she opened the nut, and took out her dress which shone like the sun, and when she had done that she went up to the festival, and everyone made way for her, for no one knew her, and thought no otherwise than that she was a king's daughter. The King came to meet her, give his hand to her, and danced with her, and thought in his heart: "My eyes have never yet seen anyone so beautiful!" When the dance was over she curtsied, and when the King looked round again she had vanished, and none knew whither. The guards who stood outside the palace were called and questioned, but no one had seen her.

She had run into her little den, however, there quickly taken off her dress, made her face and hands black again, put on the mantle of fur, and again was Allerleirauh. And now when she went into the kitchen, and was about to get to her work and sweep up the ashes, the cook said: "Leave that alone till morning, and make me the soup for the King; I, too, will go upstairs awhile, and take a look; but let no hairs fall in, or in future you shall have nothing to eat." So the cook went away, and Allerleirauh made the soup for the King, and made bread soup and the best she could, and when it was ready she fetched her golden ring from her little den, and put it in the bowl in which the soup was served. When the dancing was over, the King had his soup brought and ate it, and he liked it so much that it seemed to him he had never tasted better. But when he came to the bottom of the bowl, he found the golden ring, and could not conceive how it could have got there. Then he ordered the cook to appear before him. The cook was terrified when he heard the order, and said to Allerleirauh: "You have certainly let a hair fall into the soup, and if you have, you shall be beaten for it." When he came before the King the latter

asked who had made the soup? The cook replied: "I made it." But the King said: "That is not true, for it was much better than usual, and cooked differently." He answered: "I must acknowledge that I did not make it, it was made by the hairy animal." The King said: "Go and bid it come up here."

When Allerleirauh came, the King said: "Who are you?" "I am a poor girl who no longer has any father or mother." He asked further: "Of what use are you in my palace?" She answered: "I am good for nothing but to have boots thrown at my head." He continued: "Where did you get the ring which was in the soup?" She answered: "I know nothing about the ring." So the King could learn nothing, and had to send her away again.

After a while, there was another festival, and then, as before, Allerleirauh begged the cook for leave to go and look on. He answered: "Yes, but come back again in a half-an-hour, and make the King the bread soup which he so much likes." Then she ran into her den, washed herself quickly, and took out of the nut the dress which was as silvery as the moon, and put it on. Then she went up and was like a princess, and the King stepped forward to meet her, and rejoiced to see her once more, and as the dance was just beginning they danced it together. But when it was ended, she again disappeared so quickly that the king could not observe where she went. She, however, sprang into her den, and once more made herself a hairy animal, and went into the kitchen to prepare the bread soup. When the cook had gone upstairs, she fetched the little golden spinning-wheel, and put it in the bowl so that the soup covered it. Then it was taken to the King, who ate it, and liked it as much as before, and had the cook brought, who this time likewise was forced to confess that Allerleirauh had prepared the soup. Allerleirauh again came before the King, but she answered that she was good for nothing else but to have boots thrown at her head, and that she knew nothing at all about the little golden spinning-wheel.

When, for the third time, the King held a festival, all happened just as it had done before. The cook said: "Fur-skin, you are a witch, and always put something in the soup which makes it so good that the King likes it better than that which I cook," but as she begged so hard, he let her go up at the appointed time. And now she put on the dress which shone like the stars, and thus entered the hall. Again the King danced with the beautiful maiden, and thought that she never yet had been so beautiful. And whilst she was dancing, he contrived, without her noticing it, to slip a golden ring on her finger, and he had given orders that the dance should last a very long time. When it was ended, he wanted to hold her fast by her hands, but she tore herself loose, and sprang away so quickly through the crowd that she vanished from his sight. She ran as fast as she could into her den beneath the stairs, but as she had been too long, and had stayed more than half-an-hour she could not take off her pretty dress, but only threw over it her mantle of fur, and in her haste she did not make herself quite black, but one finger remained white. Then Allerleirauh ran into the kitchen, and cooked the bread soup for the King, and as the cook was away, put her golden reel into it. When the King found the reel at the bottom of it, he caused Allerleirauh to be summoned, and then he espied the white finger, and saw the ring which he had put on it during the dance. Then he grasped her by the hand, and held her fast, and as she tried to escape his grip and run away, her mantle of fur opened a little, and the star-dress shone forth. The King clutched the mantle and tore it off. Then her golden hair shone forth, and she stood there in full splendor, and could no longer hide herself. And when she had washed the soot and ashes from her face, she was more beautiful than anyone who had ever been seen on earth. And the King said: "You are my dear bride, and we will never more part from each other." Thereupon the marriage was solemnized, and they lived happily until their death.

How Six Men Got On in the World

There was once a man who understood all kinds of arts; he served in war, and behaved well and bravely, but when the war was over he received his dismissal, and three farthings for his expenses on the way. "Wait," said he, "I shall not be content with this. If I can only meet with the right people, the King will yet have to give me all the treasure of the country." Then full of the anger he went into the forest, and saw a man standing therein who had plucked up six trees as if they were blades of corn. He said to him: "Will you be my servant and go with me?" "Yes," he answered, "but, first, I will take this little bundle of sticks home to my mother," and he took one of the trees, and wrapped it round the five others, lifted the bundle on his back, and carried it away. Then he returned and went with his master, who said: "We two ought to be able to get through the world very well, and when they had walked on for a short while they found a huntsman who was kneeling, had shouldered his gun, and was about to fire. The master said to him: "Huntsman, what are you going to shoot?" He answered: "Two miles from here a fly is sitting on the branch of an oak-tree, and I want to shoot its eye out." "Oh, come with me," said the man, "if we three are together, we certainly ought to be able to get on in the world!" The huntsman was ready, and went with him, and they came to seven windmills whose sails were turning round with great speed, and yet no wind was blowing either on the right or the left, and no leaf was stirring. Then said the man: "I know not what is driving the windmills, not a breath of air is stirring," and he went onwards with his servants, and when they had walked two miles they saw a man sitting on a tree who was shutting one nostril, and blowing out of the other. "Good gracious! What are you doing up there?" He answered: Two miles from here are seven windmills; look, I am blowing them till they turn round." "Oh, come with me," said the man. "If we four are together, we shall carry the whole world before us!" The blower came down and went with him, and after a while they saw a man who was standing on one leg and had taken off the other, and laid it beside him. Then the master said: "You have arranged things very comfortably to have a rest." "I am a runner," he replied, "and to stop myself from running too fast, I have taken off one of my legs, for if I run with both, I go quicker than any bird can fly." "Oh, go with me. If we five are together, we shall carry the whole world before us." So he went with them, and it was not long before they met a man who wore a cap, but wore it entirely over one ear. Then the master said to him: "Gracefully, gracefully don't stick your cap on one ear, you look just like a tom-fool!" "I must not wear it otherwise," said he, "For if I set my hat straight, a terrible

frost comes on, and all the birds in the air are frozen, and drop dead on the ground." "Oh, come with me," said the master. "If we six are together, we can carry the whole world before us."

Now the six came to a town where the King had proclaimed that whosoever ran a race with his daughter and won the victory, should be her husband, but whosoever lost it, must lose his head. Then the man presented himself and said: "I will, however, let my servant run for me." The King replied: "Then his life also must be staked, so that his head and yours are both set on the victory." When that was settled and made secure, the man buckled the other leg on the runner, and said to him: "Now be nimble, and help us to win." It was fixed that the one who was the first to bring some water from a far distant well was to be the victor. The runner received a pitcher, and the King's daughter one too, and they began to run at the same time, but in an instant, when the King's daughter had got a very little way, the people who were looking on could see no more of the runner, and it was just as if the wind had whistled by. In a short time he reached the well, filled his pitcher with water, and turned back. Half-way home, however, he was overcome with fatigue, set his pitcher down, lay down himself, and fell asleep. But he had made a pillow of a horse's skull which was lying on the ground, in order that he might lie uncomfortably, and soon wake up again. In the meantime the King's daughter, who could also run very well—quite as well as any ordinary mortal can—had reached the well, and was hurrying back with her pitcher full of water, and when she saw the runner lying there asleep, she was glad and said: "My enemy is delivered over into my hands," emptied his pitcher, and ran on. And now all would have been lost if by good luck the huntsman had not been standing at the top of the castle, and had not seen everything with his sharp eyes. Then said he: "The King's daughter shall still not prevail against us; and he loaded his gun, and shot so cleverly, that he shot the horse's skull away from under the runner's head without hurting him. Then the runner awoke, leapt up, and saw that his pitcher was empty, and that the King's daughter was already far in advance. He did not lose heart, however, but ran back to the well with his pitcher, again drew some water, and was at home again a full ten minutes before the King's daughter. "Behold!" said he, "only now have I begun to use my legs; what I did before did not deserve to be called running."

But it pained the King, and still more his daughter, that she should be carried off by a common discharged soldier like that; so they took counsel with each other how to get rid of him and his companions. Then said the King to her: "I have thought of a way; don't be afraid, they shall not come back again." And he said to them: "You shall now make merry together, and eat and drink," and he conducted them to a room which had a floor of iron, and the doors also were of iron, and the windows were guarded with iron bars. There was a table in the room covered with delicious food, and the King said to them: "Go in, and enjoy yourselves." And when they were inside, he ordered the doors to be shut and bolted. Then he sent for the cook, and commanded him to make a fire under the room until the iron became red-hot. This the cook did, and the six who were sitting at table began to feel quite warm, and they thought the heat was caused by the food; but as it became still greater, and they wanted to get out, and found that the doors and windows were bolted, they became aware that the King must have an evil intention, and wanted to suffocate them. "He shall not succeed, however," said the one with the cap. "I will cause a frost to come, before which the fire shall be ashamed, and creep away." Then he put his cap on straight, and immediately there came such a frost that all heat disappeared, and the food on the dishes began to freeze. When an hour or two had passed by, and the King believed that they had perished in the heat, he had the doors opened to behold them himself. But when the doors were opened, all six were standing there, alive and well, and said that they should very much like to get out to warm themselves, for the very food was fast frozen to the dishes with the cold. Then, full of anger, the King went down to the cook, scolded him, and asked why he had not done what he had been ordered to do. But the cook replied: "There is heat enough there, just look yourself." Then the King saw that a fierce fire was burning under the iron room, and perceived that there was no getting the better of the six in this way.

Again the King considered how to get rid of his unpleasant guests, and caused their chief to be brought and said: "If you will take gold and renounce my daughter, you shall have as much as you will."

"Oh, yes, Lord King," he answered, "give me as much as my servant can carry, and I will not ask for your daughter."

On this the King was satisfied, and the other continued: "In fourteen days, I will come and fetch it." Thereupon he summoned together all the tailors in the whole kingdom, and they were to sit for fourteen days and sew a sack. And when it was ready, the strong one who could tear up trees had to take it on his back, and go with it to the King. Then said the King: "Who can that strong fellow be who is carrying a bundle of linen on his back that is as big as a house?" and he was alarmed and said: "What a lot of gold he can carry away!" Then he commanded a ton of gold to be brought, which took sixteen of his strongest men to carry, but the strong one snatched it up in one hand, put it in his sack, and said: "Why aren't you bringing me some more?—that hardly covers the bottom!" Then, little by little, the King caused all his treasure to be brought thither, and the strong one pushed it into the sack, and still the sack was not half full with it." "Bring more," cried he, "these few crumbs don't fill it." Then seven thousand carts with gold had to be gathered together in the whole kingdom, and the strong one thrust them and the oxen harnessed to them into his sack. "I will examine it no longer," said he, "but will just take what comes, so long as the sack is but full." When all that was inside, there was still room for a great deal more; then he said: "I will just make an end of the thing; people do sometimes tie up a sack even when it is not full." So he took it on his back, and went away with his comrades. When the King now saw how one single man was carrying away the entire wealth of the country, he became enraged, and bade his horsemen mount and pursue the six, and ordered them to take the sack away from the strong one. Two regiments speedily overtook the six, and called out: "You are prisoners, put down the sack with the gold, or you will all be cut to pieces!" "What say you?" cried the blower, "that we are prisoners! Rather than that should happen, all of you shall dance about in the air." And he closed one nostril, and with the other blew on the two regiments. Then they were driven away from each other, and carried into the blue sky over all the mountains—one here, the other there. One sergeant cried for mercy; he had nine wounds, and was a brave fellow who did not deserve ill-treatment. The blower stopped a little so that he came down without injury, and then the blower said to him: "Now go home to your King, and tell him he had better send some more horsemen, and I will blow them all into the air." When the King was informed of this he said: "Let the rascals go. There is magic in them." Then the six conveyed the riches home, divided it amongst them, and lived in content until their death.

Brother Lustig

There was once upon a time a great war, and when it came to an end, many soldiers were discharged. Then Brother Lustig also received his dismissal, and with it nothing but a small loaf of rationed bread, and four kreuzers in money, with which he departed. St. Peter, however, had placed himself in his way in the form of a poor beggar, and when Brother Lustig came up, he begged alms of him. Brother Lustig replied: "Dear beggar-man, what am I to give you? I have been a soldier, and have received my dismissal, and have nothing but this little loaf of rationed bread, and four kreuzers of money; when that is gone, I shall have to beg as well as you. Still I will give you something." Thereupon he divided the loaf into four parts, and gave the apostle one of them, and a kreuzer likewise. St. Peter thanked him, went onwards, and threw himself

again in the soldier's way as a beggar, but in another shape; and
when he came up begged a gift of him as before. Brother Lustig
spoke as he had done before, and again gave him a quarter of the
loaf and one kreuzer. St. Peter thanked him, and went onwards,
but for the third time placed himself in another shape as a beggar
on the road, and spoke to Brother Lustig. Brother Lustig gave him
also the third quarter of bread and the third kreuzer. St. Peter
thanked him, and Brother Lustig went onwards, and had but a
quarter of the loaf, and one kreuzer. With that he went into an
inn, ate the bread, and ordered one kreuzer's worth of beer. When
he had had it, he journeyed onwards, and then St. Peter, who had
assumed the appearance of a discharged soldier, met and spoke to
him thus: "Good day, comrade, can you not give me a bit of bread,
and a kreuzer to get a drink?" "Where am I to procure it?" answered Brother Lustig: "I have been discharged, and I got nothing
but a loaf of rationed bread and four kreuzers in money. I met
three beggars on the road, and I gave each of them a quarter of
my bread, and one kreuzer. The last quarter I ate in the inn, and
had a drink with the last kreuzer. Now my pockets are empty, and
if you also have nothing we can go a-begging together." "No,"
answered St. Peter, "we need not quite do that. I know a little about
medicine, and I will soon earn as much as I require by that." "Indeed," said Brother Lustig, "I know nothing of that, so I must go
and beg alone." "Just come with me," said St. Peter, "and if I earn
anything, you shall have half of it." "All right," said Brother Lustig, and they went away together.

Then they came to a peasant's house inside of which they heard
loud lamentations and cries; so they went in, and there the husband was lying sick unto death, and very near his end, and his
wife was crying and weeping quite loudly. "Stop that howling and
crying," said St. Peter, "I will make the man well again," and he
took a salve out of his pocket, and healed the sick man in a moment, so that he could get up, and was in perfect health. In great
delight the man and his wife said: "How can we reward you? What
shall we give you?" But St. Peter would take nothing, and the more
the peasant folks offered him, the more he refused. Brother Lustig,
however, nudged St. Peter, and said: "Take something; sure enough
we are in need of it." At length the woman brought a lamb and
said to St. Peter that he really must take that, but he would not.

Then Brother Lustig gave him a poke in the side, and said: "Do take it, you stupid fool; we are in great want of it!" Then St. Peter said at last: "Well, I will take the lamb, but I won't carry it; if you insist on having it, you must carry it." "That is nothing," said Brother Lustig, "I will easily carry it," and took it on his shoulder. Then they departed and came to a wood, but Brother Lustig had begun to feel the lamb heavy, and he was hungry, so he said to St. Peter: "Look, that's a good place, we might cook the lamb there, and eat it." "As you like," answered St. Peter, "but I can't have anything to do with the cooking; if you will cook, there is a kettle for you, and in the meantime I will walk about a little until it is ready. But you must not begin to eat until I have come back; I will come at the right time." "Well, go, then," said Brother Lustig, "I understand cookery, I will manage it." Then St. Peter went away, and Brother Lustig killed the lamb, lit a fire, threw the meat into the kettle, and boiled it. When the lamb, however, was quite ready, and the apostle Peter had not come back, Brother Lustig took it out of the kettle, cut it up, and found the heart. "That is said to be the best part," said he, and tasted it, but at last he ate it all up. At length St. Peter returned and said: "You may eat the whole of the lamb yourself, I will only have the heart, give me that." Then Brother Lustig took a knife and fork, and pretended to look anxiously about amongst the lamb's flesh, but as if unable to find the heart, and at last he said abruptly: "There is none here." "But where can it be?" said the apostle. "I don't know," replied Brother Lustig, "but look, what fools we both are, to seek for the lamb's heart, and neither of us to remember that a lamb has no heart!" "Oh," said St. Peter, "that is something quite new! Every animal has a heart, why is a lamb to have none?" "No, be assured, my brother," said Brother Lustig, "that a lamb has no heart; just consider it seriously, and then you will see that it really has none." "Well, it is all right," said St. Peter, "if there is no heart, then I want none of the lamb; you may eat it alone." "What I can't eat now, I will carry away in my knapsack," said Brother Lustig, and he ate half the lamb, and put the rest in his knapsack.

They went farther, and then St. Peter caused a great stream of water to flow right across their path, and they were obliged to pass through it. Said St. Peter: "Do go first." "No," answered Brother Lustig, "you must go first," and he thought: "if the water is too deep I will stay behind." Then St. Peter strode through it, and the water just reached to his knee. So Brother Lustig began to go through also, but the water grew deeper and reached to his throat. Then he cried: "Brother, help me!" St. Peter said: "Then will you confess that you have eaten the lamb's heart?" "No," said he, "I have not eaten it." Then the water grew deeper still and rose to his mouth. "Help me, brother," cried the soldier. St. Peter said: "Then will you confess that you have eaten the lamb's heart?" "No," he replied, "I have not eaten it." St. Peter, however, would not let him be drowned, but made the water sink and helped him through it.

Then they journeyed onwards, and came to a kingdom where they heard that the King's daughter lay sick unto death. "Hi, there, brother!" said the soldier to St. Peter, "this is a chance for us; if we can heal her we shall be provided for, for life!" But St. Peter was not half quick enough for him: "Come, lift your legs, my dear brother," said he, "that we may get there in time." But St. Peter walked slower and slower, though Brother Lustig did all he could to drive and push him on, and at last they heard that the princess was dead. "Now we are done for!" said Brother Lustig; "that comes of your sleepy way of walking!" "Just be quiet," answered St. Peter, "I can do more than cure sick people; I can bring dead ones to life again." "Well, if you can do that," said Brother Lustig, "it's all right, but you should earn at least half the kingdom for us by that." Then they went to the royal palace, where everyone was in great grief, but St. Peter told the King that he would restore his daughter to life. He was taken to her, and said: "Bring me a kettle and some water," and when that was brought, he bade everyone go out, and allowed no one to remain with him but Brother Lustig. Then he cut off all the dead girl's limbs, and threw them in the water, lighted a fire beneath the kettle, and boiled them. And when the flesh had fallen away from the bones, he took out the beautiful white bones, and laid them on a table, and arranged them together in their natural order. When he had done that, he stepped forward and said three times: "In the name of the holy Trinity, dead woman arise." And at the third time, the princess arose, living, healthy and beautiful. Then the King was in the greatest joy, and said to St. Peter: "Ask for your reward; even if it were half my kingdom, I would give it." But St. Peter said: "I want nothing for it." "Oh, you tomfool!" thought Brother Lustig to himself, and nudged his comrade's side, and said: "Don't be so stupid! If you have no need of anything, I have." St. Peter, however, would have nothing, but as the King saw that the other would very much like to have something, he ordered his treasurer to fill Brother Lustig's knapsack with gold. Then they went on their way, and when they came to a forest, St. Peter said to Brother Lustig: "Now, we will divide the gold." "Yes," he replied, "we will." So St. Peter divided the gold, and divided it into three heaps. Brother Lustig thought to himself: "What crazy idea has he got in his head now? He is making three shares, and there are only two of us!" But St. Peter said: "I have divided it exactly; there is one share for me, one for you and one for him who ate the lamb's heart."

"Oh, I ate that!" replied Brother Lustig, and hastily swept up the gold. "You may trust what I say." "But how can that be true," said St. Peter, "when a lamb has no heart?" "Eh, what, brother, what can you be thinking of? Lambs have hearts like other animals, why should only they have none?" "Well, so be it," said St. Peter, "keep the gold to yourself, but I will stay with you no longer; I will go my way alone." "As you like, dear brother," answered Brother Lustig. "Farewell."

Then St. Peter went a different road, but Brother Lustig thought: "It is a good thing that he has taken himself off, he is certainly a strange saint." Then he had money enough, but did not know how to manage it, squandered it, gave it away, and when some time had gone by, once more had nothing. Then he arrived in a certain country where he heard that the King's daughter was dead. "Oh, ho!" thought he, "that may be a good thing for me; I will bring her to life again, and see that I am paid as I ought to be." So he went to the King, and offered to raise the dead girl to life again. Now the King had heard that a discharged soldier was traveling about and bringing dead persons to life again, and thought that Brother Lustig was the man; but as he had no confidence in him, he consulted his councillors first, who said that he might give it a trial as his daughter was dead. Then Brother Lustig ordered water to be brought to him in a kettle, bade everyone go out, cut the limbs off, threw them in the water and lighted a fire beneath, just as he had seen St. Peter do. The water began to boil, the flesh fell off, and then he took the bones out and laid them on the table, but he did not know the order in which to lay them, and placed them all wrong and in confusion. Then he stood before them and said: "In the name of the most holy Trinity, dead maiden, I bid you arise," and he said this thrice, but the bones did not stir. So he said it thrice more, but also in vain: "Confounded girl that you are, get up!" cried he, "get up, or it shall be all the worse for you!" When he had said that, St. Peter suddenly appeared in his former shape as a discharged soldier; he entered by the window and said: "Godless man, what are you doing? How can the dead maiden arise, when you have thrown about her bones in such confusion?" "Dear brother, I have done everything to the best of my ability," he answered. "This once, I will help you out of your difficulty, but one thing I tell you, and that is that if ever you undertake anything of the kind again, it will be the worse for you, and also that you must neither demand nor accept the smallest thing from the King for this!" Thereupon St. Peter laid the bones in their right order, said to the maiden three times: "In the name of the most holy Trinity, dead maiden, arise," and the King's daughter arose, healthy and beautiful as before. Then St. Peter went away again by the window, and Brother Lustig was rejoiced to find that all had passed off so well, but was very much vexed to think that after all he was not to take anything for it. "I should just like to know," thought he, "what fancy that fellow has got in his head, for what he gives with one hand he takes away with the other—there is no sense whatever in it!" Then the King offered Brother Lustig whatsoever he wished to have, but he did not dare to take anything; however, by hints and cunning, he contrived to make the King order his knapsack to be filled with gold for him, and with that he departed. When he got out, St. Peter was standing by the door, and said: "Just look what a man you are; did I not forbid you to take anything, and there you have your knapsack full of gold!" "How can I help that," answered Brother Lustig, "if people will put it in for me?" "Well, I tell you this, that if ever you set about anything of this kind again you shall suffer for it!" "All right, brother, have no fear, now I have money, why should I trouble myself with washing bones?" "Faith," said St. Peter, "a long time that gold will last! In order that after this you may never tread in forbidden paths, I will bestow on your knapsack this property, namely, that whatsoever you wish to have inside it, shall be there. Farewell, you will now never see me more." "Good-bye," said Brother Lustig, and thought to himself: "I am very glad that you have taken yourself off, you strange fellow; I shall certainly not follow you." But of the magical power which had been bestowed on his knapsack, he thought no more.

Brother Lustig traveled about with his money, and squandered and wasted what he had as before. When at last he had no more than four kreuzers, he passed by an inn and thought: "The money must go," and ordered three kreuzers' worth of wine and one kreuzer's worth of bread for himself. As he was sitting there drinking, the smell of roast goose made its way to his nose. Brother Lustig looked about and peeped, and saw that the host had two geese roasting in the oven. Then he remembered that his comrade had said that whatsoever he wished to have in his knapsack should be there, so he said: "Oh, ho! I must try that with the geese." So he went out, and when he was outside the door, he said: "I wish those two roasted geese out of the oven and in my knapsack," and when he had said that, he unbuckled it and looked in, and there they were inside it. "Ah, that's right!" said he, "now I am a made man!" and went away to a meadow and took out the roast meat. When he was in the midst of his meal, two journeymen came up and looked at the second goose, which was not yet touched, with hungry eyes. Brother Lustig thought to himself: "One is enough for me," and called the two men up and said: "Take the goose, and eat it to my health." They thanked him, and went with it to the inn, ordered themselves a half bottle of wine and a loaf, took out the goose which had been given them, and began to eat. The hostess saw them and said to her husband: "Those two are eating a goose; just look and see if it is not one of ours, out of the oven." The landlord ran thither, and behold the oven was empty! "What!" cried he, "you thievish crew, you want to eat goose as cheap as that? Pay for it this moment; or I will wash you well with green hazel-sap." The two said: "We are no thieves, a discharged soldier gave us the goose, outside there in the meadow." "You shall not throw dust in my eyes that way! the soldier was here—but he went out by the door, like an honest fellow. I looked after him myself; you are the thieves and shall pay!" But as they could not pay, he took a stick, and cudgeled them out of the house.

Brother Lustig went his way and came to a place where there

was a magnificent castle, and not far from it a wretched inn. He
went to the inn and asked for a night's lodging, but the landlord
turned him away, and said: "There is no more room here, the house
is full of noble guests." "It surprises me that they should come to
you and not go to that splendid castle," said Brother Lustig. "Ah,
indeed," replied the host, "but it is no slight matter to sleep there
for a night; no one who has tried it so far, has ever come out of
it alive."

"If others have tried it," said Brother Lustig, "I will try it too."

"Leave it alone," said the host, "it will cost you your neck." "It won't kill me at once," said Brother Lustig, "just give me the key, and some good food and wine." So the host gave him the key, and food and wine, and with this Brother Lustig went into the castle, enjoyed his supper, and at length, as he was sleepy, he lay down on the ground, for there was no bed. He soon fell asleep, but during the night was disturbed by a great noise, and when he awoke, he saw nine ugly devils in the room, who had made a circle, and were dancing around him. Brother Lustig said: "Well, dance as long as you like, but none of you must come too close." But the devils pressed continually nearer to him, and almost stepped on his face with their hideous feet. "Stop, you devils' ghosts," said he, but they behaved still worse. Then Brother Lustig grew angry, and cried: "Stop! You'll soon see how I can make you quiet!" and got the leg of a chair and struck out into the midst of them with it. But nine devils against one soldier were still too many, and when he struck those in front of him, the others seized him behind by the hair, and tore it unmercifully. "Devils' crew," cried he, "this is too much, but just wait. Into my knapsack, all nine of you!" In an instant they were in it, and then he buckled it up and threw it into a corner. After this all was suddenly quiet, and Brother Lustig lay down again, and slept till it was bright day. Then came the innkeeper, and the nobleman to whom the castle belonged, to see how he had fared; but when they perceived that he was merry and well they were astonished, and asked: "Have the spirits done you no harm, then?" "The reason why they have not," answered Brother Lustig, "is because I have got the whole nine of them in my knapsack! You may once more inhabit your castle quite tranquilly, none of them will ever haunt it again." The nobleman thanked him, made him rich presents, and begged him to remain in his service, and he would provide for him as long as he lived. "No," replied Brother Lustig, "I am used to wandering about, I will travel farther." Then he went away, and entered into a smithy, laid the knapsack, which contained the nine devils on the anvil, and asked the smith and his apprentices to strike it. So they smote with their great hammers with all their strength, and the devils uttered howls which were quite pitiable. When he opened the knapsack after this, eight of them were dead, but one which had been lying in a fold of it was still alive, slipped out, and went back again to hell.

Thereupon Brother Lustig traveled a long time about the world, and those who know, can tell many a story about him. But at last he grew old, and thought of his end, so he went to a hermit who was known to be a pious man, and said to him: "I am tired of wandering about, and want now to behave in such a manner that I shall enter into the kingdom of Heaven." The hermit replied: "There are two roads, one is broad and pleasant, and leads to hell, the other is narrow and rough, and leads to heaven." "I should be a fool," thought Brother Lustig, "if I were to take the narrow, rough road." So he set out and took the broad and pleasant road, and at length came to a great black door, which was the door of Hell. Brother Lustig knocked, and the door-keeper peeped out to see who was there. But when he saw Brother Lustig, he was terrified, for he was the very same ninth devil who had been shut up in the knapsack, and had escaped from it with a black eye. So he pushed the bolt in again as quickly as he could, ran to the highest devil, and said: "There is a fellow outside with a knapsack, who wants to come in, but as you value your lives don't allow him to enter, or he will wish the whole of hell into his knapsack. He once gave me a frightful hammering when I was inside it." So they called out to Brother Lustig that he was to go away again, for he should not get in there! "If they won't have me here," thought he, "I will see if I can find a place for myself in Heaven, for I must stay somewhere." So he turned about and went onwards until he came to the door of Heaven, where he knocked. St. Peter was sitting hard by as door-keeper. Brother Lustig recognized him at once, and thought: "Here I find an old friend, I shall get on better." But St. Peter said: "I can hardly believe that you want to come into Heaven." "Let me in, brother; I must get in somewhere; if they would have taken me into Hell, I should not have come here." "No," said St. Peter, "you shall not enter." "Then if you will not let me in, take your knapsack back, for I will have nothing at all from you." "Give it here, then," said St. Peter. Then Brother Lustig gave him the knapsack into Heaven through the bars, and St. Peter took it, and hung it up beside his seat. Then said Brother Lustig: "And now I wish myself inside my knapsack," and in a second he was in it, and in Heaven, and St. Peter was forced to let him stay there.

Hans in Luck

Hans had served his master for seven years, so he said to him: "Master, my time is up; now I should be glad to go back home to my mother; give me my wages." The master answered: "You have served me faithfully and honestly; as the service was so shall the reward be"; and he gave Hans a piece of gold as big as his head. Hans pulled his handkerchief out of his pocket, wrapped up the lump in it, put it on his shoulder, and set out on the way home.

As he went on, always putting one foot before the other, he saw a horseman trotting quickly and merrily by on a lively horse. "Ah!" said Hans quite loud, "What a fine thing it is to ride! There you sit as on a chair; you stumble over no stones, you save your shoes, and cover the ground, you don't know how."

The rider, who had heard him, stopped and called out: "Hi, there, Hans! why do you go on foot, then?"

"I must," answered he, "for I have this lump to carry home; it is true that it is gold, but I cannot hold my head straight for it, and it hurts my shoulder."

"I will tell you what," said the rider, "we will exchange: I will give you my horse, and you can give me your lump."

"With all my heart," said Hans, "but I can tell you, you will have to crawl along with it."

The rider got down, took the gold, and helped Hans up; then gave him the bridle tight in his hands and said: "If you want to go at a really good pace, you must click your tongue and call out: 'Jup! Jup!'"

Hans was heartily delighted as he sat upon the horse and rode away so bold and free. After a little while he thought that it ought to go faster, and he began to click with his tongue and call out: "Jup! Jup!" The horse put himself into a sharp trot, and before Hans knew where he was, he was thrown off and lying in a ditch which separated the field from the highway. The horse would have gone off too if it had not been stopped by a countryman, who was coming along the road and driving a cow before him.

Hans pulled himself together and stood up on his legs again, but he was vexed, and said to the countryman: "It is a poor joke, this riding, especially when one gets hold of a mare like this, that kicks and throws one off, so that one has a chance of breaking one's neck. Never again will I mount it. Now I like your cow, for one can walk quietly behind her, and have, over and above, one's milk, butter and cheese every day without fail. What would I not give to have such a cow." "Well," said the countryman, "if it would give you so much pleasure, I do not mind giving the cow for the horse." Hans agreed with the greatest delight; the countryman jumped upon the horse, and rode quickly away.

Hans drove his cow quietly before him, and thought over his lucky bargain. "If only I have a morsel of bread—and that can hardly fail me—I can eat butter and cheese with it as often as I like; if I am thirsty, I can milk my cow and drink the milk. My goodness, what more can I want?"

When he came to an inn he made a halt, and in his great content ate up what he had with him—his dinner and supper—and all he had, and with his last few farthings had half a glass of beer. Then he drove his cow onwards along the road to his mother's village.

As it drew nearer mid-day, the heat was more oppressive, and Hans found himself upon a moor which it took about an hour to cross. He felt it very hot and his tongue clave to the roof of his mouth with thirst. "I can find a cure for this," thought Hans; "I will milk the cow now and refresh myself with the milk." He tied her to a withered tree, and as he had no pail he put his leather cap underneath; but try as he would, not a drop of milk came. And as he set himself to work in a clumsy way, the impatient beast at last gave him such a blow on his head with its hind foot, that he fell on the ground, and for a long time could not think where he was.

By good fortune a butcher just then came along the road with a wheel-barrow in which lay a young pig. "What sort of a trick is this?" cried he, and helped the good Hans up. Hans told him what had happened. The butcher gave him his flask and said: "Take a drink and refresh yourself. The cow will certainly give no milk, it is an old beast; at the best it is only fit for the plough, or for the butcher." "Well, well," said Hans, as he stroked his hair down on his head, "who would have thought it? Certainly it is a fine thing when one can kill a beast like that at home; what meat one has! But I do not care much for beef, it is not juicy enough for me. A young pig like that now is the thing to have; it tastes quite different; and then there are the sausages!"

"Listen, Hans," said the butcher, "out of love for you I will exchange, and will let you have the pig for the cow." "Heaven repay
you for your kindness!" said Hans as he gave up the cow, whilst
the pig was unbound from the barrow, and the cord by which it
was tied was put in his hand.

Hans went on, and thought to himself how everything was going
just as he wished; if he did meet with any vexation it was immediately set right. Presently there joined him a lad who was carrying
a fine white goose under his arm. They said good morning to each
other, and Hans began to tell of his good luck, and how he had
always made such good bargains. The boy told him that he was
taking the goose to a christening-feast. "Just lift her," added he,

and laid hold of her by the wings; "how heavy she is—she has
been fattened up for the last eight weeks. Whoever has a bit of her
when she is roasted will have to wipe the fat from both sides of
his mouth." "Yes," said Hans, as he weighed her in one hand, "she
is a good weight, but my pig is no bad one."

Meanwhile the lad looked suspiciously from one side to the other,
and shook his head. "Look here," he said at length, "it may not
be all right with your pig. In the village through which I passed,
the Mayor himself had just had one stolen out of its sty. I fear—I
fear that you have got hold of it there. They have sent out some
people and it would be a bad business if they caught you with the
pig; at the very least, you would be shut up in some dark hole."

The good Hans was terrified. "Goodness!" he said, "help me out
of this fix; you know more about this place than I do, take my pig
and leave me your goose." "I shall risk something at that game,"

answered the lad, "but I will not be the cause of your getting into trouble." So he took the cord in his hand, and drove away the pig quickly along a by-path.

The good Hans, free from care, went homewards with the goose under his arm. "When I think over it properly," said he to himself, "I have even gained by the exchange: first there is the good roast-meat, then the quantity of fat which will drip from it, and which will give me dripping for my bread for a quarter of a year, and lastly the beautiful white feathers; I will have my pillow stuffed with them, and then indeed I shall go to sleep without rocking. How glad my mother will be!"

As he was going through the last village, there stood a scissors-grinder with his barrow; as his wheel whirred he sang:

> "I sharpen scissors and quickly grind,
> My coat blows out in the wind behind."

Hans stood still and looked at him; at last he spoke to him and said: "All's well with you, as you are so merry with your grinding." "Yes," answered the scissors-grinder, "the trade has a golden foundation. A real grinder is a man who as often as he puts his hand into his pocket finds gold in it. But where did you buy that fine goose?"

"I did not buy it, but exchanged my pig for it."

"And the pig?"

"That I got for a cow."

"And the cow?"

"I took that instead of a horse."

"And the horse?"

"For that I gave a lump of gold as big as my head."

"And the gold?"

"Well, that was my wages for seven years' service."

"You have known how to look after yourself each time," said the grinder. "If you can only get on so far as to hear the money jingle in your pocket whenever you stand up, you will have made your fortune."

"How shall I manage that?" said Hans. "You must be a grinder, as I am; nothing particular is wanted for it but a grindstone, the rest finds itself. I have one here; it is certainly a little worn, but you need not give me anything for it but your goose; will you do it?"

"How can you ask?" answered Hans. "I shall be the luckiest fellow on earth; if I have money whenever I put my hand in my pocket, why should I ever worry again?" and he handed him the goose and received the grindstone in exchange. "Now," said the grinder, as he took up an ordinary heavy stone that lay by him, "here is a strong stone for you into the bargain; you can hammer well upon it, and straighten your old nails. Take it with you and keep it carefully."

Hans loaded himself with the stones, and went on with a contented heart, his eyes shining with joy. "Dame Fortune is certainly smiling on me now," he cried; "everything I want happens to me just as if I were a Sunday-child."

Meanwhile, as he had been on his legs since daybreak, he began to feel tired. Hunger also tormented him, for in his joy at the bargain by which he got the cow he had eaten up all his store of food at once. At last he could only go on with great trouble, and was forced to stop every minute; the stones, too, weighed him down dreadfully. Then he could not help thinking how nice it would be if he had not to carry them just then.

He crept like a snail to a well in a field, and there he thought that he would rest and refresh himself with a cool draught of water, but in order that he might not injure the stones in sitting down, he laid them carefully by his side on the edge of the well. Then he sat down on it, and was to stoop and drink, when he made a slip, pushed against the stones, and both of them fell into the water. When Hans saw them with his own eyes sinking to the bottom, he jumped for joy, and then knelt down, and with tears in his eyes thanked God for having shown him this favor also, and delivered him in so good a way, and without his having any need to reproach himself, from those heavy stones which had been the only things that troubled him.

"There is no man under the sun so fortunate as I," he cried out. With a light heart and free from every burden he now ran on until he was with his mother at home.

The Singing, Soaring Lark

There was once upon a time a man who was about to set out on a long journey, and on parting he asked his three daughters what he should bring back with him for them. Whereupon the eldest wished for pearls, the second wished for diamonds, but the third said: "Dear father, I should like a singing, soaring lark." The father said: "Yes, if I can get it, you shall have it," kissed all three, and set out. Now when the time had come for him to be on his way home again, he had brought pearls and diamonds for the two eldest, but he had sought everywhere in vain for a singing, soaring lark for the youngest, and he was very unhappy about it, for she was his favorite child. Then his road lay through a forest, and in the midst of it was a splendid castle, and near the castle stood a tree, but quite on the top of the tree, he saw a singing, soaring lark. "Aha, you come just at the right moment!" he said, quite delighted, and called to his servant to climb up and catch the little creature. But as he approached the tree, a lion leapt from beneath it, shook himself, and roared till the leaves on the trees trembled. "He who tries to steal my singing, soaring lark," he cried, "will I devour." Then the man said: "I did not know that the bird belonged to you. I will make amends for the wrong I have done and ransom myself with a large sum of money, only spare my life." The lion said: "Nothing can save you, unless you will promise to give me for my own what first meets you on your return home; and if you will do that, I will grant you your life, and you shall have the bird for your daughter, into the bargain." But the man hesitated and said: "That might be my youngest daughter, she loves me best, and always runs to meet me on my return home." The servant, however, was terrified and said: "Why should your daughter be the very one to meet you, it might as easily be a cat, or dog?" Then the man allowed himself to be persuaded, took the singing, soaring lark, and promised to give the lion whatsoever should first meet him on his return home.

When he reached home and entered his house, the first who met him was none other than his youngest and dearest daughter, who came running up, kissed and embraced him, and when she saw that he had brought with him a singing, soaring lark, she was beside herself with joy. The father, however, could not rejoice, but began to weep, and said: "My dearest child, I have bought the little bird dear. In return for it, I have been obliged to promise you to a savage lion, and when he has you he will tear you in pieces and devour you," and he told her all, just as it had happened, and begged her not to go there, come what might. But she consoled him and said: "Dearest father, indeed your promise must be fulfilled. I will go thither and soften the lion, so that I may return to you safely." Next morning she had the road pointed out to her, took leave, and went fearlessly out into the forest. The lion, however, was an enchanted prince and was by day a lion, and all his people were lions with him, but in the night they resumed their natural human shapes. On her arrival she was kindly received and led into the castle. When night came, the lion turned into a handsome man, and their wedding was celebrated with great magnificence. They lived happily together, remained awake at night, and slept in the daytime. One day he came and said: "To-morrow there is a feast in your father's house, because your eldest sister is to be married, and if you are inclined to go there, my lions shall conduct you." She said: "Yes, I should very much like to see my father again," and went thither, accompanied by the lions. There was great joy when she arrived, for they had all believed that she had been torn in pieces by the lion, and had long ceased to live. But she told them what a handsome husband she had, and how well off she was, remained with them while the wedding-feast lasted, and then went back again to the forest. When the second daughter was about to be married, and she was again invited to the wedding, she said to the lion: "This time I will not be alone, you must come with me." The lion, however, said that it was too dangerous for him, for if when there a ray from a burning candle fell on him, he would be changed into a dove, and for seven years long would have to fly about with the doves. She said: "Ah, but do come with me, I will take great care of you, and guard you from all light." So they went away together, and took with them their little child as well. She had a room built there, so strong and thick that no ray could pierce through it; in this he was to shut himself up when the candles were lit for the wedding-feast. But the door was made of green wood which warped and left a little crack which no one noticed. The wedding was celebrated with magnificence, but when the procession with all its candles and torches came back from church, and passed by this apartment, a ray about the breadth of a hair fell on the King's son, and when this ray touched him, he was transformed in an instant, and when she came in and looked for him, she did not see him, but a white dove was sitting there. The dove said to her: "For seven years must I fly about the world, but at every seventh step that you take I will let fall a drop of red blood and a white feather, and these will show you the way, and if you follow the trace you can release me." Thereupon the dove flew out at the door, and she followed him, and at every seventh step a red drop of blood and a little white feather fell down and showed her the way.

So she went continually further and further in the wide world, never looking about her or resting, and the seven years were almost past; then she rejoiced and thought that they would soon be saved, and yet they were so far from it! Once when they were thus moving onwards, no little feather and no drop of red blood fell, and when she raised her eyes the dove had disappeared. And as she thought to herself: "In this no man can help you," she climbed up to the sun, and said to him: "You shine into every crevice, and over every peak, have you not seen a white dove flying?" "No," said the sun, "I have seen none, but I present you with a casket, open it when you are in sorest need." Then she thanked the sun, and went on until evening came and the moon appeared; she then asked her: "You shine the whole night through, and on every field and forest, have you not seen a white dove flying?" "No," said the moon, "I have seen no dove, but here I give you an egg, break it when you are in great need." She thanked the moon, and went on until the night wind came up and blew on her, then she said to it: "You blow over every tree and under every leaf, have you not seen a white dove flying?" "No," said the night wind, "I have seen none, but I will ask the three other winds, perhaps they have seen it." The east wind and the west wind came, and had seen nothing, but the south wind said: "I have seen the white dove, it has flown to the Red Sea, where it has become a lion again, for the seven years are over, and the lion is there fighting with a dragon; the dragon, however, is an enchanted princess." The night wind then said to her: "I will advise you; go to the Red Sea, on the right bank are some tall reeds, count them, break off the eleventh, and strike the dragon with it, then the lion will be able to subdue it, and both then will regain their human form. After that, look round and you will see the griffin which is by the Red Sea; swing yourself, with your beloved, on to his back, and the bird will carry you over the sea to your own home. Here is a nut for you, when you are above the center of the sea, let the nut fall, it will immediately shoot up, and a tall nut-tree will grow out of the water on which the griffin may rest; for if he cannot rest, he will not be strong enough to carry you across, and if you forget to throw down the nut, he will let you fall into the sea."

Then she went thither, and found everything as the night wind had said. She counted the reeds by the sea, and cut off the eleventh, struck the dragon therewith, whereupon the lion conquered it, and immediately both of them regained their human shapes. But when the princess, who hitherto had been the dragon, was released from enchantment, she took the youth by the arm, seated herself on the griffin, and carried him off with her. There stood the poor maiden who had wandered so far and was again forsaken. She sat down and cried, but at last she took courage and said: "Still I will go as far as the wind blows and as long as the cock crows, until I find him," and she went forth by long, long roads, until at last she came to the castle where both of them were living together; there she heard that soon a feast was to be held, in which they would celebrate their wedding, but she said: "God still helps me," and opened the casket that the sun had given her. A dress lay therein as brilliant as the sun itself. So she took it out and put it on, and went up into the castle, and everyone, even the bride herself, looked at her with astonishment. The dress pleased the bride so well that she thought it might do for her wedding-dress, and asked if it was for sale. "Not for money or land," answered she, "but for flesh and blood." The bride asked her what she meant by that, so she said: "Let me sleep a night in the chamber where the bridegroom sleeps." The bride would not, yet wanted very much to have the dress; at last she consented, but the page was to give the prince a sleeping-draught. When it was night, therefore, and the youth was already asleep, she was led into the chamber; she seated herself on the bed and said: "I have followed after you for seven years. I have been to the sun and the moon, and the four winds, and have enquired for you, and have helped you against the dragon; will you, then, quite forget me?" But the prince slept so soundly that it only seemed to him as if the wind were whistling outside in the fir-trees. When therefore day broke, she was led out again, and had to give up the golden dress. And as that even had been of no avail, she was sad, went out into a meadow, sat down there, and wept. While she was sitting there, she thought of the egg which the moon had given her; she opened it, and there came out a clucking hen with twelve chickens all of gold, and they ran about chirping, and crept again under the old hen's wings; nothing more beautiful was ever seen in the world! Then she arose, and drove them through the meadow before her, until the bride looked out of the window. The little chickens pleased her so much that she immediately came down and asked if they were for sale. "Not for money or land, but for flesh and blood; let me sleep another night in the chamber where the bridegroom sleeps." The bride said: "Yes," intending to cheat her as on the former evening. But when the prince went to bed he asked the page what the murmuring and rustling in the night had been. On this the page told all; that he had been forced to give him a sleeping-draught, because a poor girl had slept secretly in the chamber, and that he was to give him another that night. The prince said: "Pour out the draught by the bed-side." At night, she was again led in, and when she began to relate how ill all had fared with her, he immediately recognized his beloved wife by her voice, sprang up and cried: "Now I really am released! I have been as it were in a dream, for the strange princess had bewitched me so that I have been compelled to forget you, but God has delivered me from the spell at the right time." Then they both left the castle secretly in the night, for they feared the father of the princess, who was a sorcerer, and they seated themselves on the griffin which bore them across the Red Sea, and when they were in the midst of it, she let fall the nut. Immediately a tall nut-tree grew up, whereon the bird rested, and then carried them home, where they found their child, who had grown tall and beautiful, and they lived thenceforth happily until their death.

The Goose-Girl

There was once upon a time an old Queen whose husband had been dead for many years, and she had a beautiful daughter. When the princess grew up she was betrothed to a prince who lived at a great distance. When the time came for her to be married, and she had to journey forth into the distant kingdom, the aged Queen packed up for her many costly vessels of silver and gold, and trinkets also of gold and silver, and cups and jewels; in short, everything which appertained to a royal dowry, for she loved her child with all her heart. She likewise sent her maid-in-waiting, who was to ride with her, and hand her over to the bridegroom, and each had a horse for the journey, but the horse of the King's daughter was called Falada, and could speak. So when the hour of parting had come, the aged mother went into her bedroom, took a small knife and cut her finger with it until it bled. Then she held a white handkerchief to it into which she let three drops of blood fall, gave it to her daughter and said: "Dear child, preserve this carefully, it will be of service to you on your way."

So they took a sorrowful leave of each other; the princess put the piece of cloth in her bosom, mounted her horse, and then went away to her bridegroom. After she had ridden for a while she felt a burning thirst, and said to her waiting-maid: "Dismount, and take my cup which you have brought with you for me, and get me some water from the stream, for I should like to drink." "If you are thirsty," said the waiting-maid, "get off your horse yourself, and lie down and drink out of the water, I don't choose to be your servant." So in her great thirst the princess alighted, bent down over the water in the stream and drank, and was not allowed to drink out of the golden cup. Then she said: "Ah, Heaven!" and the three drops of blood answered: "If this your mother knew, her heart would break in two." But the King's daughter was humble, said nothing, and mounted her horse again. She rode some miles further, but the day was warm, the sun scorched her, and she was thirsty once more, and when they came to a stream of water, she again cried to her waiting-maid: "Dismount, and give me some water in my golden cup," for she had long ago forgotten the girl's ill words. But the waiting-maid said still more haughtily: "If you wish to drink, get it yourself, I don't choose to be your maid." Then in her great thirst the King's daughter alighted, bent over the flowing stream, wept and said: "Ah, Heaven!" and the drops of blood again replied: "If this your mother knew, her heart would break in two." And as she was thus drinking and leaning right over the stream, the handkerchief with the three drops of blood fell out of her bosom, and floated away with the water without her observing it, so great was her trouble. The waiting-maid, however, had seen it, and she rejoiced to think that she now had power over the bride, for since the princess had lost the drops of blood, she had become weak and powerless. So now when she wanted to mount her horse again, the one that was called Falada, the waiting-maid said: "Falada is more suitable for me, and my nag will do for you," and the princess had to be content with that. Then the waiting-maid, with many hard words, bade the princess exchange her royal apparel for her own shabby clothes; and at length she was compelled to swear by the clear sky above her, that she would not say one word of this to anyone at the royal court, and if she had not taken this oath she would have been killed on the spot. But Falada saw all this, and observed it well.

The waiting-maid now mounted Falada, and the true bride the bad horse, and thus they traveled onwards, until at length they entered the royal palace. There were great rejoicings over her arrival, and the prince sprang forward to meet her, lifted the waiting-maid from her horse, and thought she was his consort. She was conducted upstairs, but the real princess was left standing below. Then the old King looked out of the window and saw her standing in the courtyard, and noticed how dainty and delicate and beautiful she was, and instantly went to the royal apartment, and asked the bride about the girl she had with her who was standing down below in the courtyard, and who she was. "I picked her up on my way for a companion; give the girl something to work at, that she may not stand idle." But the old King had no work for her, and knew of none, so he said: "I have a little boy who tends the geese, she may help him." The boy was called Conrad, and the true bride had to help him to tend the geese. Soon afterwards the false bride said to the young King: "Dearest husband, I beg you to do me a favor." He answered: "I will do so most willingly." "Then send for the knacker, and have the head of the horse on which I rode

here cut off, for it vexed me on the way." In reality, she was afraid that the horse might tell how she had behaved to the King's daughter. Then she succeeded in making the King promise that it should be done, and the faithful Falada was to die; this came to the ears of the real princess, and she secretly promised to pay the knacker a piece of gold if he would perform a small service for her. There was a great dark-looking gateway in the town, through which morning and evening she had to pass with the geese: would he be so good as to nail up Falada's head on it, so that she might see him again, more than once. The knacker's man promised to do that, and cut off the head, and nailed it fast beneath the dark gateway.

Early in the morning, when she and Conrad drove out their flock beneath this gateway, she said in passing:

"Alas, Falada, hanging there!"

Then the head answered:

"Alas, young Queen, how ill you fare!
If this your mother knew,
Her heart would break in two."

Then they went still further out of the town, and drove their geese into the country. And when they had come to the meadow, she sat down and unbound her hair which was like pure gold, and Conrad saw it and delighted in its brightness, and wanted to pluck out a few hairs. Then she said:

"Blow, blow, thou gentle wind, I say,
Blow Conrad's little hat away,
And make him chase it here and there,
Until I have braided all my hair,
And bound it up again."

And there came such a violent wind that it blew Conrad's hat far away across country, and he was forced to run after it. When he came back she had finished combing her hair and was putting it up again, and he could not get any of it. Then Conrad was angry, and would not speak to her, and thus they watched the geese until the evening, and then they went home.

Next day when they were driving the geese out through the dark gateway, the maiden said:

"Alas, Falada, hanging there!"

Falada answered:

> "Alas, young Queen, how ill you fare!
> If this your mother knew,
> Her heart would break in two."

And she sat down in the field and began to comb out her hair, and Conrad ran and tried to clutch it, so she said in haste:

> "Blow, blow, thou gentle wind, I say,
> Blow Conrad's little hat away,
> And make him chase it here and there,
> Until I have braided all my hair,
> And bound it up again."

Then the wind blew, and blew his little hat off his head and far away, and Conrad was forced to run after it, and when he came back, her hair had been put up a long time, and he could get none of it, and so they looked after their geese till evening came.

But in the evening after they had got home, Conrad went to the old King, and said: "I won't tend the geese with that girl any longer!" "Why not?" inquired the aged King. "Oh, because she vexes me the whole day long." Then the aged King commanded him to relate what it was that she did to him. And Conrad said: "In the morning when we pass beneath the dark gateway with the flock, there is a horse's head on the wall, and she says to it:

> 'Alas, Falada, hanging there!'

And the head replies:

> 'Alas, young Queen how ill you fare!
> If this your mother knew
> Her heart would break in two.' "

And Conrad went on to relate what happened on the goose pasture, and how when there he had to chase his hat.

The aged King commanded him to drive his flock out again next day, and as soon as morning came, he placed himself behind the dark gateway, and heard how the maiden spoke to the head of

Falada, and then he too went into the country, and hid himself in the thicket in the meadow. There he soon saw with his own eyes the goose-girl and the goose-boy bringing their flock, and how after a while she sat down and unplaited her hair, which shone with radiance. And soon she said:

> "Blow, blow, thou gentle wind, I say,
> Blow Conrad's little hat away,
> And make him chase it here and there,
> Until I have braided all my hair,
> And bound it up again."

Then came a blast of wind and carried off Conrad's hat, so that he had to run far away, while the maiden quietly went on combing and plaiting her hair, all of which the King observed. Then, quite unseen, he went away, and when the goose-girl came home in the evening, he called her aside, and asked why she did all these things. "I may not tell that, and I dare not lament my sorrows to any human being, for I have sworn not to do so by the heaven which is above me; if I had not done that, I should have lost my life." He urged her and left her no peace, but he could draw nothing from her. Then said he: "If you will not tell me anything, tell your sorrows to the iron-stove there," and he went away. Then she crept into the iron-stove, and began to weep and lament, and emptied her whole heart, and said: "Here am I deserted by the whole world, and yet I am a King's daughter, and a false waiting-maid has by force brought me to such a pass that I have been compelled to put off my royal apparel, and she has taken my place with my bridegroom, and I have to perform menial service as a goose-girl. If this my mother knew, her heart would break in two."

The aged King, however, was standing outside by the pipe of the stove, and was listening to what she said, and heard it. Then he came back again, and bade her come out of the stove. And royal garments were placed on her, and it was marvellous how beautiful she was! The aged King summoned his son, and revealed to him that he had got the false bride who was only a waiting-maid, but that the true one was standing there, as the former goose-girl. The young King rejoiced with all his heart when he saw her beauty and youth, and a great feast was made ready to which all the people and all good friends were invited. At the head of the table sat the bridegroom with the King's daughter on one side of him, and the waiting-maid on the other, but the waiting-maid was blinded, and did not recognize the princess in her dazzling array. When they had eaten and drunk, and were merry, the aged King asked the waiting-maid as a riddle, what punishment a person deserved who had behaved in such and such a way to her master, and at the same time related the whole story, and asked what sentence such a person merited. Then the false bride said: "She deserves no better fate than to be stripped entirely naked, and put in a barrel which is studded inside with pointed nails, and two white horses should be harnessed to it, which will drag her along through one street after another, till she is dead." "It is you," said the aged King, "and you have pronounced your own sentence, and thus shall it be done unto you." And when the sentence had been carried out, the young King married his true bride, and both of them reigned over their kingdom in peace and happiness.

The Water of Life

There was once a King who had an illness, and no one believed that he would come out of it with his life. He had three sons who were much distressed about it, and went down into the palace-garden and wept. There they met an old man who inquired as to the cause of their grief. They told him that their father was so ill that he would most certainly die, for nothing seemed to cure him. Then the old man said: "I know of one more remedy, and that is the water of life; if he drinks of it he will become well again; but it is hard to find." The eldest said: "I will manage to find it," and went to the sick King, and begged to be allowed to go forth in search of the water of life, for that alone could save him. "No," said the King, "the danger of it is too great. I would rather die." But he begged so long that the King consented. The prince thought in his heart: "If I bring the water, then I shall be best beloved of my father, and shall inherit the kingdom." So he set out, and when he had ridden forth a little distance, a dwarf stood there in the road who called to him and said: "Whither away so fast?" "Silly shrimp," said the prince, very haughtily, "it is nothing to do with you," and rode on. But the little dwarf had grown angry, and had wished an evil wish. Soon after this the prince entered a ravine, and the further he rode the closer the mountains drew together, and at last the road became so narrow that he could not advance a step further; it was impossible either to turn his horse or to dismount from the saddle, and he was shut in there as if in prison. The sick King waited long for him, but he came not. Then the second son said: "Father, let me go forth to seek the water," and thought to himself: "If my brother is dead, then the kingdom will fall to me." At first the King would not allow him to go either, but at last he yielded, so the prince set out on the same road that his brother had taken, and he too met the dwarf, who stopped him to ask, whither he was going in such haste. "Little shrimp," said the prince, "that is nothing to do with you," and rode on without giving him another look. But the dwarf bewitched him, and he, like the other, rode into a ravine, and could neither go forwards nor backwards. So fare haughty people.

As the second son also remained away, the youngest begged to be allowed to go forth to fetch the water, and at last the King was obliged to let him go. When he met the dwarf and the latter asked him whither he was going in such haste, he stopped, gave him an explanation, and said: "I am seeking the water of life, for my father is sick unto death." "Do you know then, where that is to be found?" "No," said the prince. "As you have borne yourself as is seemly, and not haughtily like your false brothers, I will give you the information and tell you how you may obtain the water of life. It springs from a fountain in the courtyard of an enchanted castle, but you will not be able to make your way to it, if I do not give you an iron wand and two small loaves of bread. Strike thrice with the wand on the iron door of the castle, and it will spring open: inside lie two lions with gaping jaws, but if you throw a loaf to each of them, they will be quieted. Then hasten to fetch some of the water of life before the clock strikes twelve, else the door will shut again, and you will be imprisoned." The prince thanked him, took the wand and the bread, and set out on his way. When he arrived, everything was as the dwarf had said. The door sprang open at the third stroke of the wand, and when he had appeased the lions with the bread, he entered the castle, and came to a large and splendid hall, wherein sat some enchanted princes whose rings he drew off their fingers. A sword and a loaf of bread were lying there, which he carried away. After this, he entered a chamber, in which was a beautiful maiden who rejoiced when she saw him, kissed him, and told him that he had set her free, and should have the whole of her kingdom, and that if he would return in a year their wedding should be celebrated; likewise she told him where the spring of the water of life was, and that he was to hasten and draw some of it before the clock struck twelve. Then he went onwards, and at last entered a room where there was a beautiful newly-made bed, and as he was very weary, he felt inclined to rest a little. So he lay down and fell asleep. When he awoke, it was striking a quarter to twelve. He sprang up in a fright, ran to the spring, drew some water in a cup which stood near, and hastened away. But just as he was passing through the iron door, the clock struck twelve, and the door fell to with such violence that it carried away a piece of his heel.

He, however, rejoicing at having obtained the water of life, went homewards, and again passed the dwarf. When the latter saw the sword and the loaf, he said: "With these you have won great wealth; with the sword you can slay whole armies, and the bread will never come to an end." But the prince would not go home to his father without his brothers, and said: "Dear dwarf, can you not tell me where my two brothers are? They went out before I did in search of the water of life, and have not returned." "They are imprisoned between two mountains," said the dwarf. "I have condemned them to stay there, because they were so haughty." Then the prince begged until the dwarf released them, but he warned him and said: "Beware of them, for they have bad hearts." When his brothers came, he rejoiced, and told them how things had gone with them, that he had found the water of life, and had brought a cupful away with him, and had rescued a beautiful princess, who was willing to wait a year for him, and then their wedding was to be celebrated, and he would obtain a great kingdom. After that they rode on together, and chanced upon a land where war and famine reigned, and the King already thought he must perish, for the scarcity was so great. Then the prince went to him and gave him the loaf, wherewith he fed and satisfied the whole of his kingdom, and then the prince gave him the sword also, wherewith he slew the hosts of his enemies, and could now live in rest and peace. The prince then took back his loaf and his sword, and the three brothers rode on. But after this they entered two more countries where war and famine reigned, and each time the prince gave his loaf and his sword to the Kings, and had now delivered three kingdoms, and after that they went on board a ship and sailed over the sea. During the passage, the two eldest conversed apart and said: "The youngest has found the water of life and not we, for that our father will give him the kingdom,—the kingdom which belongs to us, and he will rob us of all our fortune." They then began to seek revenge, and plotted with each other to destroy him. They waited until they found him fast asleep, then they poured the water of life out of the cup, and took it for themselves, but into the cup they poured salt sea-water.

Now therefore, when they arrived home, the youngest took his cup to the sick King in order that he might drink out of it, and be cured. But scarcely had he drunk a very little of the salt sea-water than he became still worse than before. And as he was lamenting over this, the two eldest brothers came, and accused the youngest of having intended to poison him, and said that they had brought him the true water of life, and handed it to him. He had scarcely tasted it, when he felt his sickness departing, and became strong and healthy as in the days of his youth. After that they both went to the youngest, mocked him, and said: "You certainly found the water of life, but you have had the pain, and we the gain; you should have been clever, and should have kept your eyes open. We took it from you whilst you were asleep at sea, and when a year is over, one of us will go and fetch the beautiful princess. But beware that you do not disclose aught of this to our father; indeed he does not trust you, and if you say a single word, you shall lose your life into the bargain, but if you keep silent, you shall have it as a gift."

The old King was angry with his youngest son, and thought he had plotted against his life. So he summoned the court together, and had sentence pronounced upon his son, that he should be secretly shot. And once when the prince was riding forth to the chase, suspecting no evil, the King's huntsman was told to go with him, and when they were quite alone in the forest, the huntsman looked so sorrowful that the prince said to him: "Dear huntsman, what ails you?" The huntsman said: "I cannot tell you, and yet I ought." Then the prince said: "Say openly what it is, I will pardon you." "Alas!" said the huntsman, "I am to shoot you dead, the King has ordered me to do it." Then the prince was shocked, and said: "Dear huntsman, let me live; there, I give you my royal garments; give me your common ones in their stead." The huntsman said: "I will willingly do that, indeed I would not have been able to shoot you." Then they exchanged clothes, and the huntsman returned home, while the prince went further into the forest. After a time three waggons of gold and precious stones came to the King for his youngest son, which were sent by the three Kings who had slain their enemies with the prince's sword, and maintained their people with his bread, and who wished to show their gratitude for it. The old King then thought: "Can my son have been innocent?" and said to his people: "Would that he were still alive, how it grieves me that I have suffered him to be killed!" "He still lives," said the huntsman, "I could not find it in my heart to carry out your command," and told the King how it had happened. Then a stone fell from the King's heart, and he had it proclaimed in every country that his son might return and be taken into favor again.

The princess, however, had a road made up to her palace which was quite bright and golden, and told her people that whosoever came riding straight along it to her, would be the right one and was to be admitted, and whoever rode by the side of it, was not the right one, and was not to be admitted. As the time was now close at hand, the eldest thought he would hasten to go to the King's daughter, and give himself out as her rescuer, and thus win her for his bride, and the kingdom to boot. Therefore he rode forth, and when he arrived in front of the palace, and saw the splendid golden road, he thought: "It would be a sin and a shame if I were to ride over that," and turned aside, and rode on the right side of it. But when he came to the door, the servants told him that he was not the right one, and was to go away again. Soon after this the second prince set out, and when he came to the golden road, and his horse had put one foot on it, he thought: "It would be a sin and a shame, a piece might be trodden off," and he turned aside and rode on the left side of it, and when he reached the door, the attendants told him he was not the right one, and he was to go away again. When at last the year had entirely expired, the third son likewise wished to ride out of the forest to his beloved, and with her forget his sorrows. So he set out and thought of her so much, that he never noticed the golden road at all. So his horse rode onwards up the middle of it, and when he came to the door, it was opened and the princess received him with joy, and said he was her savior, and lord of the kingdom, and their wedding was celebrated with great rejoicing. When it was over she told him that his father invited him to come to him, and had forgiven him. So he rode thither, and told him everything; how his brothers had betrayed him, and how he had nevertheless kept silence. The old King wished to punish them, but they had put to sea, and never came back as long as they lived.

Doctor Knowall

There was once upon a time a poor peasant called Crabb, who drove with two oxen a load of wood to the town, and sold it to a doctor for two talers. When the money was being counted out to him, it so happened that the doctor was sitting at table, and when the peasant saw how well he ate and drank, his heart desired what he saw, and he would willingly have been a doctor too. So he remained standing a while, and at length inquired if he too could not be a doctor. "Oh, yes," said the doctor, "that is soon managed." "What must I do?" asked the peasant. "In the first place buy yourself an A B C book of the kind which has a cock on the frontispiece; in the second, turn your cart and your two oxen into money, and get yourself some clothes, and whatsoever else pertains to medicine; thirdly, have a sign painted for yourself with the words: 'I am Doctor Knowall,' and have that nailed up above your house-door." The peasant did everything that he had been told to do. When he had doctored people awhile, but not long, a rich and great lord had some money stolen. Then he was told about Doctor Knowall who lived in such and such a village, and must know what had become of the money. So the lord had the horses harnessed to his carriage, drove out to the village, and asked Crabb if he were

Doctor Knowall. Yes, he was, he said. Then he was to go with him and bring back the stolen money. "Oh, yes, but Grete, my wife, must go too." The lord was willing, and let both of them have a seat in the carriage, and they all drove away together. When they came to the nobleman's castle, the table was spread, and Crabb was told to sit down and eat. "Yes, but my wife, Grete, too," said he, and he seated himself with her at the table. And when the first servant came with a dish of delicate fare, the peasant nudged his wife, and said: "Grete, that was the first," meaning that was the servant who brought the first dish. The servant, however, thought he intended by that to say: "That is the first thief," and as he actually was so, he was terrified, and said to his comrade outside: "The doctor knows all: we shall fare ill, he said I was the first." The second did not want to go in at all, but was forced. So when he went in with his dish, the peasant nudged his wife, and said: "Grete, that is the second." This servant was equally alarmed, and he got out as fast as he could. The third fared no better, for the peasant again said: "Grete, that is the third." The fourth had to carry in a dish that was covered, and the lord told the doctor that he was to show his skill, and guess what was beneath the cover. Actually, there were crabs. The doctor looked at the dish, had no idea what to say, and cried: "Ah, poor Crabb." When the lord heard that, he cried: "There! he knows it; he must also know who has the money!"

On this the servants looked terribly uneasy, and made a sign to the doctor that they wished him to step outside for a moment. When therefore he went out, all four of them confessed to him that they had stolen the money, and said that they would willingly restore it and give him a heavy sum into the bargain, if he would not denounce them, for if he did they would be hanged. They led him to the spot where the money was concealed. With this the doctor was satisfied, and returned to the hall, sat down to the table, and said: "My lord, now will I search in my book where the gold is hidden." The fifth servant, however, crept into the stove to hear if the doctor knew still more. But the doctor sat still and opened his A B C book, turned the pages backwards and forwards, and looked for the cock. As he could not find it immediately he said: "I know you are there, so you had better come out!" Then the fellow in the stove thought that the doctor meant him, and full of terror, sprang out, crying: "That man knows everything!" Then Doctor Knowall showed the lord where the money was, but did not say who had stolen it, and received from both sides much money in reward, and became a renowned man.

The Spirit in the Bottle

There was once a poor woodcutter who toiled from early morning till late at night. When at last he had laid by some money he said to his boy: "You are my only child, I will spend the money which I have earned with the sweat of my brow on your education; if you learn some honest trade you can support me in my old age, when my limbs have grown stiff and I am obliged to stay at home." Then the boy left home to study and learned diligently so that his masters praised him, and he remained there a long time. When he had worked through two classes, but was still not yet perfect in everything, the little pittance which the father had earned was all spent, and the boy was obliged to return home to him. "Ah," said the father, sorrowfully, "I can give you no more, and in these hard times I cannot earn a farthing more than will suffice for our daily bread." "Dear father," answered the son, "don't trouble yourself about it, if it is God's will, it will turn to my advantage. I shall soon accustom myself to it." When the father wanted to go into the forest to earn money by helping to chop and stack wood, the son said: "'I will go with you and help you." "Nay, my son," said the father, "that would be hard for you; you are not accustomed to rough work, and will not be able to bear it. Besides, I have only one axe and no money left wherewith to buy another." "Just go to the neighbor," answered the son, "he will lend you his axe until I have earned one for myself."

The father then borrowed an axe of the neighbor, and next morning at break of day they went out into the forest together. The son helped his father and was quite merry and brisk about it. But when the sun was right over their heads, the father said: "We will rest, and have our dinner, and then we shall work twice as well." The son took his bread in his hands, and said: "Just you rest, father, I am not tired; I will walk up and down a little in the forest, and look for birds' nests." "Oh, you fool," said the father, "why should you want to run about there? Afterwards you will be tired, and no longer able to raise your arm; stay here, and sit down beside me."

The son, however, went into the forest, ate his bread, was very merry and peered in among the green branches to see if he could discover a bird's nest anywhere. So he walked to and fro until at last he came to a great dangerous-looking oak, which certainly was already many hundred years old, and which five men could not have spanned. He stood still and looked at it, and thought: "Many a bird must have built its nest in that." Then all at once it seemed to him that he heard a voice. He listened and became aware that someone was crying in a very smothered voice: "Let me out, let me out!" He looked around, but could discover nothing; then he fancied that the voice came out of the ground. So he cried: "Where are you?" The voice answered: "I am down here amongst the roots of the oak-tree. Let me out! Let me out!" The student began to loosen the earth under the tree, and search among the roots, until at last he found a glass bottle in a little hollow. He lifted it up and held it against the light, and then saw a creature shaped like a frog, springing up and down in it. "Let me out! Let me out!" it cried anew, and the boy, thinking no evil, drew the cork out of the bottle. Immediately a spirit ascended from it, and began to grow, and grew so fast that in a very few moments he stood before the boy, a terrible fellow as big as half the tree. "Do you know," he cried in an awful voice, "what your reward is for having let me out?" "No," replied the boy fearlessly, "how should I know that?" "Then I will tell you," cried the spirit; "I must strangle you for it." "You should have told me that sooner," said the boy, "for I should then have left you shut up, but my head shall stand fast for all you can do; more than one person must be consulted about that." "More people here, more people there," said the spirit. "You shall have the reward you have earned. Do you think that I was shut up there for such a long time as a favor? No, it was a punishment for me. I am the mighty Mercurius. Whosoever releases me, him must I strangle." "Just a moment," answered the boy, "not so fast. I must first know that you really were shut up in that little bottle, and that you are the right spirit. If, indeed, you can get in again, I will

believe, and then you may do as you will with me." The spirit said haughtily: "That is a very trifling feat," drew himself together, and made himself as small and slender as he had been at first, so that he crept through the same opening, and right through the neck of the bottle in again. Scarcely was he within than the boy thrust the cork back into the bottle, and threw it among the roots of the oak into its old place, and the spirit was deceived.

And now the student was about to return to his father, but the spirit cried very piteously: "Ah, do let me out! ah, do let me out!" "No," answered the boy, "not a second time! He who has once tried to take my life shall not be set free by me, now that I have caught him again." "If you will set me free," said the spirit, "I will give you so much that you will have plenty all the days of your life." "No," answered the boy, "you would cheat me as you did the first time." "You are spurning your own good luck," said the spirit; "I will do you no harm, but will reward you richly." The boy thought: "I will venture it, perhaps he will keep his word, and anyhow he shall not get the better of me." Then he took out the cork, and the spirit rose up from the bottle as he had done before, stretched himself out and became as big as a giant. "Now you shall have your reward," said he, and handed the boy a little rag just like sticking-plaster, and said: "If you spread one end of this over a wound it will heal, and if you rub steel or iron with the other end it will be changed into silver." "I must just try that," said the boy, and went to a tree, tore off the bark with his axe, and rubbed it with one end of the plaster. It immediately closed together and was healed. "Now, it is all right," he said to the spirit, "and we can part." The spirit thanked him for his release, and the boy thanked the spirit for his present, and went back to his father.

"Where have you been racing about?" said the father; "why have you forgotten your work? I always said that you would never come to anything." "Be easy, father, I will make it up." "Make it up indeed," said the father angrily, "that's no use." "Take care, father, I will soon hew that tree there, so that it will split." Then he took his plaster, rubbed the axe with it, and dealt a mighty blow, but as the iron had changed into silver, the edge bent: "Hi, father, just look what a bad axe you've given me, it has become quite crooked." The father was shocked and said: "Ah, what have you done? now I shall have to pay for that, and have not the where-withal, and that is all the good I have got by your work." "Don't get angry," said the son, "I will soon pay for the axe." "Oh, you blockhead," cried the father, "wherewith will you pay for it? You have nothing but what I give you. These are students' tricks that are sticking in your head, you have no idea of woodcutting." After a while the boy said: "Father, I can really work no more, we had better call it a day." "Eh, what!" answered he. "Do you think I will sit with my hands in my pockets like you? I must go on working, but you may take yourself off home." "Father, I am here in this wood for the first time, I don't know my way alone. Do go with me." As his anger had now abated, the father at last let himself be persuaded and went home with him. Then he said to the son: "Go and sell your damaged axe, and see what you can get for it, and I must earn the difference, in order to pay the neighbor." The son took the axe, and carried it into town to a goldsmith, who tested it, laid it in the scales, and said: "It is worth four hundred talers, I have not so much as that by me." The son said: "Give me what you have, I will lend you the rest." The goldsmith gave him three hundred talers, and remained a hundred in his debt. The son thereupon went home and said: "Father, I have got the money, go and ask the neighbor what he wants for the axe." "I know that already," answered the old man, "one taler, six groschen." "Then give him two talers, twelve groschen, that is double and enough; see, I have money in plenty," and he gave the father a hundred talers, and said: "You shall never know want, live as comfortably as you like." "Good heavens!" said the father, "how have you come by these riches?" The boy then told how all had come to pass, and how he, trusting in his luck, had made such a bundle. But with the money that was left, he went back to his studies and went on learning more, and as he could heal all wounds with his plaster, he became the most famous doctor in the whole world.

Bearskin

There was once a young fellow who enlisted as a soldier, conducted himself bravely, and was always the foremost when it rained bullets. So long as the war lasted, all went well, but when peace was made, he received his dismissal, and the captain said he might go where he liked. His parents were dead, and he had no longer a home, so he went to his brothers and begged them to take him in, and keep him until war broke out again. The brothers, however, were hard-hearted and said: "What can we do with you? You are of no use to us; go and make a living for yourself." The soldier had nothing left but his gun; so he took that on his shoulder, and went forth into the world. He came to a wide heath, on which nothing was to be seen but a circle of trees; under these he sat sorrowfully down, and began to think over his fate. "I have no money," thought he, "I have learnt no trade but that of fighting, and now that they have made peace they don't want me any longer; I can see in advance that I shall have to starve." All at once he heard a rustling, and when he looked round, a strange man stood before him, who wore a green coat and looked right stately, but had a hideous cloven foot. "I know already what you are in need of," said the man; "gold and possessions shall you have, as much as you can make away with, do what you will, but first I must know if you are fearless, that I may not bestow my money in vain." "A soldier and fear—how can those two things go together?" he answered; "you can put me to the proof." "Very well, then," answered the man, "look behind you." The soldier turned round, and saw a large bear, which came growling towards him. "Oho!" cried the soldier, "I will tickle your nose for you, so that you shall soon lose your fancy for growling," and he aimed at the bear and shot it through the muzzle; it fell down and never stirred again. "I see quite well," said the stranger, "that you are not wanting in courage, but there is still another condition which you will have to fulfil." "If it does not endanger my salvation," replied the soldier, who knew very well who was standing by him. "If it does, I'll have nothing to do with it." "You will look to that for yourself," answered Greencoat; "you shall for the next seven years neither wash yourself, nor comb your beard, nor your hair, nor cut your nails, nor once say the Lord's prayer. I will give you a coat and a cloak, which during this time you must wear. If you die during these seven years, you are mine; if you remain alive, you are free, and rich to boot, for all the rest of your life." The soldier thought of the great extremity in which he now found himself, and as he so often had gone to meet death, he resolved to risk it now also, and agreed to the terms. The Devil took off his green coat, and gave it to the soldier, and said: "If you have this coat on your back and put your hand into the pocket, you will always find it full of money." Then he pulled the skin off the bear and said: "This shall be your cloak, and your bed also, for thereon shall you sleep, and in no other bed shall you lie, and because of this apparel shall you be called Bearskin." Whereupon the Devil vanished.

The soldier put the coat on, felt at once in the pocket, and found that the thing was really true. Then he put on the bearskin and went forth into the world, and enjoyed himself, refraining from nothing that did him good and his money harm. During the first year his appearance was passable, but during the second he began to look like a monster. His hair covered nearly the whole of his face, his beard was like a piece of coarse felt, his fingers had claws, and his face was so covered with dirt that if cress had been sown on it, it would have come up. Whosoever saw him, ran away, but as he everywhere gave the poor money to pray that he might not die during the seven years, and as he paid well for everything he still always found shelter. In the fourth year, he entered an inn where the landlord would not receive him, and would not even let him have a place in the stable, because he was afraid the horses would be scared. But as Bearskin thrust his hand into his pocket and pulled out a handful of ducats, the host let himself be persuaded and gave him a room in an outhouse. Bearskin, however, was obliged to promise not to let himself be seen, lest the inn should get a bad name.

As Bearskin was sitting alone in the evening, and wishing from the bottom of his heart that the seven years were over, he heard a loud lamenting in a neighboring room. He had a compassionate heart, so he opened the door, and saw an old man weeping bitterly, and wringing his hands. Bearskin went nearer, but the man sprang to his feet and tried to escape from him. At last when the man perceived that Bearskin's voice was human he let himself be prevailed upon, and by kind words Bearskin succeeded so far that the old man revealed the cause of his grief. His property had dwindled away by degrees, he and his daughters would have to starve, and he was so poor that he could not pay the innkeeper, and was to be put in prison. "If that is your only trouble," said Bearskin, "I have plenty of money." He caused the innkeeper to be brought thither, paid him and even put a purse full of gold into the poor old man's pocket.

When the old man saw himself set free from all his troubles he did not know how to show his gratitude. "Come with me," said he to Bearskin; "my daughters are all miracles of beauty, choose one of them for yourself as a wife. When she hears what you have done for me, she will not refuse you. You do in truth look a little strange, but she will soon put you to rights again." This pleased Bearskin well, and he went. When the eldest saw him she was so terribly alarmed at his face that she screamed and ran away. The second stood still and looked at him from head to foot, but then she said: "How can I accept a husband who no longer has a human form? The shaven bear that once was here and passed itself off for a man pleased me far better, for at any rate it wore a hussar's dress and white gloves. If he were only ugly, I might get used to that." The youngest, however, said: "Dear father, that must be a good man to have helped you out of your trouble, so if you have promised him a bride for doing it, your promise must be kept." It was a pity that Bearskin's face was covered with dirt and with hair, for if not they might have seen how delighted he was when he heard these words. He took a ring from his finger, broke it in two, and gave her one half, the other he kept for himself. Then he wrote his name on her half, and hers on his, and begged her to keep her piece carefully. Then he took his leave and said: "I must still wander about for three years, and if I do not return then, you are free, for I shall be dead. But pray to God to preserve my life."

The poor betrothed bride dressed herself entirely in black, and when she thought of her future bridegroom, tears came into her eyes. Nothing but contempt and mockery fell to her lot from her sisters. "Take care," said the eldest, "if you give him your hand, he will strike his claws into it." "Beware!" said the second. "Bears like sweet things, and if he takes a fancy to you, he will eat you up." "You must always do as he likes," began the elder again, "or else he will growl." And the second continued: "But the wedding will be a merry one, for bears dance well." The bride was silent, and did not let them vex her. Bearskin, however, traveled about the world from one place to another, did good where he was able, and gave generously to the poor that they might pray for him.

At length, as the last day of the seven years dawned, he went once more out on to the heath, and seated himself beneath the circle of trees. It was not long before the wind whistled, and the Devil stood before him and looked angrily at him; then he threw Bearskin his old coat, and asked for his own green one back. "We have not got so far as that yet," answered Bearskin, "you must first make me clean." Whether the Devil liked it or not, he was forced to fetch water, and wash Bearskin, comb his hair, and cut his nails. After this, he looked like a brave soldier, and was much handsomer than he had ever been before.

When the Devil had gone away, Bearskin was quite light-hearted. He went into the town, put on a magnificent velvet coat, seated himself in a carriage drawn by four white horses, and drove to his bride's house. No one recognized him. The father took him for a distinguished general, and led him into the room where his daughters were sitting. He was forced to place himself between the two eldest, who helped him to wine, gave him the best pieces of meat, and thought that in all the world they had never seen a handsomer man. The bride, however, sat opposite to him in her black dress, and never raised her eyes, nor spoke a word. When at length he asked the father if he would give him one of his daughters to wife, the two eldest jumped up, ran into their bedrooms to put on splendid dresses, for each of them fancied she was the chosen one. The stranger, as soon as he was alone with his bride, brought out his half of the ring, and threw it in a glass of wine which he handed across the table to her. She took the wine, but when she had drunk it, and found the half ring lying at the bottom, her heart began to beat. She got the other half, which she wore on a ribbon round her neck, joined them, and saw that the two pieces fitted exactly together. Then said he: "I am your betrothed bridegroom, whom you saw as Bearskin, but through God's grace I have again received my human form, and have once more become clean." He went up to her, embraced her, and gave her a kiss. In the meantime the two sisters came back in full dress, and when they saw that the handsome man had fallen to the share of the youngest, and heard that he was Bearskin, they ran out full of anger and rage. One of them drowned herself in the well, the other hanged herself on a tree. In the evening, someone knocked at the door, and when the bridegroom opened it, it was the Devil in his green coat, who said: "You see, I have now got two souls in the place of your one!"

The Willow-Wren and the Bear

Once in summer-time the bear and the wolf were walking in the forest, and the bear heard a bird singing so beautifully that he said: "Brother wolf, what bird is it that sings so well?" "That is the King of birds," said the wolf, "before whom we must bow down." In reality the bird was the willow-wren. "If that's the case," said the bear, "I should very much like to see his royal palace; come, take me thither." "That is not done quite as you seem to think," said the wolf; "you must wait until the Queen comes." Soon afterwards, the Queen arrived with some food in her beak, and the lord King came too, and they began to feed their young ones. The bear would have liked to go at once, but the wolf held him back by the sleeve, and said: "No, you must wait until the lord and lady Queen have gone away again." So they took stock of the hole where the nest lay, and trotted away. The bear, however, could not rest until he had seen the royal palace, and when a short time had passed, went to it again. The King and Queen had just flown out, so he peeped in and saw five or six young ones lying there. "Is that the royal palace?" cried the bear; "it is a wretched palace, and you are not King's children, you are disreputable children!" When the young wrens heard that, they were frightfully angry, and screamed: "No, that we are not! Our parents are honest people! Bear, you will have to pay for that!"

The bear and the wolf grew uneasy, and turned back and went into their holes. The young willow-wrens, however, continued to cry and scream, and when their parents again brought food they said: "We will not so much as touch one fly's leg, no, not if we were dying of hunger, until you have settled whether we are respectable children or not; the bear has been here and has insulted us!" Then the old King said: "Be still, he shall be punished," and he at once flew with the Queen to the bear's cave, and called in: "Old Growler, why have you insulted my children? You shall suffer for it—we will punish you by a bloody war." Thus war was announced to the Bear, and all four-footed animals were summoned to take part in it, oxen, asses, cows, deer, and every other animal the earth contained. And the willow-wren summoned everything which flew in the air, not only birds, large and small, but midges, and hornets, bees and flies had to come.

When the time came for the war to begin, the willow-wren sent out spies to discover who was the enemy's commander-in-chief. The gnat, who was the most crafty, flew into the forest where the enemy was assembled, and hid herself beneath a leaf of the tree where the password was to be announced. There stood the bear, and he called the fox before him and said: "Fox, you are the most cunning of all animals, you shall be general and lead us." "Good," said the fox, "but what signal shall we agree upon?" Since no one knew, the fox said: "I have a fine long bushy tail, which almost looks like a plume of red feathers. When I lift my tail up quite high, all is going well, and you must charge; but if I let it hang down, run away as fast as you can." When the gnat had heard that, she flew away again, and revealed everything, down to the minutest detail, to the willow-wren. When day broke, and the battle was to begin, all the four-footed animals came running up with such a noise that the earth trembled. The willow-wren with his army also came flying through the air with such a humming, and whirring, and swarming that everyone was uneasy and afraid, and on both sides they advanced against each other. But the willow-wren sent down the hornet, with orders to settle beneath the fox's tail, and sting with all his might. When the fox felt the first sting, he started so that he lifted one leg, from pain, but he bore it, and still kept his tail high in the air; at the second sting, he was forced to put it down for a moment; at the third, he could hold out no longer, screamed, and put his tail between his legs. When the animals saw that, they thought all was lost, and began to flee, each into his hole, and the birds had won the battle.

Then the King and Queen flew home to their children and cried: "Children, rejoice, eat and drink to your heart's content, we have won the battle!" But the young wrens said: "We will not eat yet, the bear must come to the nest, and beg for pardon and say that we are honorable children, before we will do that." Then the willow-wren flew to the bear's hole and cried: "Growler, you are to come to the nest to my children, and beg their pardon, or else every rib of your body shall be broken." So the bear crept thither in the greatest fear, and begged their pardon. And now at last the young wrens were satisfied, and sat down together and ate and drank, and made merry till quite late into the night.

Sweet Porridge

There was a poor but good little girl who lived alone with her mother, and they no longer had anything to eat. So the child went into the forest, and there an aged woman met her who was aware of her sorrow, and presented her with a little pot, which when she said: "Cook, little pot, cook," would cook good, sweet porridge, and when she said: "stop, little pot," it ceased to cook. The girl took the pot home to her mother, and now they were freed from their poverty and hunger, and ate sweet porridge as often as they chose. Once on a time when the girl had gone out, her mother said: "Cook, little pot, cook." And it did cook and she ate till she was satisfied, and then she wanted the pot to stop cooking, but did not know the word. So it went on cooking and the porridge rose over the edge, and still it cooked on until the kitchen and whole house were full, and then the next house, and then the whole street, just as if it wanted to satisfy the hunger of the whole world, and there was the greatest distress, but no one knew how to stop it. At last when only one single house remained, the child came home and just said: "stop, little pot," and it stopped and gave up cooking, and whosoever wished to return to the town had to eat his way back.

Hans the Hedgehog

There was once a country man who had money and land in plenty, but however rich he was, his happiness was still lacking in one respect—he had no children. Often when he went into the town with the other peasants they mocked him and asked why he had no

children. At last he became angry, and when he got home he said:
"I will have a child, even if it be a hedgehog." Then his wife had
a child that was a hedgehog in the upper part of his body and a
boy in the lower, and when she saw the child, she was terrified,
and said: "See, there you have brought ill-luck on us." Then said
the man: "What can be done now? The boy must be christened,
but we shall not be able to get a godfather for him." The woman
said: "And we cannot call him anything else but Hans the Hedgehog."

When he was christened, the parson said: "He cannot go into
any ordinary bed because of his spikes." So a little straw was put
behind the stove, and Hans the Hedgehog was laid on it. His mother
could not suckle him, for he would have pricked her with his quills.
So he lay there behind the stove for eight years, and his father was
tired of him and thought: "If he would but die!" He did not die,
however, but remained lying there. Now it happened that there was
a fair in the town, and the peasant was about to go to it, and asked
his wife what he should bring back with him for her. "A little meat
and a couple of white rolls which are wanted for the house," said
she. Then he asked the servant, and she wanted a pair of slippers
and some stockings with clocks. At last he said also: "And what
will you have, Hans my Hedgehog?" "Dear father," he said, "do
bring me bagpipes." When, therefore, the father came home again,
he gave his wife what he had bought for her, meat and white rolls;
and then he gave the maid the slippers, and the stockings with
clocks; and, lastly, he went behind the stove, and gave Hans the
Hedgehog the bagpipes. And when Hans the Hedgehog had the
bagpipes, he said: "Dear father, do go to the forge and get the cock
shod, and then I will ride away, and never come back again." At
this, the father was delighted to think that he was going to get rid
of him, and had the cock shod for him, and when it was done,
Hans the Hedgehog got on it, and rode away, but took swine and
asses with him which he intended to keep in the forest. When they
got there he made the cock fly on to a high tree with him, and
there he sat for many a long year, and watched his asses and swine
until the herd was quite large, and his father knew nothing about
him. And while he was sitting in the tree, he played his bagpipes,
and made music which was very beautiful. Once a King came
traveling by who had lost his way and heard the music. He was

astonished at it, and sent his servant forth to look all round and see from whence this music came. He spied about, but saw nothing but a little animal sitting up aloft on the tree, which looked like a cock with a hedgehog on it which made this music. Then the King told the servant he was to ask why he sat there, and if he knew the road which led to his kingdom. So Hans the Hedgehog descended from the tree, and said he would show the way if the King would write a bond and promise him whatever he first

met in the royal courtyard as soon as he arrived at home. Then the King thought: "I can easily do that, Hans the Hedgehog understands nothing, and I can write what I like." So the King took pen and ink and wrote something, and when he had done it, Hans the Hedgehog showed him the way, and he got safely home. But his daughter, when she saw him from afar, was so overjoyed that she ran to meet him, and kissed him. Then he remembered Hans the Hedgehog, and told her what had happened, and that he had been forced to promise whatsoever first met him when he got home, to a very strange animal which sat on a cock as if it were a horse, and made beautiful music, but that instead of writing that he should have what he wanted, he had written that he should not have it. Thereupon the princess was glad, and said he had done well, for she never would have gone away with the Hedgehog.

Hans the Hedgehog, however, looked after his asses and pigs, and was always merry and sat on the tree and played his bagpipes.

Now it came to pass that another King came journeying by with his attendants and runners, and he also had lost his way, and did not know how to get home again because the forest was so large. He likewise heard the beautiful music from a distance, and asked his runner what that could be, and told him to go and see. Then the runner went under the tree, and saw the cock sitting at the top of it, and Hans the Hedgehog on the cock. The runner asked him what he was doing up there. "I am keeping my asses and my pigs; but what is your desire?" The messenger said that they had lost their way, and could not get back into their own kingdom, and asked if he would not show them the way. Then Hans the Hedgehog descended the tree with the cock, and told the aged King that he would show him the way, if he would give him for his own whatsoever first met him in front of his royal palace. The King said: "Yes," and wrote a promise to Hans the Hedgehog that he should have this. That done, Hans rode on before him on the cock, and pointed out the way, and the King reached his kingdom again in safety. When he got to the courtyard, there were great rejoicings. Now he had an only daughter who was very beautiful; she ran to meet him, threw her arms round his neck, and was delighted to have her old father back again. She asked him where in the world he had been so long. So he told her how he had lost his way, and had very nearly not come back at all, but that as he was traveling through a great forest, a creature, half hedgehog, half man, who was sitting astride a cock in a high tree, and making music, had shown him the way and helped him to get out, but that in return he had promised him whatsoever first met him in the royal courtyard, and how that was she herself, which made him unhappy now. But on this she promised that, for love of her father, she would willingly go with this Hans if he came.

Hans the Hedgehog, however, took care of his pigs, and the pigs became more pigs until there were so many in number that the whole forest was filled with them. Then Hans the Hedgehog resolved not to live in the forest any longer, and sent word to his father to have every stye in the village emptied, for he was coming with such a great herd that all might kill who wished to do so. When his father heard that, he was troubled, for he thought Hans the Hedgehog had died long ago. Hans the Hedgehog, however, seated himself on the cock, and drove the pigs before him into the village, and ordered the slaughter to begin. Ha!—then there was a butchery and a chopping that might have been heard two miles off! After this Hans the Hedgehog said: "Father, let me have the cock shod once more at the forge, and then I will ride away and never come back as long as I live." Then the father had the cock shod once more, and was pleased that Hans the Hedgehog would never return again.

Hans the Hedgehog rode away to the first kingdom. There the King had commanded that whosoever came mounted on a cock and had bagpipes with him should be shot at, cut down, or stabbed by everyone, so that he might not enter the palace. When, therefore, Hans the Hedgehog came riding thither, they all pressed forward against him with their pikes, but he spurred the cock and it flew up over the gate in front of the King's window and lighted there, and Hans cried that the King must give him what he had promised, or he would take both his life and his daughter's. Then the King began to speak to his daughter, and to beg her to go away with Hans in order to save her own life and her father's. So she dressed herself in white, and her father gave her a carriage with six horses and magnificent attendants together with gold and possessions. She seated herself in the carriage, and placed Hans the Hedgehog beside her with the cock and the bagpipes, and then they took leave and drove away, and the King thought he should never see her again. But he was deceived in his expectation, for when they were at a short distance from the town, Hans the Hedgehog took her pretty clothes off, and pierced her with his hedgehog's spikes until she bled all over. "That is the reward of your falseness," said he, "go on your way, I will not have you!" and on that he chased her home again, and she was disgraced for the rest of her life.

Hans the Hedgehog, however, rode on further with the cock and his bagpipes, to the dominions of the second King to whom he had shown the way. But this one had arranged that if anyone resembling Hans the Hedgehog should come, they were to present arms, give him safe conduct, cry long life to him, and lead him to the royal palace.

But when the King's daughter saw him she was terrified, for he really looked too strange. Then she remembered that she could not change her mind, for she had given her promise to her father. So Hans the Hedgehog was welcomed by her, and married to her, and had to go with her to the royal table, and she seated herself by his side, and they ate and drank. When the evening came and they wanted to go to sleep, she was afraid of his quills, but he told her she was not to fear, for no harm would befall her, and he told the old King that he was to appoint four men to watch by the door of the chamber, and light a great fire, and when he entered the room and was about to get into bed, he would creep out of his hedgehog's skin and leave it lying there by the bedside, and that the men were to run nimbly to it, throw it in the fire, and stay by it until it was consumed. When the clock struck eleven, he went into the chamber, stripped off the hedgehog's skin, and left it lying by the bed. Then came the men and fetched it swiftly, and threw it in the fire; and when the fire had consumed it, he was saved, and lay there in bed in human form, but he was coal-black as if he had been burnt. The King sent for his physician who washed him with precious salves and anointed him, and he became white, and was a handsome young man. When the King's daughter saw that she was glad, and the next morning they arose joyfully, ate and drank, and then the marriage was properly solemnized, and Hans the Hedgehog received the kingdom from the aged King.

When several years had passed he went with his wife to his father, and said that he was his son. The father, however, declared he had no son—he had never had but one, and he had been born like a hedgehog with spikes, and had gone forth into the world. Then Hans made himself known, and the old father rejoiced and went with him to his kingdom.

My tale is done,
And away it has run
To little Augusta's house.

The Blue Light

There was once on a time a soldier who for many years had served the King faithfully, but when the war came to an end could serve no longer because of the many wounds which he had received. The King said to him: "You may return to your home, I need you no longer, and you will not receive any more money, for he only receives wages who renders me service for them." Then the soldier did not know how to earn a living, went away greatly troubled, and walked the whole day, until in the evening he entered a forest. When darkness came on, he saw a light, which he went up to, and came to a house wherein lived a witch. "Do give me one night's lodging, and a little to eat and drink," said he to her, "or I shall starve." "Oho!" she answered, "who gives anything to a run-away soldier? Yet will I be compassionate, and take you in, if you will do what I wish." "What do you wish?" said the soldier. "That you should dig all round my garden for me, tomorrow." The soldier consented, and next day labored with all his strength, but could not finish it by the evening. "I see well enough," said the witch, "that you can do no more today, but I will keep you yet another night, in payment for which you must tomorrow chop me a load of wood, and chop it small." The soldier spent the whole day in doing it, and in the evening the witch proposed that he should stay one night more. "Tomorrow, you shall only do me a very trifling piece of work. Behind my house, there is an old dry well, into which my light has fallen, it burns blue, and never goes out, and you shall bring it up again." Next day the old woman took him to the well, and let him down in a basket. He found the blue light, and made her a signal to draw him up again. She did draw him up, but when he came near the edge, she stretched down her hand and wanted to take the blue light away from him. "No," said he, perceiving her evil intention, "I will not give you the light until I am standing with both feet upon the ground." The witch fell into a passion, let him fall again into the well, and went away.

The poor soldier fell without injury on the moist ground, and the blue light went on burning, but of what use was that to him? He saw very well that he could not escape death. He sat for a while very sorrowfully, then suddenly he felt in his pocket and found his tobacco pipe, which was still half full. "This shall be my last pleasure," thought he, pulled it out, lit it at the blue light and began to smoke. When the smoke had circled about the cavern, suddenly a little black dwarf stood before him, and said: "Lord, what are your commands?" "What my commands are?" replied the soldier, quite astonished. "I must do everything you bid me," said the little man. "Good," said the soldier; "then in the first place help me out of this well." The little man took him by the hand, and led him through an underground passage, but he did not forget to take the blue light with him. On the way the dwarf showed him the treasures which the witch had collected and hidden there, and the soldier took as much gold as he could carry. When he was above, he said to the little man: "Now go and bind the old witch, and carry her before the judge." In a short time she came by like the wind, riding on a wild tom-cat and screaming frightfully. Nor was it long before the little man re-appeared. "It is all done," said he, "and the witch is already hanging on the gallows. What further commands has my lord?" inquired the dwarf. "At this moment, none," answered the soldier; "you can return home, only be at hand immediately, if I summon you." "Nothing more is needed than that you should light your pipe at the blue light, and I will appear before you at once." Thereupon he vanished from his sight.

The soldier returned to the town from which he had come. He went to the best inn, ordered himself handsome clothes, and then bade the landlord furnish him a room as handsome as possible. When it was ready and the soldier had taken possession of it, he summoned the little black mannikin and said: "I have served the King faithfully, but he has dismissed me, and left me to hunger, and now I want to take my revenge." "What am I to do?" asked the little man. "Late at night, when the King's daughter is in bed, bring her here in her sleep; she shall do servant's work for me." The mannikin said: "That is an easy thing for me to do, but a very dangerous thing for you, for if it is discovered, you will fare ill." When twelve o'clock had struck, the door sprang open, and the mannikin carried in the princess. "Aha! are you there?" cried the soldier, "get to your work at once! Fetch the broom and sweep the chamber." When she had done this, he ordered her to come to his chair, and then he stretched out his feet and said: "Pull off my boots," and then he threw them in her face, and made her pick them up again, and clean and brighten them. She, however, did everything he bade her, without opposition, silently and with half-shut eyes. When the first cock crowed, the mannikin carried her back to the royal palace, and laid her in her bed.

Next morning when the princess arose she went to her father, and told him that she had had a very strange dream. "I was carried through the streets with the rapidity of lightning," said she, "and taken into a soldier's room, and I had to wait upon him like a servant, sweep his room, clean his boots, and do all kinds of menial work. It was only a dream, and yet I am just as tired as if I really had done everything." "The dream may have been true," said the King, "I will give you a piece of advice. Fill your pocket full of peas, and make a small hole in the pocket, and then if you are carried away again, they will fall out and leave a track in the streets." But unseen by the King, the mannikin was standing beside him when he said that, and heard all. At night when the sleeping princess was again carried through the streets, some peas certainly did fall out of her pocket, but they made no track, for the crafty mannikin had just before scattered peas in every street there was. And again the princess was compelled to do servant's work until cock-crow.

Next morning the King sent his people out to seek the track, but it was all in vain, for in every street poor children were sitting, picking up peas, and saying: "It must have rained peas, last night." "We must think of something else," said the King; "keep your shoes on when you go to bed, and before you come back from the place where you are taken, hide one of them there, I will soon contrive to find it." The black mannikin heard this plot, and at night when the soldier again ordered him to bring the princess, revealed it to him, and told him that he knew of no expedient to counteract this stratagem, and that if the shoe were found in the soldier's house it would go badly with him. "Do what I bid you," replied the soldier, and again this third night the princess was obliged to work like a servant, but before she went away, she hid her shoe under the bed.

Next morning the King had the entire town searched for his daughter's shoe. It was found at the soldier's, and the soldier himself, who at the entreaty of the dwarf had gone outside the gate, was soon brought back, and thrown into prison. In his flight he had forgotten the most valuable things he had, the blue light and the gold, and had only one ducat in his pocket. And now loaded with chains, he was standing at the window of his dungeon, when he chanced to see one of his comrades passing by. The soldier tapped at the pane of glass, and when this man came up, said to him: "Be so kind as to fetch me the small bundle I have left lying in the inn, and I will give you a ducat for doing it." His comrade ran thither and brought him what he wanted. As soon as the soldier was alone again, he lighted his pipe and summoned the black mannikin. "Have no fear," said the latter to his master. "Go wheresoever they take you, and let them do what they will, only take the blue light with you." Next day the soldier was tried, and though he had done nothing wicked, the judge condemned him to death. When he was led forth to die, he begged a last favor of the King. "What is it?" asked the King. "That I may smoke one more pipe on my way." "You may smoke three," answered the King, "but do not imagine that I will spare your life." Then the soldier pulled out his pipe and lighted it at the blue light, and as soon as a few wreaths of smoke had ascended, the mannikin was there with a small cudgel in his hand, and said: "What does my lord command?" "Strike down to earth that false judge there, and his constable, and spare not the King who has treated me so ill." Then the mannikin fell on them like lightning, darting this way and that way, and whosoever was so much as touched by his cudgel fell to earth, and did not venture to stir again. The King was terrified; he threw himself on the soldier's mercy, and merely to be allowed to live at all, gave him his kingdom for his own, and his daughter to wife.

The Seven Swabians

Seven Swabians were once together. The first was Master Schulz; the second, Jackli; the third, Marli; the fourth, Jergli; the fifth, Michal; the sixth, Hans; the seventh, Veitli: all seven had made up their minds to travel about the world to seek adventures and perform great deeds. But in order that they might go in safety and with arms in their hands, they thought it would be advisable that they should have one solitary, but very strong, and very long spear made for them. This spear all seven of them took in their hands at once; in front walked the boldest and bravest, and that was Master Schulz; all the others followed in a row and Veitli was the last. Then it came to pass one day in the hay month, when they had walked a long distance, and still had a long way to go before they reached the village where they were to pass the night, that as they were in a meadow in the twilight a great beetle or hornet flew by them from behind a bush, and hummed in a menacing manner. Master Schulz was so terrified that he all but dropped the spear, and a cold sweat broke out over his whole body. "Hark! hark!" cried he to his comrades, "Good heavens! I hear a drum." Jackli, who was behind him holding the spear, and into whose nose some smell had risen, said: "Something is most certainly going on, for I smell the powder and the match." At these words Master Schulz began to take to flight, and in a trice jumped over a hedge, but as he just happened to jump on to the teeth of a rake which had been left lying there after the hay-making, the handle of it struck against his face and gave him a tremendous blow. "O dear! O dear!" screamed Master Schulz. "Take me prisoner; I surrender! I surrender!" The other six all leapt over, one on the top of the other, crying: "If you surrender, I surrender too! If you surrender, I surrender too!" At length, as no enemy was there to bind and take them away, they saw that they had been mistaken, and in order that the story might not be known, and they be treated as fools and ridiculed, they all swore to each other to hold their peace about it until one of them should speak of it by mistake.

Then they journeyed onwards. The second danger which they survived cannot be compared with the first. Some days afterwards, their path led them through a fallow-field where a hare was sitting sleeping in the sun. Her ears were standing straight up, and her great glassy eyes were wide open. All of them were alarmed at the sight of the horrible wild beast, and they consulted together as to what it would be the least dangerous to do. For if they were to run away, they knew that the monster would pursue and swallow them whole. So they said: "We must go through a great and dangerous struggle. Boldly ventured, is half won," and all seven grasped the spear, Master Schulz in front, and Veitli behind. Master Schulz was always trying to keep the spear back, but Veitli had become quite brave while behind, and wanted to dash forward and cried:

> "Strike home, in every Swabian's name,
> Or else I wish you may be lame."

But Hans knew how to meet this, and said:

> "Thunder and lightning, it's fine to prate,
> But for dragon-hunting you are always late."

Michal cried:

> "Nothing is missing, not even a hair,
> Be sure the Devil himself is there."

Then it was Jergli's turn, and he said:

> "If it be not he, it's at least his mother,
> Or else the Devil's own step-brother."

And now Marli had a bright thought, and said to Veitli:

> "Advance, Veitli, advance, advance,
> And I behind will hold the lance."

Veitli, however, did not obey, and Jackli said:

> "'Tis Schulz's place the first to be,
> No one deserves that honor but he."

Then Master Schulz plucked up his courage, and said, gravely:

> "Then let us boldly advance to the fight,
> Thus we shall show our valor and might."

Hereupon they all together set on the dragon. Master Schulz crossed himself and prayed for God's assistance, but as all this was of no avail, and he was getting nearer and nearer to the enemy, he screamed: "Oho! Oho! ho! ho! ho!" in the greatest anguish. This awakened the hare, which in great alarm darted swiftly away. When

Master Schulz saw her thus flying from the field of battle, he cried in his joy:

"Quick, Veitli, quick, look there, look there,
The monster's nothing but a hare!"

So the Swabian allies went in search of further adventures, and came to the Moselle, a mossy, quiet, deep river, over which there are few bridges, and which in many places people have to cross in boats. As the seven Swabians did not know this, they called to a man who was working on the opposite side of the river, to know how people contrived to get across. The distance and their way of speaking made the man unable to understand what they wanted, and he said: "What? what?" in the way people speak in the neighborhood of Treves. Master Schulz thought he was saying: "Wade, wade through the water," and as he was the first, began to set out and went into the Moselle. It was not long before he sank in the mud and the deep waves which drove against him, but his hat was blown on the opposite shore by the wind, and a frog sat down beside it, and croaked: "Wat, wat, wat." The other six on the opposite side heard that, and said: "Oho, comrades, Master Schulz is calling us; if he can wade across, why cannot we?" So they all jumped into the water together in a great hurry, and were drowned, and thus one frog took the lives of all six of them, and not one of the Swabian allies ever reached home again.

One-Eye, Two-Eyes, and Three-Eyes

There was once a woman who had three daughters, the eldest of whom was called One-eye, because she had only one eye in the middle of her forehead, and the second, Two-eyes, because she had two eyes like other folks, and the youngest, Three-eyes, because she had three eyes; and her third eye was also in the center of her forehead. However, as Two-eyes saw just as other human beings did, her sisters and her mother could not endure her. They said to her: "You, with your two eyes, are no better than the common people; you do not belong to us!" They pushed her about, and threw old clothes to her, and gave her nothing to eat but what they left, and did everything that they could to make her unhappy.

It came to pass that Two-eyes had to go out into the fields and tend the goat, but she was still quite hungry, because her sisters had given her so little to eat. So she sat down on a ridge and began to weep, and so bitterly that two streams ran down from her eyes. And once when she looked up in her grief, a woman was standing beside her, who said: "Why are you weeping, little Two-eyes?" Two-eyes answered: "Have I not reason to weep, when I have two eyes like other people, and my sisters and mother hate me for it, and push me from one corner to another, throw old clothes to me, and give me nothing to eat but the scraps they leave? To-day they have given me so little that I am still quite hungry." Then the wise woman said: "Wipe away your tears, Two-eyes, and I will tell you something to stop your ever suffering from hunger again; just say to your goat:

'Bleat, my little goat, bleat,
Cover the table with something to eat,'

and then a clean well-spread little table will stand before you, with the most delicious food upon it of which you may eat as much as you are inclined to, and when you have had enough, and have no more need of the little table, just say,

'Bleat, bleat, my little goat, I pray,
And take the table quite away,'

and then it will vanish again from your sight." Hereupon the wise woman departed. But Two-eyes thought: "I must instantly make a trial, and see if what she said is true, for I am far too hungry," and she said:

"Bleat, my little goat, bleat,
Cover the table with something to eat,"

and scarcely had she spoken the words than a little table, covered with a white cloth, was standing there, and on it was a plate with a knife and fork, and a silver spoon; and the most delicious food was there also, warm and smoking as if it had just come out of the kitchen. Then Two-eyes said the shortest prayer she knew: "Lord God, be our Guest forever, Amen," and helped herself to some food, and enjoyed it. And when she was satisfied, she said, as the wise woman had taught her:

"Bleat, bleat, my little goat, I pray,
And take the table quite away,"

and immediately the little table and everything on it was gone again. "That is a delightful way of keeping house!" thought Two-eyes, and was quite glad and happy.

In the evening, when she went home with her goat, she found a small earthenware dish with some food, which her sisters had set ready for her, but she did not touch it. Next day she again went out with her goat, and left the few bits of broken bread which had been handed to her, lying untouched. The first and second time that she did this, her sisters did not notice it at all, but as it happened every time, they did observe it, and said: "There is something wrong about Two-eyes, she always leaves her food untasted, and she used to eat up everything that was given her; she must have discovered other ways of getting food." In order that they might learn the truth, they resolved to send One-eye with Two-eyes when she went to drive her goat to the pasture, to observe what Two-eyes did when she was there, and whether anyone brought her anything to eat and drink.

So when Two-eyes set out the next time, One-eye went to her and said: "I will go with you to the pasture, and see that the goat is well taken care of, and driven where there is food." But Two-eyes knew what was in One-eye's mind, and drove the goat into high grass and said: "Come, One-eye, we will sit down, and I will sing something to you." One-eye sat down and was tired with the unaccustomed walk and the heat of the sun, and Two-eyes sang constantly:

> "One-eye, are you waking?
> One-eye, are you sleeping?"

until One-eye shut her one eye, and fell asleep, and as soon as Two-eyes saw that One-eye was fast asleep, and could discover nothing, she said:

> "Bleat, my little goat, bleat,
> Cover the table with something to eat,"

and seated herself at her table, and ate and drank until she was satisfied, and then she again cried:

> "Bleat, bleat, my little goat, I pray,
> And take the table quite away,"

and in an instant all had vanished. Two-eyes now awakened One-eye, and said: "One-eye, you want to take care of the goat, and go to sleep while you are doing it, but in the meantime the goat might run all over the world. Come, let us go home again." So they went home, and again Two-eyes let her little dish stand untouched, and One-eye could not tell her mother why she would not eat it, and to excuse herself said: "I fell asleep while I was out."

Next day the mother said to Three-eyes: "This time you shall go and observe if Two-eyes eats anything when she is out, and if anyone fetches her food and drink, for she must eat and drink in secret." So Three-eyes went to Two-eyes, and said: "I will go with you and see if the goat is taken proper care of, and driven where there is food." But Two-eyes knew what was in Three-eyes' mind, and drove the goat into high grass and said: "We will sit down, and I will sing something to you, Three-eyes." Three-eyes sat down and was tired with the walk and with the heat of the sun, and Two-eyes began the same song as before, and sang:

> "Three-eyes, are you waking?"

but then, instead of singing:

> "Three-eyes, are you sleeping?"

as she ought to have done, she thoughtlessly sang:

> "Two-eyes, are you sleeping?"

and sang all the time:

> "Three-eyes, are you waking?
> Two-eyes, are you sleeping?"

Then two of the eyes which Three-eyes had, shut and fell asleep, but the third, as it had not been named in the song, did not sleep. It is true that Three-eyes shut it, but only in her cunning, to pretend it was asleep too, but it blinked, and could see everything very well. And when Two-eyes thought that Three-eyes was fast asleep, she used her little charm:

> "Bleat, my little goat, bleat,
> Cover the table with something to eat,"

and ate and drank as much as her heart desired, and then ordered the table to go away again,

> "Bleat, bleat, my little goat, I pray,
> And take the table quite away,"

and Three-eyes had seen everything. Then Two-eyes came to her, woke her and said: "Have you been asleep, Three-eyes? You keep watch very well! Come, we will go home." And when they got home, Two-eyes again did not eat, and Three-eyes said to the mother: "Now, I know why that haughty thing there does not eat. When she is out, she says to the goat:

'Bleat, my little goat, bleat,
Cover the table with something to eat,'

and then a little table appears before her covered with the best of food, much better than any we have here, and when she has eaten all she wants, she says:

'Bleat, bleat, my little goat, I pray,
And take the table quite away,'

and all disappears. I watched everything closely. She put two of my eyes to sleep by means of a charm, but luckily the one in my forehead kept awake." Then the envious mother cried: "Do you want to fare better than we do? The desire shall pass from you," and she fetched a butcher's knife, and thrust it into the heart of the goat, which fell down dead.

When Two-eyes saw that, she went out full of sadness, seated herself on the ridge of grass at the edge of the field, and wept bitter tears. Suddenly the wise woman once more stood by her side, and said: "Two-eyes, why are you weeping?" "Have I not reason to weep?" she answered. "The goat which covered the table for me every day when I spoke your charm, has been killed by my mother, and now I shall again have to bear hunger and want." The wise woman said: "Two-eyes, I will give you a piece of good advice; ask your sisters to give you the entrails of the slaughtered goat, and bury them in the ground in front of the house, and your fortune will be made." Then she vanished, and Two-eyes went home and said to her sisters: "Dear sisters, do give me some part of my goat; I don't wish for what is good, but give me the entrails." Then they laughed and said: "If that's all you want, you can have it." So Two-eyes took the entrails and buried them quietly in the evening, in front of the house-door, as the wise woman had counseled her to do.

Next morning, when they all awoke, and went to the house-door, there stood a strangely magnificent tree with leaves of silver, and fruit of gold hanging among them, so that in all the wide world there was nothing more beautiful or precious. They did not know how the tree could have come there during the night, but Two-eyes saw that it had grown up out of the entrails of the goat, for it was standing on the exact spot where she had buried them. Then the mother said to One-eye: "Climb up, my child, and gather some of the fruit of the tree for us." One-eye climbed up, but when she was about to get hold of one of the golden apples, the branch escaped from her hands, and that happened each time, so that she could not pluck a single apple, let her do what she might. Then said the mother: "Three-eyes, you climb up; you with your three eyes can look about you better than One-eye." One-eye slipped down, and Three-eyes climbed up. Three-eyes was not more skillful, and might try as she would, but the golden apples always escaped her. At length the mother grew impatient, and climbed up herself, but could get hold of the fruit no better than One-eye and Three-eyes, for she always clutched empty air. Then said Two-eyes: "Let me go up, perhaps I may succeed better." The sisters cried: "You indeed, with your two eyes, what can you do?" But Two-eyes climbed up, and the golden apples did not avoid her, but came into her hand of their own accord, so that she could pluck them one after the other, and brought a whole apronful down with her. The mother took them away from her, and instead of treating poor Two-eyes any better for this, she and One-eye and Three-eyes were only envious, because Two-eyes alone had been able to get the fruit, and they treated her still more cruelly.

It so happened that once when they were all standing together by the tree, a young knight came up. "Quick, Two-eyes," cried the two sisters, "creep under this, and don't disgrace us!" and with all speed they turned an empty barrel which was standing close by the tree over poor Two-eyes, and they swept the golden apples which she had been gathering, under it too. When the knight came nearer he was a handsome lord, who stopped and admired the magnificent gold and silver tree, and said to the two sisters: "To whom does this fine tree belong? Anyone who would bestow one branch of it on me might in return for it ask whatsoever he desired." Then One-eye and Three-eyes replied that the tree belonged to them, and that they would give him a branch. They both took great trouble, but they were not able to do it, for the branches and fruit both moved away from them every time. Then said the knight: "It is

very strange that the tree should belong to you, and that you should not have the power to break a piece off." They again asserted that the tree was their property. Whilst they were saying so, Two-eyes rolled out a couple of golden apples from under the barrel to the feet of the knight, for she was vexed with One-eye and Three-eyes, for not speaking the truth. When the knight saw the apples he was astonished, and asked where they came from. One-eye and Three-eyes answered that they had another sister, who was not allowed to show herself, for she had only two eyes like any common person. The knight, however, desired to see her, and cried: "Two-eyes, come forth." Then Two-eyes, quite comforted, came from beneath the barrel, and the knight was surprised at her great beauty, and said: "You, Two-eyes, can certainly break off a branch from the tree for me." "Yes," replied Two-eyes, "that I certainly shall be able to do, for the tree belongs to me." And she climbed up, and with the greatest ease broke off a branch with beautiful silver leaves and golden fruit, and gave it to the knight. Then said the knight: "Two-eyes, what shall I give you for it?" "Alas!" answered Two-eyes, "I suffer from hunger and thirst, grief and want, from early morning till late night; if you would take me with you, and rescue me, I should be happy." So the knight lifted Two-eyes on to his horse, and took her home with him to his father's castle, and there he gave her beautiful clothes, and meat and drink to her heart's content, and as he loved her so much he married her, and the wedding was solemnized with great rejoicing.

When Two-eyes was thus carried away by the handsome knight, her sisters begrudged her her good fortune in downright earnest. "The wonderful tree, however, still remains with us," thought they, "and even if we can gather no fruit from it, still everyone will stand still and look at it, and come to us and admire it. Who knows what good things may be in store for us?" But next morning, the tree had vanished, and all their hopes along with it. And when Two-eyes looked out of the window of her own little room, to her great delight it was standing in front of it, and so it had followed her.

Two-eyes lived a long time in happiness. Once two poor women came to her in her castle, and begged for alms. She looked in their faces, and recognized her sisters, One-eye, and Three-eyes, who had fallen into such poverty that they had to wander about and beg their bread from door to door. Two-eyes, however, made them welcome, and was kind to them, and took care of them, so that they both with all their hearts repented the evil that they had done their sister in their youth.

The Shoes That Were Danced to Pieces

There was once upon a time a King who had twelve daughters, each one more beautiful than the other. They all slept together in one chamber, in which their beds stood side by side, and every night when they were in them the King locked the door, and bolted it. But in the morning when he unlocked the door, he saw that their shoes were worn out with dancing, and no one could find out how that had come to pass. Then the King caused it to be proclaimed that whosoever could discover where they danced at night, should choose one of them for his wife and be King after his death, but that whosoever came forward and had not discovered it within three days and nights, should have forfeited his life. It was not long before a King's son presented himself, and offered to undertake the enterprise. He was well received, and in the evening was led into a room adjoining the princesses' sleeping-chamber. His bed was placed there, and he was to observe where they went and danced, and in order that they might do nothing secretly or go away to some other place, the door of their room was left open.

But the eyelids of the prince grew heavy as lead, and he fell asleep, and when he awoke in the morning, all twelve had been to the dance, for their shoes were standing there with holes in the soles. On the second and third nights there was no difference, and then his head was struck off without mercy. Many others came after this and undertook the enterprise, but all forfeited their lives. Now it came to pass that a poor soldier, who had a wound, and could serve no longer, found himself on the road to the town where the King lived. There he met an old woman, who asked him where he was going. "I hardly know myself," answered he, and added in jest: "I had half a mind to discover where the princesses danced their shoes into holes, and thus become King." "That is not so difficult," said the old woman, "you must not drink the wine which will be brought to you at night, and must pretend to be sound asleep." With that she gave him a little cloak, and said: "If you wear this, you will be invisible, and then you can steal after the twelve." When the soldier had received this good advice, he fell to in earnest, took heart, went to the King, and announced himself as a suitor. He was as well received as the others, and royal garments were put upon him. He was conducted that evening at bedtime into the antechamber, and as he was about to go to bed, the eldest came and brought him a cup of wine, but he had tied a sponge under his chin, and let the wine run down into it, without drinking a drop. Then he lay down and when he had lain a while, he began to snore, as if in the deepest sleep. The twelve princesses heard that, and laughed, and the eldest said: "He, too, might as well have saved his life." With that they got up, opened wardrobes, presses, cupboards, and brought out pretty dresses; dressed themselves before the mirrors, sprang about, and rejoiced at the prospect of the dance. Only the youngest said: "I know not how it is; you are very happy, but I feel very strange; some misfortune is certainly about to befall us." "You are a goose, who are always frightened," said the eldest. "Have you forgotten how many Kings' sons have already come here in vain? I had hardly any need to give the soldier a sleeping-draught, the booby would not have awakened anyway." When they were all ready they looked carefully at the soldier, but he had closed his eyes and did not move or stir, so they felt themselves safe enough. The eldest then went to her bed and tapped it; whereupon it immediately sank into the earth, and one after the other they descended through the opening, the eldest going first. The soldier, who had watched everything, tarried no longer, put on his little cloak, and went down last with the youngest. Half-way down the steps, he just trod a little on her dress; she was terrified at that, and cried out: "What is that? who is pulling at my dress?" "Don't be so silly!" said the eldest, "you have caught it on a nail."

Then they went all the way down, and when they were at the bottom, they were standing in a wonderfully pretty avenue of trees, all the leaves of which were of silver, and shone and glistened. The soldier thought: "I must carry a token away with me," and broke off a twig from one of them, on which the tree cracked with a loud report. The youngest cried out again: "Something is wrong, did you hear the crack?" But the eldest said: "It is a gun fired for joy, because we have got rid of our prince so quickly." After that they came into an avenue where all the leaves were of gold, and lastly into a third where they were of bright diamonds; he broke off a twig from each, which made such a crack each time that the youngest started back in terror, but the eldest still maintained that they were salutes. They went on and came to a great lake whereon stood twelve little boats, and in every boat sat a handsome prince, all of whom were waiting for the twelve, and each took one of them with him, but the soldier seated himself by the youngest. Then her prince said: "I wonder why the boat is so much heavier to-day; I shall have to row with all my strength, if I am to get it across." "What should cause that," said the youngest, "but the warm weather? I feel very warm too." On the opposite side of the lake stood a splendid, brightly-lit castle, from whence resounded the joyous music of trumpets and kettle-drums. They rowed there, entered, and each prince danced with the girl he loved, but the soldier danced with them unseen, and when one of them had a cup of wine in her hand he drank it up, so that the cup was empty when she carried it to her mouth; the youngest was alarmed at this, but the eldest always silenced her. They danced there till three o'clock in the morning when all the shoes were danced into holes, and they were forced to leave off; the princes rowed them back again over the lake, and this time the soldier seated himself by the eldest. On the shore they took leave of their princes, and promised to return the following night. When they reached the stairs the soldier ran on in front and lay down in his bed, and when the twelve had come up slowly and wearily, he was already snoring so loudly that they could all hear him, and they said: "So far as he is concerned, we are safe." They took off their beautiful dresses, laid them away, put the worn-out shoes under the bed, and lay down. Next morning the soldier was resolved not to speak, but to watch the wonderful goings-on, and again went with them a second and a third night. Then everything was just as it had been the first time, and each time they danced until their shoes were worn to pieces. But the third time he took a cup away with him as a token. When the hour had arrived for him to give his answer, he took the three twigs and the cup, and went to the King, but the twelve stood behind the door, and listened for what he was going to say. When the King put the question: "Where have my twelve daughters danced their shoes to pieces in the night?" he answered: "In an underground castle with twelve princes," and related how it had come to pass, and brought out the tokens. The King then summoned his daughters, and asked them if the soldier had told the truth, and when they saw that they were betrayed, and that falsehood would be of no avail, they were obliged to confess all. Thereupon the King asked which of them he would have to wife? He answered: "I am no longer young, so give me the eldest." Then the wedding was celebrated on the self-same day, and the kingdom was promised him after the King's death. But the princes were bewitched for as many days as they had danced nights with the twelve.

Iron Hans

There was once upon a time a King who had a great forest near his palace, full of all kinds of wild animals. One day he sent out a huntsman to shoot him a roe, but he did not come back. "Perhaps some accident has befallen him," said the King, and the next day he sent out two more huntsmen who were to search for him, but they too stayed away. Then on the third day, he sent for all his huntsmen, and said: "Scour the whole forest through, and do not give up until you have found all three." But of these also, none came home again, and of the pack of hounds which they had taken with them, none were seen again. From that time forth, no one would any longer venture into the forest, and it lay there in deep stillness and solitude, and nothing was seen of it, but sometimes an eagle or a hawk flying over it. This lasted for many years, when an unknown huntsman announced himself to the King as seeking a situation, and offered to go into the dangerous forest. The King, however, would not give his consent, and said: "It is not safe in there; I fear it would fare with you no better than with the others, and you would never come out again." The huntsman replied: "Lord, I will venture it at my own risk, of fear I know nothing."

The huntsman therefore betook himself with his dog to the forest. It was not long before the dog fell in with some game on the way, and wanted to pursue it; but hardly had the dog run two steps when it stood before a deep pool, could go no farther, and a naked arm stretched itself out of the water, seized it, and drew it under. When the huntsman saw that, he went back and fetched three men to come with buckets and bale out the water. When they could see to the bottom there lay a wild man whose body was brown like rusty iron, and whose hair hung over his face down to his knees. They bound him with cords, and led him away to the castle. There was great astonishment over the wild man; the King, however, had him put in an iron cage in his court-yard, and forbade the door to be opened on pain of death, and the Queen herself was to take the key into her keeping. And from this time forth everyone could again go into the forest with safety.

The King had a son of eight years, who was once playing in the court-yard, and while he was playing, his golden ball fell into the cage. The boy ran thither and said: "Give me my ball out." "Not till you have opened the door for me," answered the man. "No," said the boy, "I will not do that; the King has forbidden it," and ran away. The next day he again went and asked for his ball; the wild man said: "Open my door," but the boy would not. On the third day the King had ridden out hunting, and the boy went once more and said: "I cannot open the door even if I wished, for I have not the key." Then the wild man said: "It lies under your mother's pillow, you can get it there." The boy, who wanted to have his ball back, cast all thought to the winds, and brought the key. The door opened with difficulty, and the boy pinched his fingers. When it was open the wild man stepped out, gave him the golden ball, and hurried away. The boy had become afraid; he called and cried after him: "Oh, wild man, do not go away, or I shall be beaten!" The wild man turned back, took him up, set him on his shoulder, and went with hasty steps into the forest. When the King came home, he observed the empty cage, and asked the Queen how that had happened. She knew nothing about it, and sought the key, but it was gone. She called the boy, but no one answered. The King sent out people to seek for him in the fields, but they did not find him. Then he could easily guess what had happened, and much grief reigned in the royal court.

When the wild man had once more reached the dark forest, he took the boy down from his shoulder, and said to him: "You will never see your father and mother again, but I will keep you with me, for you have set me free, and I have compassion on you. If you do all I bid you, you shall fare well. Of treasure and gold have I enough, and more than anyone in the world." He made a bed of moss for the boy on which he slept, and the next morning the man took him to a well, and said: "Behold, the gold well is as bright and clear as crystal, you shall sit beside it, and take care that nothing falls into it, or it will be polluted. I will come every evening to see if you have obeyed my order." The boy placed himself by the brink of the well, and often saw a golden fish or a golden snake show itself therein, but took care that nothing fell in. As he was thus sitting, his finger hurt him so violently that he involuntarily put it in the water. He drew it quickly out again, but saw that it was quite gilded, and whatsoever pains he took to wash the gold off again, all was to no purpose. In the evening Iron Hans came back, looked at the boy, and said: "What has happened to the well?" "Nothing, nothing," he answered, and held his finger behind his back, that the man might not see it. But he said: "You have dipped your finger into the water, this time it may pass, but take care you do not again let anything go in." By daybreak the boy was already sitting by the well and watching it. His finger hurt him again and he passed it over his head, and then unhappily a hair fell down into the well. He took it quickly out, but it was already quite gilded. Iron Hans came, and already knew what had happened. "You have let a hair fall into the well," said he. "I will allow you to watch by it once more, but if this happens for the third time then the well is polluted, and you can no longer remain with me."

On the third day, the boy sat by the well, and did not stir his finger, however much it hurt him. But the time was long to him, and he looked at the reflection of his face on the surface of the water. And as he still bent down more and more while he was doing so, and trying to look straight into the eyes, his long hair fell down from his shoulders into the water. He raised himself up quickly, but the whole of the hair of his head was already golden and shone like the sun. You can imagine how terrified the poor boy was! He took his pocket-handkerchief and tied it round his head, in order that the man might not see it. When he came he already knew everything, and said: "Take the handkerchief off." Then the golden hair streamed forth, and let the boy excuse himself as he might, it was of no use. "You have not stood the trial, and can stay here no longer. Go forth into the world, there you will learn what poverty is. But as you have not a bad heart, and as I mean well by you, there is one thing I will grant you; if you fall into any difficulty, come to the forest and cry: 'Iron Hans,' and then I will come and help you. My power is great, greater than you think, and I have gold and silver in abundance."

Then the King's son left the forest, and walked by beaten and unbeaten paths ever onwards until at length he reached a great city. There he looked for work, but could find none, and he had learnt nothing by which he could help himself. At length he went to the palace, and asked if they would take him in. The people about court did not at all know what use they could make of him, but they liked him, and told him to stay. At length the cook took him into his service, and said he might carry wood and water, and rake the cinders together. Once when it so happened that no one else was at hand, the cook ordered him to carry the food to the royal table, but as he did not like to let his golden hair be seen, he kept his little cap on. Such a thing as that had never yet come under the King's notice, and he said: "When you come to the royal table you must take your hat off." He answered: "Ah, Lord, I cannot; I have a bad sore on my head." Then the King had the cook called before him and scolded him, and asked how he could take such a boy as that into his service; and that he was to send him away at once. The cook, however, had pity on him, and exchanged him for the gardener's boy.

And now the boy had to plant and water the garden, hoe and dig, and bear the wind and bad weather. Once in summer when he was working alone in the garden, the day was so warm he took his little cap off that the air might cool him. As the sun shone on his hair it glittered and flashed so that the rays fell into the bedroom of the King's daughter, and up she sprang to see what that could be. Then she saw the boy, and cried to him: "Boy, bring me a wreath of flowers." He put his cap on with all haste, and gathered wild field-flowers and bound them together. When he was ascending the stairs with them, the gardener met him, and said: "How can you take the King's daughter a garland of such common flowers? Go quickly, and get another, and seek out the prettiest and rarest." "Oh, no," replied the boy, "the wild ones have more scent, and will please her better." When he got into the room, the King's daughter said: "Take your cap off, it is not seemly to keep it on in my presence." He again said: "I may not, I have a sore head." She, however, caught at his cap and pulled it off, and then his golden hair rolled down on his shoulders, and it was splendid to behold.

He wanted to run out, but she held him by the arm, and gave him a handful of ducats. With these he departed, but he cared nothing for the gold pieces. He took them to the gardener, and said: "I present them to your children, they can play with them." The following day the King's daughter again called to him that he was to bring her a wreath of field-flowers, and when he went in with it, she instantly snatched at his cap, and wanted to take it away from him, but he held it fast with both hands. She again gave him a handful of ducats, but he would not keep them, and gave them to the gardener for playthings for his children. On the third day things went just the same; she could not get his cap away from him, and he would not have her money.

Not long afterwards, the country was overrun by war. The King gathered together his people, and did not know whether or not he could offer any opposition to the enemy, who was superior in strength and had a mighty army. Then said the gardener's boy: "I am grown up, and will go to the wars also, only give me a horse." The others laughed, and said: "Seek one for yourself when we are gone, we will leave one behind us in the stable for you." When they had gone forth, he went into the stable, and led the horse out; it was lame of one foot, and limped hobblety jig, hobblety jig; nevertheless he mounted it, and rode away to the dark forest. When he came to the outskirts, he called "Iron Hans" three times so loudly that it echoed through the trees. Thereupon the wild man appeared immediately, and said: "What do you desire?" "I want a strong steed, for I am going to the wars." "That you shall have, and still more than you ask for." Then the wild man went back into the forest, and it was not long before a stable-boy came out of it, who led a horse that snorted with its nostrils, and could hardly be restrained, and behind them followed a great troop of warriors entirely equipped in iron, and their swords flashed in the sun. The youth made over his three-legged horse to the stable-boy, mounted the other, and rode at the head of the soldiers. When he got near the battle-field a great part of the King's men had already fallen, and little was wanting to make the rest give way. Then the youth galloped thither with his iron soldiers, broke like a hurricane over the enemy, and beat down all who opposed him. They began to flee, but the youth pursued, and never stopped, until there was not a single man left. Instead of returning to the King, however, he conducted his troop by byways back to the forest, and called forth Iron Hans. "What do you desire?" asked the wild man. "Take back your horse and your troops, and give me my three-legged horse again." All that he asked was done, and soon he was riding on his three-legged horse. When the King returned to his palace, his daughter went to meet him, and wished him joy of his victory. "I am not the one who carried away the victory," said he, "but a strange knight who came to my assistance with his soldiers." The daughter wanted to hear who the strange knight was, but the King did not know, and said: "He followed the enemy, and I did not see him again." She inquired of the gardener where his boy was, but he smiled, and said: "He has just come home on his three-legged horse, and the others have been mocking him, and crying: 'Here comes our hobblety jig back again!' They asked, too: 'Under what hedge have you been lying sleeping all the time?' So he said: 'I did the best of all, and it would have gone badly without me.' And then he was still more ridiculed."

The King said to his daughter: "I will proclaim a great feast that shall last for three days, and you shall throw a golden apple. Perhaps the unknown man will show himself." When the feast was announced, the youth went out to the forest, and called Iron Hans. "What do you desire?" asked he. "That I may catch the King's daughter's golden apple." "It is as safe as if you had it already," said Iron Hans. "You shall likewise have a suit of red armor for the occasion, and ride on a spirited chestnut-horse." When the day came, the youth galloped to the spot, took his place amongst the knights, and was recognized by no one. The King's daughter came forward, and threw a golden apple to the knights, but none of them caught it but he, only as soon as he had it he galloped away.

On the second day Iron Hans equipped him as a white knight, and gave him a white horse. Again he was the only one who caught the apple, and he did not linger an instant, but galloped off with it. The King grew angry, and said: "That is not allowed; he must appear before me and tell his name." He gave the order that if the knight who caught the apple, should go away again they should pursue him, and if he would not come back willingly, they were to cut him down and stab him.

On the third day, he received from Iron Hans a suit of black armor and a black horse, and again he caught the apple. But when he was riding off with it, the King's attendants pursued him, and one of them got so near him that he wounded the youth's leg with the point of his sword. The youth nevertheless escaped from them, but his horse leapt so violently that the helmet fell from the youth's head, and they could see that he had golden hair. They rode back and announced this to the King.

The following day the King's daughter asked the gardener about his boy. "He is at work in the garden; the queer creature has been at the festival too, and only came home yesterday evening; he has likewise shown my children three golden apples which he has won."

The King had him summoned into his presence, and he came and again had his little cap on his head. But the King's daughter went up to him and took it off, and then his golden hair fell down over his shoulders, and he was so handsome that all were amazed. "Are you the knight who came every day to the festival, always in different colors, and who caught the three golden apples?" asked the King. "Yes," answered he, "and here the apples are," and he took them out of his pocket, and returned them to the King. "If you desire further proof, you may see the wound which your people gave me when they followed me. But I am likewise the knight who helped you to your victory over your enemies." "If you can perform such deeds as that, you are no gardener's boy; tell me, who is your father?" "My father is a mighty King, and gold have I in plenty as great as I require." "I well see," said the King, "that I owe thanks to you; can I do anything to please you?" "Yes," answered he, "that indeed you can. Give me your daughter to wed." The maiden laughed, and said: "He does not stand much on ceremony, but I have already seen by his golden hair that he was no gardener's boy," and then she went and kissed him. His father and mother came to the wedding, and were in great delight, for they had given up all hope of ever seeing their dear son again. And as they were sitting at the marriage-feast, the music suddenly stopped, the doors opened, and a stately King came in with a great retinue. He went up to the youth, embraced him and said: "I am Iron Hans, and was by enchantment a wild man, but you have set me free; all the treasures which I possess, shall be your property."

The Star-Money

There was once upon a time a little girl whose father and mother were dead, and she was so poor that she no longer had a room to live in, or bed to sleep in, and at last she had nothing else but the clothes she was wearing and a little bit of bread in her hand which some charitable soul had given her. She was good and pious, however. And as she was thus forsaken by all the world, she went forth into the open country, trusting in the good God. Then a poor man met her, who said: "Ah, give me something to eat, I am so hungry!" She handed him the whole of her piece of bread, and said: "May God bless you," and went onwards. Then came a child who moaned and said: "My head is so cold, give me something to cover it with." So she took off her hood and gave it to him; and when she had walked a little farther, she met another child who had no jacket and was frozen with cold. Then she gave it her own; and a little farther on one begged for a frock, and she gave away that also. At length she got into a forest and it had already become dark, and there came yet another child, and asked for a shirt, and the good little girl thought to herself: "It is a dark night and no one sees you, you can very well give your shirt away," and took it off, and gave away that also. And as she so stood, and had not one single thing left, suddenly some stars from heaven fell down, and they were nothing else but hard smooth pieces of money, and although she had just given her shirt away, she had a new one which was of the very finest linen. Then she put the money into it, and was rich all the days of her life.

Snow-White and Rose-Red

There was once a poor widow who lived in a lonely cottage. In front of the cottage was a garden wherein stood two rose-trees, one of which bore white and the other red roses. She had two children who were like the two rose-trees, and one was called Snow-white, and the other Rose-red. They were as good and happy, as busy and cheerful as ever two children in the world were, only Snow-white was more quiet and gentle than Rose-red. Rose-red liked better to run about in the meadows and fields seeking flowers and catching butterflies; but Snow-white sat at home with her mother, and helped her with her house-work, or read to her when there was nothing to do.

The two children were so fond of one another that they always held each other by the hand when they went out together, and when Snow-white said: "We will not leave each other," Rose-red answered; "Never so long as we live," and their mother would add: "What one has she must share with the other."

They often ran about the forest alone and gathered red berries, and no beasts did them any harm, but came close to them trustfully. The little hare would eat a cabbage-leaf out of their hands, the roe grazed by their side, the stag leapt merrily by them, and the birds sat still upon the boughs, and sang whatever they knew.

No mishap overtook them; if they had stayed too late in the forest, and night came on, they laid themselves down near one another upon the moss, and slept until morning came, and their mother knew this and did not worry on their account.

Once when they had spent the night in the wood and the dawn had roused them, they saw a beautiful child in a shining white dress sitting near their bed. He got up and looked quite kindly at them, but said nothing and went away into the forest. And when they looked round they found that they had been sleeping quite close to a precipice, and would certainly have fallen into it in the darkness if they had gone only a few paces further. And their mother told them that it must have been the the angel who watches over good children.

Snow-white and Rose-red kept their mother's little cottage so neat that it was a pleasure to look inside it. In the summer Rose-red took care of the house, and every morning laid a wreath of flowers by her mother's bed before she awoke, in which was a rose from each tree. In the winter Snow-white lit the fire and hung the kettle on the hob. The kettle was of brass and shone like gold, so brightly was it polished. In the evening, when the snowflakes fell, the mother said: "Go, Snow-white, and bolt the door," and then they sat round the hearth, and the mother took her spectacles and read aloud out of a large book, and the two girls listened as they sat and spun.

And close by them lay a lamb upon the floor, and behind them upon a perch sat a white dove with its head hidden beneath its wings.

One evening, as they were thus sitting comfortably together, someone knocked at the door as if he wished to be let in. The mother said: "Quick, Rose-red, open the door, it must be a traveler who is seeking shelter." Rose-red went and pushed back the bolt, thinking that it was a poor man, but it was not; it was a bear that stretched his broad, black head within the door.

Rose-red screamed and sprang back, the lamb bleated, the dove fluttered, and Snow-white hid herself behind her mother's bed. But the bear began to speak and said: "Do not be afraid, I will do you no harm! I am half-frozen, and only want to warm myself a little beside you."

"Poor bear," said the mother, "lie down by the fire, only take care that you do not burn your coat." Then she cried:"Snow-white, Rose-red, come out, the bear will do you no harm, he means well." So they both came out, and by-and-by the lamb and dove came nearer, and were not afraid of him. The bear said: "Here, children, knock the snow out of my coat a little;" so they brought the broom and swept the bear's hide clean; and he stretched himself by the fire and growled contentedly and comfortably. It was not long before they grew quite at home, and played tricks with their clumsy guest. They tugged his hair with their hands, put their feet upon his back and rolled him about, or they took a hazel-switch and beat him, and when he growled they laughed. But the bear took it all in good part, only when they were too rough he called out: "Leave me alive, children,

> Snow-white, Rose-red
> Will you beat your wooer dead?"

When it was bed-time, and the others went to bed, the mother said to the bear: "You can lie there by the hearth, and then you will be safe from the cold and the bad weather." As soon as day dawned the two children let him out, and he trotted across the snow into the forest.

Henceforth the bear came every evening at the same time, laid himself down by the hearth, and let the children amuse themselves with him as much as they liked; and they got so used to him that the doors were never fastened until their black friend had arrived.

When spring had come and all outside was green, the bear said one morning to Snow-white: "Now I must go away, and cannot come back for the whole summer." "Where are you going, then, dear bear?" asked Snow-white. "I must go into the forest and guard my treasures from the wicked dwarfs. In the winter, when the earth is frozen hard, they are obliged to stay below and cannot work their way through; but now, when the sun has thawed and warmed the earth, they break through it, and come out to pry and steal; and what once gets into their hands, and in their caves, does not easily see daylight again."

Snow-white was quite sorry at his departure, and as she unbolted the door for him, and the bear was hurrying out, he caught against the bolt and a piece of his hairy coat was torn off, and it seemed to Snow-white as if she had seen gold shining through it, but she was not sure about it. The bear ran away quickly, and was soon out of sight behind the trees.

A short time afterwards the mother sent her children into the forest to get fire-wood. There they found a big tree which lay felled on the ground, and close by the trunk something was jumping backwards and forwards in the grass, but they could not make out what it was. When they came nearer they saw a dwarf with an old withered face and a snow-white beard a yard long. The end of the beard was caught in a crevice of the tree, and the little fellow was jumping about like a dog tied to a rope, and did not know what to do.

He glared at the girls with his fiery red eyes and cried: "Why do you stand there? Can you not come here and help me?" "What are you up to, little man?" asked Rose-red. "You stupid, prying goose!" answered the dwarf; "I was going to split the tree to get a little wood for cooking. The little bit of food that we people get is immediately burnt up with heavy logs; we do not swallow so much as you coarse, greedy folk. I had just driven the wedge safely in, and everything was going as I wished; but the cursed wedge was too smooth and suddenly sprang out, and the tree closed so quickly that I could not pull out my beautiful white beard; so now it is tight in and I cannot get away, and the silly, sleek, milk-faced things laugh! Ugh! how odious you are!"

The children tried very hard, but they could not pull the beard out, it was caught too fast. "I will run and fetch someone," said Rose-red. "You senseless goose!" snarled the dwarf; "why should you fetch someone? You are already two too many for me; can you not think of something better?" "Don't be impatient," said Snow-white "I will help you," and she pulled her scissors out of her pocket, and cut off the end of the beard.

As soon as the dwarf felt himself free he laid hold of a bag which lay amongst the roots of the tree, and which was full of gold, and lifted it up, grumbling to himself: "Uncouth people, to cut off a piece of my fine beard. Bad luck to you!" and then he swung the bag upon his back, and went off without even once looking at the children.

Some time afterwards Snow-white and Rose-red went to catch a dish of fish. As they came near the brook they saw something like a large grasshopper jumping towards the water, as if it were going to leap in. They ran to it and found it was the dwarf. "Where are you going?" said Rose-Red; "you surely don't want to go into the water?" "I am not such a fool!" cried the dwarf; "don't you see that the accursed fish wants to pull me in?" The little man had been sitting there fishing, and unluckily the wind had tangled up his beard with the fishing-line; a moment later a big fish made a bite and the feeble creature had not strength to pull it out; the fish kept the upper hand and pulled the dwarf towards him. He held on to all the reeds and rushes, but it was of little good, for he was forced to follow the movements of the fish, and was in urgent danger of being dragged into the water.

The girls came just in time; they held him fast and tried to free his beard from the line, but all in vain, beard and line were entangled fast together. There was nothing to do but to bring out the scissors and cut the beard, whereby a small part of it was lost. When the dwarf saw that he screamed out: "Is that civil, you toadstool, to disfigure a man's face? Was it not enough to clip off the end of my beard? Now you have cut off the best part of it. I cannot let myself be seen by my people. I wish you had been made to run the soles off your shoes!" Then he took out a sack of pearls which lay in the rushes, and without another word he dragged it away and disappeared behind a stone.

It happened that soon afterwards the mother sent the two chil-

dren to the town to buy needles and thread, and laces and ribbons. The road led them across a heath upon which huge pieces
of rock lay strewn about. There they noticed a large bird hovering
in the air, flying slowly round and round above them; it sank lower
and lower, and at last settled near a rock not far away. Immediately they heard a loud, piteous cry. They ran up and saw with
horror that the eagle had seized their old acquaintance the dwarf,
and was going to carry him off.

The children, full of pity, at once took tight hold of the little man, and pulled against the eagle so long that at last he let his booty go. As soon as the dwarf had recovered from his first fright he cried with his shrill voice: "Could you not have done it more carefully! You dragged at my brown coat so that it is all torn and full of holes, you clumsy creatures!" Then he took up a sack full of precious stones, and slipped away again under the rock into his hole. The girls, who by this time were used to his ingratitude, went on their way and did their business in the town.

As they crossed the heath again on their way home they surprised the dwarf, who had emptied out his bag of precious stones in a clean spot, and had not thought that anyone would come there so late. The evening sun shone upon the brillant stones; they glittered and sparkled with all colors so beautifully that the children stood still and stared at them. "Why do you stand gaping there?" cried the dwarf, and his ashen-gray face became copper-red with rage. He was still cursing when a loud growling was heard, and a black bear came trotting towards them out of the forest. The dwarf sprang up in a fright, but he could not reach his cave, for the bear was already close. Then in the dread of his heart he cried: "Dear Mr. Bear, spare me, I will give you all my treasures; look, the beautiful jewels lying there! Grant me my life; what do you want with a slender little fellow like me? You would not feel me between your teeth. Come, take these two wicked girls, they are tender morsels for you, fat as young quails; for mercy's sake eat them!" The bear took no heed of his words, but gave the wicked creature a single blow with his paw, and he did not move again.

The girls had run away, but the bear called to them: "Snow-white and Rose-red, do not be afraid; wait, I will come with you." Then they recognised his voice and waited, and when he came up to them suddenly his bearskin fell off, and he stood there a handsome man, clothed all in gold. "I am a King's son," he said, "and I was bewitched by that wicked dwarf, who had stolen my treasures; I have had to run about the forest as a savage bear until I was freed by his death. Now he has got his well-deserved punishment."

Snow-white was married to him, and Rose-red to his brother, and they divided between them the great treasure which the dwarf had gathered together in his cave. The old mother lived peacefully and happily with her children for many years. She took the two rose-trees with her, and they stood before her window, and every year bore the most beautiful roses, white and red.

The Glass Coffin

Let no one ever say that a poor tailor cannot do great things and win high honors; all that is needed is that he should go to the right smithy, and what is of most consequence, that he should have good luck. A quick-witted tailor's apprentice once went out traveling, and came into a great forest, and, as he did not know the way, he lost himself. Night fell and nothing was left for him to do in this painful solitude but to seek a bed. He might certainly have found a good bed on the soft moss, but the fear of wild beasts let him have no rest there, and at last he made up his mind to spend the night in a tree. He sought out a high oak, climbed up to the top of it, and thanked God that he had his goose with him, for otherwise the wind which blew over the top of the tree would have carried him away.

After he had spent some hours in the darkness, not without fear and trembling, he saw at a very short distance the glimmer of a light, and as he thought that a human habitation might be there, where he would be better off than on the branches of a tree, he got carefully down and went towards the light. It guided him to a small hut that was woven together of reeds and rushes. He knocked boldly, the door opened, and by the light which came forth he saw a little hoary old man who wore a coat made of bits of colored stuff sewn together. "Who are you, and what do you want?" asked the man in a grumbling voice. "I am a poor tailor," he answered, "whom night has surprised here in the wilderness, and I earnestly beg you to take me into your hut until morning." "Go your way," replied the old man in a surly voice, "I will have nothing to do with tramps; seek for yourself a shelter elsewhere." Having said this, he was about to slip into his hut again, but the tailor held him so tightly by the corner of his coat, and pleaded so piteously, that the old man, who was not so ill-natured as he wished to appear, was at last softened, and took him into the hut with him where he gave him something to eat, and then offered him a very good bed in a corner.

The weary tailor needed no rocking; but slept sweetly till morning, but even then would not have thought of getting up, if he had not been aroused by a great noise. A violent sound of screaming and roaring forced its way through the thin walls of the hut. The tailor, full of unwonted courage, jumped up, put his clothes on in haste, and hurried out. Then close by the hut, he saw a great black bull and a beautiful stag, which were just preparing for a violent struggle. They rushed at each other with such extreme rage that the ground shook with their trampling, and the air resounded with their cries. For a long time it was uncertain which of the two would gain the victory; at length the stag thrust his horns into his adversary's body, whereupon the bull fell to the earth with a terrific roar, and was finished off by a few strokes from the stag.

The tailor, who had watched the fight with astonishment, was still standing there motionless when the stag bounded up to him at full speed, and before he could escape, caught him up on his great horns. He had not much time to collect his thoughts, for it went in a swift race over stock and stone, mountain and valley, wood and meadow. He held with both hands to the ends of the horns, and resigned himself to his fate. It seemed to him just as if he were flying away. At length the stag stopped in front of a wall of rock, and gently let the tailor down. The tailor, more dead than alive, required some time to come to himself. When he had in some degree recovered, the stag, which had remained standing by him, pushed its horns with such force against a door in the rock, that it sprang open. Flames of fire shot forth, after which followed a great smoke, which hid the stag from his sight. The tailor did not know what to do, or whither to turn, in order to get out of this desert and back to human beings again. Whilst he was standing thus undecided, a voice sounded out of the rock, which cried to him: "Enter without fear, no evil shall befall you." He hesitated, but driven by a mysterious force, he obeyed the voice and went through the iron door into a large spacious hall, whose ceiling, walls and floor were made of shining polished square stones, on each of which were carved signs which were unknown to him. He looked at everything full of admiration, and was on the point of going out again, when he once more heard the voice which said to him: "Step on the stone which lies in the middle of the hall, and great good fortune awaits you."

His courage had already grown so great that he obeyed the order. The stone began to give way under his feet, and sank slowly down into the depths. When it was once more firm, and the tailor looked round, he found himself in a hall which in size resembled the former. Here, however, there was more to look at and to admire. Hollow places were cut in the walls, in which stood vases of transparent glass and filled with colored spirit or with a bluish vapor. On the floor of the hall two great glass chests stood opposite each other, which at once excited his curiosity. When he went to one of them he saw inside it a handsome structure like a castle surrounded by farm-buildings, stables and barns, and a quantity of other good things. Everything was small, but exceedingly carefully and delicately made, and seemed to be carved out by a dexterous hand with the greatest precision.

He might not have turned away his eyes from the consideration of this rarity for some time, had not the voice once more made itself heard. It ordered him to turn round and look at the glass chest which was standing opposite. How his admiration increased when he saw therein a maiden of the greatest beauty! She lay as if asleep, and was wrapped in her long fair hair as in a precious mantle. Her eyes were closely shut, but the brightness of her complexion and a ribbon which her breathing moved to and fro, left no doubt that she was alive. The tailor was looking at the beauty with beating heart, when she suddenly opened her eyes, and started up at the sight of him with a shock of joy. "Divine Providence!" cried she, "my deliverance is at hand! Quick, quick help me out of my prison; if you push back the bolt of this glass coffin, then I shall be free." The tailor obeyed without delay, and she immediately raised up the glass lid, came out and hastened into the corner of the hall, where she covered herself with a large cloak. Then she seated herself on a stone, ordered the young man to come to her, and after she had planted a friendly kiss on his lips, she said: "My long-desired deliverer, kind Heaven has guided you to me, and put an end to my sorrows. On the self-same day when they end, shall your happiness begin. You are the husband chosen for me by Heaven, and shall pass your life in unbroken joy, loved by me, and rich to overflowing in every earthly possession. Seat yourself, and listen to the story of my life:

"I am the daughter of a rich count. My parents died when I was still in my tender youth, and recommended me in their last will to my elder brother, by whom I was brought up. We loved each other so tenderly, and were so alike in our way of thinking and our inclinations, that we both embraced the resolution never to marry, but to stay together to the end of our lives. In our house there was no lack of company; neighbors and friends visited us often, and we showed the greatest hospitality to everyone. So it came to pass one evening that a stranger came riding to our castle, and, under pretext of not being able to get on to the next place, begged for shelter for the night. We granted his request with ready courtesy, and he entertained us in the most agreeable manner during supper by conversation intermingled with stories. My brother liked the stranger so much that he begged him to spend a couple of days with us, to which, after some hesitation, he consented. We did not rise from table until late in the night, the stranger was shown to a room, and I hastened, as I was tired, to lay my limbs in my soft bed. Hardly had I fallen off to sleep, when the sound of faint and delightful music awoke me. As I could not conceive from whence it came, I wanted to summon my waiting-maid who slept in the next room, but to my astonishment I found that speech was taken away from me by an unknown force. I felt as if a nightmare were weighing down my breast, and was unable to make the very slightest sound. In the meantime, by the light of my night-lamp, I saw the stranger enter my room through two doors which were fast bolted. He came to me and said that, by magic arts which were at his command, he had caused the lovely music to sound in order to awaken me, and that he now forced his way through all fastenings with the intention of offering his hand and heart. My dislike of his magic arts was so great, however, that I refused to answer him. He remained for a time standing without moving, apparently with the idea of waiting for a favorable decision, but as I continued to keep silence, he angrily declared he would revenge himself and find means to punish my pride, and left the room. I passed the night in the greatest disquietude, and fell asleep only towards morning. When I awoke, I hurried to my brother, but did not find him in his room, and the attendants told me that he had ridden forth with the stranger to the chase at daybreak.

"I at once suspected nothing good. I dressed myself quickly, ordered my palfrey to be saddled, and accompanied only by one servant, rode full gallop to the forest. The servant fell with his horse, and could not follow me, for the horse had broken its foot. I pursued my way without halting, and in a few minutes I saw the stranger coming towards me with a beautiful stag which he led by a cord. I asked him where he had left my brother, and how he had come by this stag, out of whose great eyes I saw tears flowing. Instead of answering me, he began to laugh loudly. I fell into a great rage at this, pulled out a pistol and discharged at the monster; but the ball rebounded from his breast and went into my horse's head. I fell to the ground, and the stranger muttered some words which deprived me of consciousness.

"When I came to my senses again I found myself in this underground cave in a glass coffin. The magician appeared once again, and said he had changed my brother into a stag, my castle with all that belonged to it, diminished in size by his arts, he had shut up in the other glass chest, and my people, who were all turned into smoke, he had confined in glass bottles. He told me that if I would now comply with his wish, it would be an easy thing for him to put everything back in its former state, as he had nothing to do but open the vessels, and everything would return once more to its natural form. I answered him as little as I had done the first time. He vanished and left me in my prison, in which a deep sleep came on me. Among the visions which passed before my eyes, the most comforting was that in which a young man came and set me free, and when I opened my eyes to-day I saw you, and beheld my dream fulfilled. Help me to accomplish the other things which happened in those visions. The first is that we lift the glass chest in which my castle is enclosed, on to that broad stone."

As soon as the stone was laden, it began to rise up on high with the maiden and the young man, and mounted through the opening of the ceiling into the upper hall, from whence they then could easily reach the open air. Here the maiden opened the lid, and it was marvellous to behold how the castle, the houses, and the farm buildings which were enclosed, stretched themselves out and grew to their natural size with the greatest rapidity. After this, the maiden and the tailor returned to the cave beneath the earth, and had the vessels which were filled with smoke carried up by the stone. The maiden had scarcely opened the bottles when the blue smoke rushed out and changed itself into living men, in whom she recognized her servants and her people. Her joy was still more increased when her brother, who had killed the magician in the form of the bull, came out of the forest towards them in his human form, and on the self-same day the maiden, in accordance with her promise, gave her hand at the altar to the lucky tailor.

The Hare and the Hedgehog

This story, my dear young folks, seems to be false, but it really is true, for my grandfather, from whom I have it, used always, when relating it, to say: "It must be true, my son, or else no one could tell it to you." The story is as follows. One Sunday morning about harvest time, just as the buckwheat was in bloom, the sun was shining brightly in heaven, the east wind was blowing warmly over the stubble-fields, the larks were singing in the air, the bees buzzing among the buckwheat, the people in their Sunday clothes were all going to church, and all creatures were happy, and the hedgehog was happy too.

The hedgehog, however, was standing by his door with his arms akimbo, enjoying the morning breezes, and slowly trilling a little song to himself, which was neither better nor worse than the songs which hedgehogs are in the habit of singing on a blessed Sunday morning. Whilst he was thus singing half aloud to himself, it suddenly occurred to him that, while his wife was washing and drying the children, he might very well take a walk into the field, and see how his turnips were getting on. The turnips, in fact, were close beside his house, and he and his family were accustomed to eat them, for which reason he looked upon them as his own. No sooner said than done. The hedgehog shut the house-door behind him, and took the path to the field. He had not gone very far from home,

and was just turning around the sloe-bush which stands there outside the field, to go up into the turnip-field, when he observed the
hare who had gone out on business of the same kind, namely, to
visit his cabbages. When the hedgehog caught sight of the hare, he
bade him a friendly good morning. But the hare, who was in his
own way a distinguished gentleman, and frightfully haughty, did
not return the hedgehog's greeting, but said to him, assuming at
the same time a very contemptuous manner: "How do you happen to be running about here in the field so early in the morning?"
"I am taking a walk," said the hedgehog. "A walk!" said the hare,
with a smile. "It seems to me that you might use your legs for a
better purpose." This answer made the hedgehog furiously angry,
for he can bear anything but a reference to his legs, just because
they are crooked by nature. So now the hedgehog said to the hare:
"You seem to imagine that you can do more with your legs than
I with mine." "That is just what I do think," said the hare. "That
can be put to the test," said the hedgehog. "I wager that if we run
a race, I will outstrip you." "That is ridiculous! You with your
short legs!" said the hare, "but for my part I am willing, if you
have such a monstrous fancy for it. What shall we wager?" "A
golden louis-d'or and a bottle of brandy," said the hedgehog.
"Done," said the hare. "Shake hands on it, and then we may as
well begin at once." "Nay," said the hedgehog, "there is no such
great hurry! I am still fasting, I will go home first, and have a little
breakfast. In half-an-hour I will be back again at this place."

Hereupon the hedgehog departed, for the hare was quite satisfied with this. On his way the hedgehog thought to himself: "The
hare relies on his long legs, but I will contrive to get the better of
him. He may be a great man, but he is a very silly fellow, and he
shall pay for what he has said." So when the hedgehog reached
home, he said to his wife: "Wife, dress yourself quickly, you must
go out to the field with me." "What is going on, then?" said his
wife. "I have made a wager with the hare, for a gold louis-d'or
and a bottle of brandy. I am to run a race with him, and you must
be present." "Good heavens, husband," the wife now cried, "are
you not right in your mind, have you completely lost your wits?
What can make you want to run a race with the hare?" "Hold
your tongue, woman," said the hedgehog, "that is my affair. Don't

begin to discuss things which are matters for men. Be off, dress yourself, and come with me." What could the hedgehog's wife do? She was forced to obey him, whether she liked it or not.

So when they had set out on their way together, the hedgehog said to his wife: "Now pay attention to what I am going to say. Look you, I will make the long field our race-course. The hare shall run in one furrow, and I in another, and we will begin to run from the top. Now all that you have to do is to place yourself here below in the furrow, and when the hare arrives at the end of the furrow on the other side of you, you must cry out to him: 'I am here already!' "

Then they reached the field, and the hedgehog showed his wife her place, and then walked up the field. When he reached the top, the hare was already there. "Shall we start?" said the hare. "Certainly," said the hedgehog. "Then both at once." So saying, each placed himself in his own furrow. The hare counted: "Once, twice, thrice, and away!" and went off like a whirlwind down the field. The hedgehog, however, only ran about three paces, and then he crouched down in the furrow, and stayed quietly where he was.

When the hare therefore arrived at full speed at the lower end of the field, the hedgehog's wife met him with the cry: "I am here already!" The hare was shocked and wondered not a little, he thought no other than that it was the hedgehog himself who was calling to him, for the hedgehog's wife looked just like her husband. The hare, however, thought to himself: "That has not been done fairly," and cried: "It must be run again, let us have it again." And once more he went off like the wind in a storm, so that he seemed to fly. But the hedgehog's wife stayed quietly in her place. So when the hare reached the top of the field, the hedgehog himself cried out to him: "I am here already." The hare, however, quite beside himself with anger, cried: "It must be run again, we must have it again." "All right," answered the hedgehog, "for my part we'll run as often as you choose." So the hare ran seventy-three times more, and the hedgehog always held out against him, and every time the hare reached either the top or the bottom, either the hedgehog or his wife said: "I am here already."

At the seventy-fourth time, however, the hare could no longer reach the end. In the middle of the field he fell to the ground, blood streamed out of his mouth, and he lay dead on the spot. But the

hedgehog took the louis-d'or which he had won and the bottle of brandy, called his wife out of the furrow, and both went home together in great delight, and if they are not dead, they are living there still.

This is how it happened that the hedgehog made the hare run races with him on the Heath of Buxtehude till he died, and since that time no hare has ever had any fancy for running races with a Buxtehude hedgehog.

The moral of this story is, firstly, that no one, however great he may be, should permit himself to jest at anyone beneath him, even if he be only a hedgehog. And secondly, it teaches, that when a man marries, he should take a wife in his own position, who looks just as he himself looks. So whosoever is a hedgehog let him see to it that his wife is a hedgehog also, and so forth.

The Peasant and the Devil

There was once upon a time a far-sighted, crafty peasant whose tricks were much talked about. The best story, however, is how he once got hold of the Devil, and made a fool of him.

The peasant had one day been working in his field, and as twilight had set in, was making ready for the journey home, when he saw a heap of burning coals in the middle of his field, and when, full of astonishment, he went up to it, a little black Devil was sitting on the live coals. "Are you sitting upon a treasure?" said the peasant. "Yes, in truth," replied the Devil, "on a treasure which contains more gold and silver than you have ever seen in your life!" "The treasure lies in my field and belongs to me," said the peasant. "It is yours," answered the Devil, "if you will for two years give me one half of everything your field produces. Money I have enough, but I have a desire for the fruits of the earth." The peasant agreed to the bargain. "In order, however, that no dispute may arise about the division," said he, "everything that is above ground shall belong to you, and what is under the earth to me." The Devil was quite satisfied with that, but the cunning peasant had sown turnips.

Now when the time for harvest came, the Devil appeared and wanted to take away his crop; but he found nothing but the yellow withered leaves, while the peasant, full of delight, was digging up his turnips. "You have had the best of it for once," said the Devil, "but the next time that won't do. What grows above ground shall be yours, and what is under it, mine." "I am willing," replied the peasant; but when the time came to sow, he did not again sow turnips, but wheat. The grain became ripe, and the peasant went into the field and cut the full stalks down to the ground. When the Devil came, he found nothing but the stubble, and went away in a fury down into a cleft in the rocks. "That is the way to cheat the Devil," said the peasant, and went and fetched away the treasure.

The Master-Thief

One day an old man and his wife were sitting in front of a miserable house resting a while from their work. Suddenly a splendid carriage with four black horses came driving up, and a richly-dressed man descended from it. The peasant stood up, went to the great man, and asked what he wanted, and in what way he could serve him. The stranger stretched out his hand to the old man, and said:

"I want nothing but to enjoy for once a country dish; cook me some potatoes, in the way you always have them, and then I will sit down at your table and eat them with pleasure." The peasant smiled and said: "You are a count or a prince, or perhaps even a duke; noble gentlmen often have such fancies, but you shall have your wish." The wife went into the kitchen, and began to wash and rub the potatoes, and to make them into balls, as they are eaten by the country-folks. Whilst she was busy with this work, the peasant said to the stranger: "Come into my garden with me for a while, I have still something to do there." He had dug some holes in the garden, and now wanted to plant trees in them. "Have you no children," asked the stranger, "who could help you with your work?" "No," answered the peasant, "I had a son, it is true, but it is long since he went out into the world. He was a ne'er-do-well; clever and knowing, but he would learn nothing and was full of bad tricks. At last he ran away from me, and since then I have heard nothing of him."

The old man took a young tree, put it in a hole, drove in a post beside it, and when he had shovelled in some earth and had tramp-led it firmly down, he tied the stem of the tree above, below, and in the middle, fast to the post by a rope of straw. "But tell me," said the stranger, "why you don't tie that crooked knotted tree, which is lying in the corner there, bent down almost to the ground, to a post also that it may grow straight, as well as these?" The old man smiled and said: "Sir, you speak according to your knowl-edge, it is easy to see that you are not familiar with gardening. That tree there is old, and mis-shapen, no one can make it straight now. Trees must be trained while they are young." "That is how it was with your son," said the stranger, "if you had trained him while he was still young, he would not have run away; now he too must have grown hard and mis-shapen." "Truly it is a long time since he went away," replied the old man, "he must have changed." "Would you know him again if he were to come to you?" asked the stranger. "Hardly by his face," replied the peasant, "but he has a mark about him, a birth-mark on his shoulder, that looks like a bean." When he had said that the stranger pulled off his coat, bared his shoulder, and showed the peasant the bean. "Good God!" cried the old man, "you are really my son!" and love for his child stirred in his heart. "But," he added, "how can you be my son, you have become a great lord and live in wealth and luxury? How have you contrived to do that?" "Ah, father," answered the son, "the young tree was bound to no post and has grown crooked. Now it is too old, it will never be straight again. How have I come by all this? I have become a thief, but do not be alarmed, I am a master-thief. For me there are neither locks nor bolts, whatsoever I desire is mine. Do not imagine that I steal like a common thief, I only take some of the superfluity of the rich. Poor people are safe, I would rather give to them than take anything from them. It is the same with anything which I can have without trouble, cunning and dexterity—I never touch it." "Alas, my son," said the father, "it still does not please me, a thief is still a thief, I tell you it will end badly." He took him to his mother, and when she heard that was her son, she wept for joy, but when he told her that he had become a master-thief, two streams flowed down over her face. At length she said: "Even if he has become a thief, he is still my son, and my eyes have beheld him once more."

They sat down to table, and once again he ate with his parents the wretched food which he had not eaten for so long. The father said: "If our lord, the count up there in the castle, learns who you are, and what trade you follow, he will not take you in his arms and cradle you in them as he did when he held you at the font, but will cause you to swing from a halter." "Be easy, father, he will do me no harm, for I understand my trade. I will go to him myself this very day." When evening drew near, the master-thief seated himself in his carriage, and drove to the castle. The count received him civilly, for he took him for a distinguished man. When, however, the stranger made himself known, the count turned pale and was quite silent for some time. At length he said: "You are my godson, and on that account mercy shall take the place of justice, and I will deal leniently with you. Since you pride yourself on being a master-thief, I will put your art to the proof, but if you do not stand the test, you must marry the rope-maker's daughter, and the croaking of the raven must be your music on the occasion." "Lord Count," answered the master-thief, "think of three things, as difficult as you like, and if I do not perform your tasks, do with me what you will." The count reflected for some minutes, and then said: "Well, then, in the first place, you shall steal the horse I keep for my own riding, out of the stable; in the next, you shall steal the sheet from beneath the bodies of my wife and myself when we are asleep, without our observing it, and the wedding-ring of my wife as well; thirdly and lastly, you shall steal away out of the church, the parson and clerk. Mark what I am saying, for your life depends on it."

The master-thief went to the nearest town; there he bought the clothes of an old peasant woman, and put them on. Then he stained his face brown, and painted wrinkles on it as well, so that no one could have recognized him. Then he filled a small cask with old Hungarian wine in which was mixed a powerful sleeping-drink. He put the cask in a basket, which he took on his back, and walked with slow and tottering steps to the count's castle. It was already dark when he arrived. He sat down on a stone in the court-yard and began to cough, like an asthmatic old woman, and to rub his hands as if he were cold. In front of the door of the stable some soldiers were lying round a fire; one of them observed the woman, and called out to her: "Come nearer, old mother, and warm yourself beside us. After all, you have no bed for the night, and must take one where you can find it." The old woman tottered up to them, begged them to lift the basket from her back, and sat down beside them at the fire. "What have you got in your little cask, old hag?" asked one. "A good mouthful of wine," she answered. "I live by trade, for money and fair words I am quite ready to let you have a glass." "Let us have it here, then," said the soldier, and when he had tasted one glass he said: "When wine is good, I like another glass," and had another poured out for himself, and the rest followed his example. "Hallo, comrades," cried one of them to those who were in the stable, "here is an old girl who has wine that is as old as herself; take a draught, it will warm your stomachs far better than our fire." The old woman carried her cask into the stable. One of the soldiers had seated himself on the saddled riding-horse, another held its bridle in his hand, a third had laid hold of its tail. She poured out as much as they wanted until the spring ran dry. It was not long before the bridle fell from the hand of the one, and he fell down and began to snore, the other left hold of the tail, lay down and snored still louder. The one who was sitting in the saddle, did remain sitting, but bent his head almost down to the horse's neck, and slept and blew with his mouth like the bellows of a forge. The soldiers outside had already been asleep for a long time, and were lying on the ground motionless, as if dead. When the master-thief saw that he had succeeded, he gave the first a rope in his hand instead of the bridle, and the other who had been holding the tail, a wisp of straw, but what was he to do with the one who was sitting on the horse's back? He did not want to throw him down, for he might have awakened and have uttered a cry. He had a good idea; he unbuckled the girths of the saddle, tied a couple of ropes which were hanging to a ring on the wall fast to the saddle, and drew the sleeping rider up into the air on it, then he twisted the rope round the posts, and made it fast. He soon unloosed the horse from the chain, but if he had ridden over the stony pavement of the yard they would have heard the noise in the castle. So he wrapped the horse's hoofs in old rags, led him carefully out, leapt upon him, and galloped off.

When day broke, the master galloped to the castle on the stolen horse. The count had just got up, and was looking out of the window. "Good morning, Sir Count," he cried to him, "here is the horse, which I have got safely out of the stable! Just look, how beautifully your soldiers are lying there sleeping; and if you will but go into the stable, you will see how comfortable your watchers have made it for themselves." The count could not help laughing. Then he said: "For once you have succeeded, but things won't go so well the second time, and I warn you that if you come before me as a thief, I will handle you as I would a thief."

When the countess went to bed that night, she closed her hand with the wedding-ring tightly together, and the count said: "All the doors are locked and bolted, I will keep awake and wait for the thief, but if he gets in by the window, I will shoot him." The master-thief, however, went in the dark to the gallows, cut a poor sinner who was hanging there down from the halter, and carried him on his back to the castle. Then he set a ladder up to the bedroom, put the dead body on his shoulders, and began to climb up. When he had got so high that the head of the dead man showed at the window, the count, who was watching in his bed, fired a pistol at him, and immediately the master let the poor sinner fall down, descended the ladder, and hid himself in one corner. The night was sufficiently lighted by the moon, for the master to see distinctly how the count got out of the window on to the ladder, came down, carried the dead body into the garden, and began to

dig a hole in which to lay it. "Now," thought the thief, "the favorable moment has come," stole nimbly out of his corner, and
climbed up the ladder straight into the countess's bedroom. "Dear
wife," he began in the count's voice, "the thief is dead, but, after
all, he is my godson, and has been more of a scape-grace than a
villain. I will not put him to open shame; besides, I am sorry for
the parents. I will bury him myself before daybreak in the garden,
that the thing may not be known. So give me the sheet, I will wrap
up the body in it, and not bury him like a dog." The countess gave
him the sheet. "I tell you what," continued the thief, "I'm having
a fit of magnanimity, give me the ring too; the unhappy man risked
his life for it, so he may take it with him into his grave." She would
not gainsay the count, and although she did it unwillingly she drew
the ring from her finger, and gave it to him. The thief made off
with both these things, and reached home safely before the count
in the garden had finished his work of burying.

What a long face the count did pull when the master came next
morning, and brought him the sheet and the ring. "Are you a wiz-
ard?" said he. "Who has fetched you out of the grave in which I
myself laid you, and brought you to life again?" "You did not bury
me," said the thief, "but the poor sinner on the gallows," and he
told him exactly how everything had happened, and the count was
forced to own to him that he was a clever, crafty thief. "But you
have not reached the end yet," he added, "you have still to perform the third task, and if you do not succeed in that, all is of no
use." The master smiled and returned no answer.

When night had fallen he went with a long sack on his back, a
bundle under his arms, and a lantern in his hand to the village-
church. In the sack he had some crabs, and in the bundle short
wax-candles. He sat down in the churchyard, took out a crab, and
stuck a wax-candle on his back. Then he lighted the little light,
put the crab on the ground, and let it creep about. He took a second out of the sack, and treated it in the same way, and so on
until the last was out of the sack. Hereupon he put on a long black
garment that looked like a monk's cowl, and stuck a gray beard
on his chin. When at last he was quite unrecognizable, he took the
sack in which the crabs had been, went into the church, and ascended the pulpit. The clock in the tower was just striking twelve;
when the last stroke had sounded, he cried with a loud and pierc-

ing voice: "Hearken, sinful men, the end of all things has come! The last day is at hand! Hearken! Hearken! Whosoever wishes to go to heaven with me must creep into the sack. I am Peter, who opens and shuts the gate of heaven. Behold how the dead outside there in the churchyard are wandering about collecting their bones. Come, come, and creep into the sack; the world is about to be destroyed!" The cry echoed through the whole village. The parson and clerk who lived nearest to the church heard it first, and when they saw the lights which were moving about the churchyard, they observed that something unusual was going on, and went into the church. They listened to the sermon for a while, and then the clerk nudged the parson and said: "It would not be amiss if we were to use the opportunity together, and before the dawning of the last day, find an easy way of getting to heaven." "To tell the truth," answered the parson, "that is what I myself have been thinking, so if you are inclined, we will set out on our way." "Yes," answered the clerk, "but you, the pastor have the precedence, I will follow." So the parson went first, and ascended the pulpit where the master opened his sack. The parson crept in first, and then the clerk. The master immediately tied up the sack tightly, seized it by the middle, and dragged it down the pulpit-steps, and whenever the heads of the two fools bumped against the steps, he cried: "We are going over the mountains." Then he drew them through the village in the same way, and when they were passing through puddles, he cried: "Now we are going through wet clouds," and when at last he was dragging them up the steps of the castle, he cried: "Now we are on the steps of heaven, and will soon be in the outer court." When he had got to the top, he pushed the sack into the pigeon-house, and when the pigeons fluttered about, he said: "Hark how glad the angels are, and how they are flapping their wings!" Then he bolted the door upon them, and went away.

Next morning he went to the count, and told him that he had performed the third task also, and had carried the parson and clerk out of the church. "Where have you left them?" asked the lord. "They are lying upstairs in a sack in the pigeon-house, and imagine that they are in heaven." The count went up himself, and convinced himself that the master had told the truth. When he had delivered the parson and clerk from their captivity, he said: "You are an archthief, and have won your wager. For once you escape with a whole skin, but see that you leave my land, for if ever you set foot on it again, you may count on your elevation to the gallows." The archthief took leave of his parents, once more went forth into the wide world, and no one has ever heard of him since.

The Boots of Buffalo-Leather

A soldier who is afraid of nothing, troubles himself about nothing. One of this kind had received his discharge, and as he had learnt no trade and could earn nothing, he traveled about and begged alms of kind people. He had an old raincoat on his back, and a pair of riding-boots of buffalo-leather which were still left to him. One day he was walking he knew not where, straight out into the open country, and at length came to a forest. He did not know where he was, but saw sitting on the trunk of a tree, which had been cut down, a man who was well dressed and wore a green shooting-coat. The soldier shook hands with him, sat down on the grass by his side, and stretched out his legs. "I see you have good boots on, which are well blacked," said he to the huntsman: "but if you had to travel about as I have, they would not last long. Look at mine, they are of buffalo-leather, and have been worn for a long time, but in them I can go through thick and thin." After a while the soldier got up and said: "I can stay no longer, hunger drives me onwards; but, Brother Brightboots, where does this road lead to?" "I don't know that myself," answered the huntsman, "I have lost my way in the forest." "Then you are in the same plight as I," said the soldier; "birds of a feather flock together, let us remain together, and seek our way." The huntsman smiled a little, and they walked on further and further, until night fell. "We do not get out of the forest," said the soldier, "but there in the distance I see a light shining; there we might find something to eat." They found a stone house, knocked at the door, and an old woman opened it. "We are looking for quarters for the night," said the soldier, "and some lining for our stomachs, for mine is as empty as an old knapsack." "You cannot stay here," answered the old woman; "this is a robbers' house, and you would do wisely to get away before they come home, or you will be lost." "It won't be so bad as that," answered the soldier, "I have not had a mouthful for two days, and whether I am murdered here or die of hunger in the forest is all the same to me. I shall come in." The huntsman would not follow, but the soldier drew him in with him by the sleeve. "Come, my dear brother, we shall not come to an end so quickly as that!" The old woman had pity on them and said: "Creep

in here behind the stove, and if they leave anything, I will give it to you on the sly when they are asleep." Scarcely were they in the corner before twelve robbers came bursting in, seated themselves at the table which was already laid, and vehemently demanded some food. The old woman brought in some great dishes of roast meat, and the robbers enjoyed that thoroughly. When the soldier smelled the food, he said to the huntsman: "I cannot hold out any longer, I shall seat myself at the table, and eat with them." "You will bring us to destruction," said the huntsman and held him back by the arm. But the soldier began to cough loudly. When the robbers heard that, they threw away their knives and forks, leapt up, and discovered the two who were behind the stove. "Aha, gentlemen, are you in the corner?" cried they. "What are you doing here? Have you been sent as spies? Wait a while, and you shall learn how to fly on a dry bough." "But do be civil," said the soldier, "I am hungry, give me something to eat, and then you can do what you like with me." The robbers were astonished, and the captain said: "I see that you have no fear; well, you shall have some food, but after that you must die." "We shall see," said the soldier, and seated himself at the table, and began to cut away valiantly at the roast meat. "Brother Brightboots come and eat," cried he to the huntsman; "you must be as hungry as I am, and cannot have better roast meat at home," but the huntsman would not eat. The robbers looked at the soldier in astonishment, and said: "The rascal uses no ceremony." After a while he said: "I have had enough food, now get me something good to drink." The chief of the robbers was in the mood to humor him in this also, and called to the old woman: "Bring a bottle out of the cellar, and mind it be of the best." The soldier drew the cork out with a loud noise, and then went with the bottle to the huntsman and said: "Watch this, brother, and you shall see something that will surprise you; I am now going to drink the health of the whole clan." Then he brandished the bottle over the heads of the robbers, and cried: "Long life to you all, but with your mouths open and your right hands lifted up," and then he drank a hearty draught. Scarcely were the words said than they all sat motionless as if made of stone, and their mouths were open and their right hands stretched up in the air. The huntsman said to the soldier: "I see that you are acquainted with tricks of another kind, but now come and let us go home." "Oho, my dear brother, but that would be marching away far too soon; we have conquered the enemy, and must first take the booty. Those men there are sitting fast, and are opening their mouths with astonishment, but they will not be allowed to move until I permit them. Come, eat and drink." The old woman had to bring another bottle of the best wine, and the soldier would not stir until he had eaten enough to last for three days. At last when day came, he said: "Now it is time to strike our tents, and in order that our march may be a short one, the old woman shall show us the nearest way to the town."

When they had arrived there, he went to his old comrades, and said: "Out in the forest I have found a nest full of gallows' birds, come with me and we will take it." The soldier led them, and said to the huntsman: "You must go back again with me to see how they flutter when we seize them by the feet." He placed the men round about the robbers, and then he took the bottle, drank a mouthful, brandished it above them, and cried: "Long life to you all." Instantly they all regained the power of movement, but were thrown down and bound hand and foot with cords. Then the soldier ordered them to be thrown into a cart as if they had been so many sacks, and said: "Now drive them straight to prison." The huntsman, however, took one of the men aside and gave him another commission as well.

"Brother Brightboots," said the soldier, "we have safely routed the enemy and been well fed, now we will quietly walk behind them as if we were stragglers!" When they approached the town, the soldier saw a crowd of people pouring through the gate of the town who were raising loud cries of joy, and waving green boughs in the air. Then he saw that the entire body-guard was coming up. "What can this mean?" said he to the huntsman. "Don't you know," he replied, "that the King has for a long time been absent from his kingdom, and that today he is returning, and everyone is going to meet him?" "But where is the King?" said the soldier; "I do not see him." "Here he is," answered the huntsman, "I am the King, and have announced my arrival." Then he opened his hunting-coat, and his royal garments were visible. The soldier was alarmed, and fell on his knees and begged him to forgive him for having in his ignorance treated him as an equal, and spoken to him by such a name. But the King shook hands with him, and said: "You are a brave soldier, and have saved my life. You shall never again be in want, I will take care of you. And if ever you would like to eat a piece of roast meat, as good as that in the robbers' house, come to the royal kitchen. But if you would drink a health, you must first ask my permission."

Puss-in-Boots

A miller had three sons, his mill, a donkey, and a cat. The sons had to run the mill, the donkey had to fetch the grain and haul away the meal, and the cat had to catch mice. When the miller died, the three sons divided up the legacy: the eldest inherited the mill, the second son inherited the donkey, and the third inherited the cat since nothing else was left over. So he was sad and said to himself, "I have, after all, fared worst of all. My oldest brother can run the mill, my other brother can ride his donkey, but what can I do with the cat? If I have myself a pair of fur gloves made from his pelt, it is all used up." The cat, who had understood everything, started in by saying, "Listen, you do not need to kill me just to get a miserable pair of gloves from my pelt. Simply have a pair of boots made for me so I can go out and be seen among the people, and then there will soon be help for us. The miller's son was astonished that the cat spoke in this manner, but since the cobbler just happened to be passing by, he called him in and had the cat measured for a pair of boots. When they were finished, the cat put them on, took a sack, filled the bottom of the sack with corn, but put a cord at the top so it could be closed. He then tossed the sack on his back and walked out of the door on two legs like a human being.

At that time the country was ruled by a king who very much liked to eat pheasant. Since times were hard, none were to be had. The entire forest was full of them, but they were so shy that no hunter could catch them. The cat knew this and intended to fare better at his task. When he reached the forest, he opened up the sack, spread the corn about, but put the cord in the grass with its end leading into a hedge. There he himself hid, crept about, and lay in wait. The pheasants soon came running, found the corn, and one after the other hopped into the sack. When a goodly number were inside, the cat pulled the cord, ran to the sack, and wrung their necks. He then put the sack on his back and immediately walked to the king's palace. The guard shouted: "Halt! Where are you going?" "To the king," the cat answered bluntly. "Are you crazy? A cat going to the king?"—"Just let him go," said another, "the king is often bored. Perhaps the cat's growling and purring will amuse him." When the cat came before the king, he bowed and said, "My master, the Earl," mentioning in doing so a long and elegant name, "commends himself to the king and sends him pheasants that he just caught in a trap." The king was astonished about the beautiful fat pheasants, was beside himself with joy, and commanded that the cat be given as much money from the treasury as he was able to carry in the sack: "Bring that to your master and thank him again very much for his present."

The poor miller's son, though, was sitting at home at the window, his head resting on his hands, thinking that he had now given away his last money for the cat's boots and thinking about what great thing the cat could bring him in return. The cat then walked in, cast the sack from his back, opened it up, and dumped out the money in front of the miller. "There you have something for the boots. The king also sends his greetings and much gratitude." The miller was happy about his wealth without, however, really being able to comprehend how it had come about. The cat, though, told him everything while removing his boots. Then he said, "Now you in fact have money enough, but that is not all there is to the matter. Tomorrow I shall again put on my boots. You should become still wealthier. I also told the king that you are an earl."

The next morning the well-shod cat again went hunting and brought the king a rich catch. This continued every day, and every day the cat brought money. And he became a great favorite of the king and could go in and out of the palace and prowl around as he pleased. The cat was once standing in the king's kitchen, warming himself at the stove, when the coachman entered and cursed, "I wish that the king and the princess were at the hangman's! For once I would like to go to the inn and drink and play cards, but I am supposed to drive them to the lake." When the cat heard that, he crept home and said to his master, "If you want to become an earl and wealthy, come out with me to the lake and go for a swim there." The miller did not know what he should say to that, but he followed the cat, went with him, took off all his clothes, and leaped into the water. The cat, though, took his clothing, carried it away and hid it. Hardly was he finished with that when the king came riding by. The cat immediately started to lament pitiably. "Oh, most merciful king! My master was swimming here in the lake. A thief came along and stole his clothes that were lying on the shore, and now the earl is in the water and cannot come out, and if he remains in the water any longer, he will freeze and die." When the king heard that, he stopped and had one of his people gallop back to fetch some of the king's clothes. The earl put on the most magnificent clothes, and since the king was already kindly disposed toward him because of the pheasants, which he believed had come from him, he was obliged to join him in the carriage. The princess was also not angry about that, for the earl was young and handsome, and she quite liked him.

The cat, however, had gone on ahead and arrived at a large meadow where more than a hundred people were making hay. "Tell me, you people, who owns this meadow?" "The great magician."—"Listen, soon the king is going to ride past. When he asks whose meadow this is, answer, 'It belongs to the earl.' And if you do not do that, you will all be beaten to death." The cat then walked on and came to a corn field so large that no one could see the end of it. More than two hundred people were harvesting corn there. "Tell me, you people, who owns this field?"—"The magician." "Listen, the king is now going to ride past. When he asks who owns this corn, answer, 'The earl.' And if you do not do that, you will all be beaten to death."—Finally the cat came to a magnificent forest where more than three hundred people were cutting large oaks and making timber. "Tell me, you people, whose forest is this?" "The magician's." "Listen, the king is going to ride by soon. When he asks who owns the forest, answer 'The earl.' And if you do not do that, you will all be killed." As the cat continued on his way, all the people looked around at him, and since he looked so strange and walked along in his boots like a human being, they were afraid of him. Soon he came to the magician's palace, boldly entered, and stood before him. The magician looked at him contemptuously and asked him what he wanted. The cat bowed and said, "I have heard that you are capable of transforming yourself as you please into any animal. Now when it comes to a dog, a fox, or even a wolf, I am ready to believe it, but when it comes to an elephant, that seems to me entirely impossible, and for that reason I have come to convince myself." The magician said proudly, "For me that is a small matter," and was at that moment transformed into an elephant. "That is a lot, but can you also transform yourself into a lion?" "That, too, is nothing," said the magician, who appeared as a lion in front of the cat. The cat pretended surprise and shouted, "That is unbelievable and unprecedented. Not even in a dream would I have come upon such ideas. But it would be better still if you were able to transform yourself into an animal as small as a mouse. You are certainly capable of more than any magician in the world, but that will be too much even for you." The magician became quite friendly from the pleasing words and said, "Oh, yes, dear pussy-cat, I can do that, too," and ran about the room in the form of a mouse. The cat gave chase and with one leap caught and ate the mouse.

The king, however, had continued his ride with the earl and the princess and came to the large meadow: "Who owns the hay?" asked the king. All shouted, as commanded by the cat, "The earl." "You have a nice piece of property there, Earl," he said. Next they came to the large corn field: "Tell me, you people, who owns the corn?" "The earl." "Oh, Earl, large fine holdings!" Next they came to the forest. "Tell me, you people, who owns this wood?" "The earl." The king was even more astonished and said, "You must be a wealthy man, Earl. I do not believe that I have such a magnificent forest." Finally they arrived at the palace. The cat was standing at the top of the stairs, and when the carriage stopped down below, he leaped down, opened the door, and said: "Sire, you have arrived here at the palace of my master, the Earl. This honor will make him happy for the rest of his life." The king climbed out and was astonished at the magnificent building, which was almost larger and more beautiful than his palace. The earl, however, led the princess up the steps into the hall that fairly glistened with gold and precious jewels. The princess was then betrothed to the earl, and when the king died, the earl became king. Puss-in-Boots, however, became his prime-minister.

Translated by Martha Humphreys

The Pied Piper of Hamelin

In the year 1284, a wondrous man appeared in the town of Hamelin. He wore a coat of many bright colors and for this reason was called the Pied Piper. Claiming to be a ratcatcher, he promised to rid the city of all mice and rats in exchange for a certain sum. The citizens came to terms with him and promised him a certain sum of money.

The ratcatcher then took out a small fife and began playing. The rats and mice immediately came creeping out of all the houses and gathered around him. When he was certain that none remained behind, he left, followed by the entire pack, which he led down to the Weser River. There he rolled up his clothes and marched into the water, followed by all the animals that then drowned.

After the citizens had been freed of this plague, they regretted having promised the payment. Using all kinds of excuses, they withheld it from the man, causing him to become angry and to go away feeling embittered. On June 26, St. John's and St. Paul's Day— some say at seven in the morning, others say at noon—he reappeared as a hunter. He had a terrifying expression on his face and was wearing a strange red hat. Once again the sounds of his fife were heard in the alleys. This time, though, instead of rats and mice, children—boys and girls from age four on—came running in great numbers, among them the grown daughter of the town mayor. The whole swarm followed him, and he led them out of the village into a mountain where he vanished with them. This had been witnessed by a nursemaid with a child in her arms who had followed from afar and had then turned around and brought the rumour to the city. The parents ran to the gates in droves, seeking their children with grieving hearts. The mothers started weeping and wailing. From that hour on, messengers were dispatched by land and sea to all towns to inquire whether anyone had seen the children or at least some of them, but in vain. Altogether one hundred and thirty were lost. Some say that two had later returned, but one was blind and the other mute. The blind one could not point out the place where the children had followed the minstrel but was probably able to tell about it; the mute, although unable to have heard anything, was able to point out the place. A lad in his nightshirt had joined the others and turned back to get his coat. He thus escaped the misfortune, for when he came back the others had already disappeared in a pit in the hillside that people still point out today.

The street through which the children marched toward the gate was still called the Silent Street in the middle of the eighteenth century (and probably still is), because no one was permitted to dance or play a musical instrument in it. In fact, if a bride was accompanied by music on the way to the church, the musicians had to cross that street in complete silence. The name of the mountain near Hamelin where the children disappeared is Poppenberg. Two stones in the shape of the cross have been erected to the right and to the left of the mountain. Some people say the children had been led into a cave and had reemerged in Transylvania.

The citizens of Hamelin had the incident recorded in their city registry and got into the habit of dating their announcements from the day they lost their children. The following lines were inscribed on the City Hall:

> In the year of our Lord 1284
> From Hamelin were led away
> 130 children who here were born
> Lost by a piper inside the mountain.

And on the new gate:

> *Centum ter denos cum magnus ab urbe puellos*
> *Duxerat ante annon CCLXXII condita porta fuit.*

(This gate was built 272 years after the sorcerer abducted 130 children from the city.)

In the year 1572 the town mayor had the story illustrated in the church windows with an accompanying text inscription. This has become largely illegible. A coin commemorating the event was also issued.

Translated by Martha Humphreys

Ludwig Bechstein

The Swabian Who Devoured the Liver

When our Lord and Savior was still on earth and moved about from one city to the other preaching the gospel and making many signs, a good, simple-minded Swabian once came to him and asked, "My companion in suffering, where are you going?" Our Lord answered him, "I am moving about and making the people happy." Then the Swabian said: "Do you want me to go with you?" "Yes," answered our Lord, "if you want to be good and pray diligently." The Swabian said that he did. While they then were walking together and were between two villages, they heard bells ringing. The Swabian, who liked to chatter, asked our Lord, "My companion in suffering, what does the ringing of the bells mean?" Our savior, who knew the answer to all things, answered: "In one village the bells are being rung for a wedding, in the other for a funeral." "You go to the funeral," said the Swabian. "Then I'll go the the wedding."

Whereupon our Lord entered the village and made the dead person alive and was given a hundred gulden. The Swabian bestirred himself with the wedding, helped in pouring for one guest after the other and for himself, too, and when the wedding was over, he was given a kreuzer. The Swabian was pleased about that, went on his way, and again came to our Lord. As soon as the Swabian glimpsed Him from a distance, he held up his little kreuzer and shouted, "Look, my companion in suffering! I have money, and what do you have?" and engaged in much boasting about his little kreuzer. Our God, for his part, laughed and said, "Oh, I surely have more than you!" opened his sack and let the Swabian see the hundred gulden. He was not lacking in adroitness, however, and quickly tossed his miserable little kreuzer among the hundred gulden and shouted, "Let's share! Let's share! We want to share everything with one another'!" That was agreeable with our Lord.

As they walked on together, it happened that they came upon a herd of sheep. Then the Lord said to the Swabian, "Go to the shepherd, Swabian. Have him give us a lamb, and cook us the offal, or the heart, lungs, and liver for a meal. "Yes," said the Swabian, who did as he was told by the Lord, went to the shepherd, had the shepherd give him a lamb, took it and prepared the entrails to be eaten. During the simmering process the liver always floated to the top. The Swabian pushed it down with the spoon, but it refused to stay down, which vexed the Swabian beyond all telling. So he took a knife, cut off the liver while it was still whole, and ate it. When the meal was put on the table, our Lord then asked what had happened to the liver. The Swabian, though, had a ready answer, that the lamb had none. "What!" said our Lord, "how can it have been alive without a liver?" Then the Swabian swore by all that was holy, "By God and by all God's holiness, it had none!" What was our Lord to do? If he wanted the Swabian to remain silent, he had to hold his peace.

It then came to pass that they were again walking with one another, and once again bells were ringing in two villages. The Swabian asked, "Dear companion, what is the meaning of the bells?" "In one village the bells are for a funeral, in the other for a wedding," said our Lord. "Well," said the Swabian, "I was already at a wedding, so I now want to go to a funeral!" (meaning that he, too, wanted to earn a hundred gulden). He inquired further of the Lord, "Dear companion, what did you do to waken the dead?" The Lord answered, "Well, I said to him, 'Arise in the name of the Father, the Son, and the Holy Ghost!' Then he arose." "Fine, fine!" shouted the Swabian. "Now I know what to do!" and went to the village where the dead man was being borne along toward him. When the Swabian saw that, he shouted in a cheerful voice, "Stop, stop! I want to make him alive, and if I do not make him alive, you can hang me without verdict and justice."

The good people were happy, promised him a hundred gulden,

and set down the bier on which the dead person lay. The Swabian opened the coffin and started to speak, "Rise up, in the name of the Holy Trinity!" The dead person, however, did not arise. The Swabian became anxious. He spoke his blessing a second and a third time, but when the dead still failed to arise, he shouted very furiously: "Then, in the name of a thousand devils, remain lying!" When the people heard the godless talk and saw that they had been deceived by the jackanapes, they let go the coffin, seized the Swabian, and hastened immediately with him to the gallows, propped up the ladder, and led the Swabian onto it.

Our Lord was strolling down the street in quite a leisurely manner, since he certainly knew how the Swabian would fare, and wanted to see how he would behave. He now came upon the proceedings and shouted, "Oh, good companion, what have you done? In what shape do I see you?" The Swabian was enraged and began to scold the master for not having taught him the blessing correctly. "I taught you correctly," said the master. "You, however, did not learn it correctly and acted, but be that as it may. I want you to tell me what happened to the liver, then I will deal with your situation." "Oh," said the Swabian, "the lamb really had no liver! What are you accusing me of?" "Oh, you just do not want to admit it!" spoke the Lord. "Come on. If you admit it, I will make the dead person alive!" The Swabian, though, began to scream: "Hang me, hang me! In that way, I will get away from the torture. He wants to force me with the liver, but believe me, the lamb really had no liver. Just hang me right away!"

When our Lord heard that the Swabian sooner wanted to let himself be hanged than to admit the truth, he commanded them to let him down and himself now brought the dead to life.

As they went on their way with one another, our Lord spoke to the Swabian: "Come here, we want to divide with one another the money we won and then separate, for if I constantly had to save you from the gallows everywhere, that would be too much for me." So he took the two hundred gulden and divided them into three parts. When the Swabian saw that, he asked, "Oh, dear Companion, why are you dividing it into three parts when there are only two of us?" "Well," answered our dear God, "one part is mine, the second part is yours, and the third part belongs to the one who devoured the liver!" When the Swabian heard that, he cheerily shouted: "By God and by all that is holy, I devoured it!" He said that and also pocketed the third part and thus separated from our dear Lord.

Translated by Martha Humphreys

The Tale of the Man in the Moon

In ancient times a man once went into the forest on a beautiful Sunday morning, chopped himself a large bundle of wood, tied it up, inserted a staff, lifted the bundle, and carried it home.

Along the way he encountered a handsome man dressed in his Sunday clothes, probably on his way to church. He stopped, spoke to the man carrying the bundle, and said: "Do you not know that everywhere on earth it is Sunday, the day the dear Lord rested after he had created the world and all the animals and people? Do you not know that it is written in the Third Commandment that you should observe the holiday?" The inquirer, however, was the dear Lord himself. That woodcutter, though, was quite defiant and answered, "Sunday on earth or Moonday in heaven, what concern of that is mine, and what concern is that of yours?"

"Then you shall carry your bundle of wood forever!" spoke the dear Lord, "and since Sunday on earth is of so little value to you, from now on every day into eternity shall be Mo(o)nday for you, and you shall stand in the moon to serve as a warning to those who desecrate Sunday with work."

From this time on, the man with the bundle of wood is still standing in the moon and probably will remain standing there into all eternity.

Translated by Martha Humphreys

The Tale of the Land of Milk and Honey

Listen carefully. I want to tell you about a good country to which many people would emigrate if in fact they knew its location and knew of a good passage by ship. But the route there is long for youth and for the elderly, for whom winter is too hot and summer too cold. This beautiful region is called the Land of Milk and Honey, or Cucagna in the Romance languages. The houses there are covered with spoonbread, the doors and walls are made of gingerbread, and the beams of roast pork. Things that cost us a ducat are only a penny there. Around each house is a fence made of woven bratwurst and Bavarian sausages—some roasted, some freshly simmered, according to the preference of the one person or the next. All fountains are full of Malvasier and other sweet wines as well as champagne, which simply flow into one's mouth when placed at the pipes. So anyone who likes to drink such wines should hasten to make certain of entry into the Land of Milk and Honey. Freshly baked rolls grow on the birch trees and meadows there, and beneath the trees flow brooks of milk into which the rolls fall and soften for those who like them crumbled. It is something for women and children, for knaves and maids. Hello there, Greta! Hello there, Stefan! Do you not want to emigrate? Hasten off to the brook of fresh rolls, and do not forget to bring along a large dipper for the milk.

In the Land of Milk and Honey the fish swim on the surface of the water. They are also already baked or poached and swim quite close to the banks. Anyone who is too lazy, though, and is a real native of the Land of Milk and Honey need only call pst! pst!, and the fish walk out onto the ground and hop into the hands of the good native so there is no need to bend down.

You can believe it that there the birds—geese and pheasants, doves and capons, larks and fieldfare—fly around in the air already roasted. They fly straight into the jaws of anyone who finds it too much effort to reach out for them. Suckling pigs are excellent there every year; they run around already roasted, and each one carries a carving knife in its back so that whoever wishes to do so can cut off a fresh juicy piece.

In the Land of Milk and Honey cheese grows like stones, large and small. The stones themselves are veritable pigeon craws with stuffing, or they are small meat pies. When it rains in winter, it simply rains sweet drops of honey. People can lick and lap it up, so it is a pleasure; and when it snows, it snows clear sugar; and when it hails, it hails cube sugar mixed with figs, raisins, and almonds.

There are no horse-droppings in the Land of Milk and Honey. The horses instead leave eggs, whole large baskets full and piles of them, so a thousand cost only one penny. And money can be shaken from the trees like Spanish chestnuts. Anyone is permitted to shake down the best and leave pieces of lesser value lying on the ground.

In that country there are also large forests. There the most beautiful clothes—skirts, coats, cloaks, pants, and jerkins of all colors—black, green, yellow (for the postillions), blue or red—grow in the shrubbery and on trees, and anyone needing a new garment goes into the forest and knocks it down with a stone or shoots at it with a crossbow. Ladies' dresses made of velvet, atlas, Italian silk, barège, madras, taffeta, nanking, etc., grow on the heath. The grass consists of ribbons of all colors, even moiré. Juniper branches hold brooches and golden needles for chemisettes and capes, and the juniper berries, instead of being black, are genuine pearls. Ladies' watches and very artful chatelaines hang from the fir trees. On the bushes there grow boots and shoes, men's and women's hats, hats made of rice straw, and marabout, and there is all manner of head-dress decorated with birds of paradise, humming birds, diamond beetles, pearls, enamels, and gold braid.

This noble country also has two large fairs and markets with beautiful liberties. Anyone who has an old wife and no longer likes her because she is not young and pretty enough can exchange her there for a young and beautiful one and is even given additional payment. The country is blessed with a fountain of youth that possesses great powers. Old and ugly women are placed in its waters (for a saying has it that people who get old become ugly) and, after bathing in them for three days or four at the most, emerge as attractive lasses of seventeen or eighteen.

In the Land of Milk and Honey there is also much entertainment of many kinds. Anyone in these parts who has no luck has it there in games and in the sport of shooting as well as in journeymen's tournaments. Many people who go through life here shooting just short of or far off the mark hit the target there, even the bull's eye, regardless of how far away it is. That country is also splendid for the lazybones and sleepyheads who here become poor from their indolence, causing them to go bankrupt and to have to beg. Each hour of sleep there is awarded with a gulden, each yawn with a double taler. Any money lost in gambling falls back into the loser's pocket. Drinkers get the best wine for free, and both male and female tipplers receive a wage of three silver coins for every sip and swallow. Whoever can best tease and make a fool out of the people receives a gulden for each such achievement. No one is permitted to do anything for nothing, and the person who tells the biggest lie is always rewarded with a crown.

Many people in these parts tell bald-faced lies and get nothing for their effort; there, however, lying is considered the best art. For this reason, many a fool of a lawyer, many a fool of a doctor, other fools, horse-swindlers, and *** craftsmen who constantly hassle their customers and never keep their word surely lie their way into the country.

Anyone wishing to be an academician there must have studied with a boor. In our country, we also have such students, but they are given neither gratitude nor honors. There, in addition to being boorish, it is necessary to be lazy and gluttonous, for churlishness, indolence, and gluttony are considered the three fine arts. I know someone who can become a professor any day.

Anyone who enjoys work, does good, and shuns evil is disdained by everyone there and is denied entrance to the Land of Milk and Honey. But anyone who is an oaf, incapable of doing anything, and is at the same time full of stupid opinions is considered a nobleman there. Anyone incapable of anything but sleeping, eating, drinking, dancing, and gambling is made an earl. The person, though, who is recognized by universal suffrage as the laziest and the most unsuited for anything good becomes king of the entire country and has a large income.

You now know about the characteristics and ways of the Land of Milk and Honey. So all persons wishing to bestir themselves and travel there but not knowing which route to take should inquire of a blind person. A mute person is also suited for this purpose, for there is no danger of hearing a wrong route mentioned.

The entire country is surrounded by a wall of rice pudding as high as a mountain. Persons wishing to enter or leave must first devour their route by eating through the wall crossways.

Translated by Martha Humphreys

Irving Fetscher

Anti-Fairy Tale:
The Goat and the Seven Small Wolves

Once upon a time there was a happy and contented family of
wolves—Father Wolf, Mother Wolf, and seven small wolves that
had been born as septuplets and were not yet permitted to go into
the forest alone.

One day when Father Wolf had already left for work, Mother
Wolf said to her children: "Children, today I must go to the mat-
tress store 'Moss and Matting' to buy you new beds, for the old
ones are completely sagging and no longer comfortable, not to
mention their other shortcomings. Be good and do not leave the
cave while I am away. You never know who may be coming through
the forest—hunters, policemen, soldiers, and other people bearing
arms who do not mean well by young wolves. I will return some
time in the afternoon and will bring something nice for all those
who have been good."

"Yes, yes, of course, of course," answered the seven small wolves
impatiently, for they wanted the mother finally to be on her way
so they could romp about and hold moss battles without any in-
terference. As soon as Mother Wolf had left, the small wolves began to play boisterously. But after perhaps an hour had passed,
there was a shuffling sound at the entrance to the cave, and a voice
shouted: "Come out, you dear children, your mama is back and
has brought something splendid for each of you, but hurry so you
can see it well in bright daylight." But as she was saying this, her

voice sounded so querulous and bleating that the small wolves called out: "No, we will not come out. You are not our mama, you are the old grouchy goat. Our mama has a beautiful deep voice!" The evil goat then became cross and thought about what she should do to make her voice as deep and pleasing as Mama Wolf's.

In its perplexity, it went—as do many animals in the forest—to an old owl that was known far and wide as the wisest animal. "Dear owl," said the wolf, "what can I do to make my voice as deep and pleasing as Mother Wolf's?" The old owl cocked his head and reflected for a moment. Then he said, "The best thing for you to do is to take voice lessons with me, but I cannot do it free of charge."

"Just let that be my concern," said the goat. "You can have from me a liter of the finest rich milk for making genuine goat cheese."

"One liter is not enough," said the old owl, "but I will probably do it for two."

"Well, fine," said the goat, "if you are intent on ruining your stomach with so much cheese, let it be two liters," and they started the voice lesson.

The old owl, however, was such a good teacher and the goat, due to her interest in deceiving the small wolves, such an attentive student that within a half-hour the goat had acquired a beautiful, deep bass voice that would have been acceptable in any church choir. After she had paid the owl, she went back to the cave of the small wolves. Once again she shouted, "Come out, you dear children, your mama is back and has brought something splendid for each of you, but do hurry so you can see it well in bright daylight."

And this time the voice sounded so deep and beautiful that the small wolves were completely deceived and blinked their eyes as they ran out into the bright morning sun. But hardly were they outside when they were lifted onto the horns of the evil goat and thrown high up into a fir tree where they anxiously clung to the branches. For, as you know, wolves cannot climb.

The opening to the wolves' cave was so small that only one wolf at a time could exit, and since the others were pushing, the ones at the front could no longer turn back after they had recognized who was standing outside. Only the last and weakest of the small wolves that had no one pushing him was able to save himself in time before the goat had noticed it. The goat, however, who had always been poor in arithmetic, thought she had already hurled all seven small wolves into the branches of the fir tree and, profoundly satisfied, moved on.

If you were to ask me why the goat was altogether so angry at the small wolves, then I could only say that she begrudged the wolves their free, untrammeled existence in the forest and—precisely like her owner whose attitude she had gradually adopted—countered with envious hate everything that deviated from the bourgeois lifestyle. Examined more closely, therefore, it was not at all its own hatred but the hatred of the petty bourgeois goat owner that was being expressed. This hatred of everything free had been whipped into her during years of being confined in a stall, and she now naturally took it out on the weakest—on small wolves and on other children.

When Mama Wolf, laden with beautiful, deep, moss beds, finally came home though, only one lone small wolf came out of the cave and told her what had happened. Soon she also heard from the fir branches above her the six-voiced weeping of the small wolves who, already quite weak from holding on for a long time, shouted: "Please, please, dear Mama, please fetch us down!" But Mama Wolf was of course also unable to climb, just as little as Papa Wolf, who anyway was not expected back before evening. So Mama Wolf went into the neighboring cave where an old climbing bear was sleeping, wakened him, and asked for help. The old climbing bear was jolted from the middle of his most beautiful dreams of honey, but since he was a kind fellow who moreover was a vegetarian, he got up immediately and in no time fetched the six small wolves down from the tree. That was a joy. From sheer excitement, Mama Wolf even forgot to rebuke her children.

But when Papa Wolf returned home in the evening and heard of the incident, he became very furious and, growling, said angrily: "Just wait, I will pay the goat back!" In vain Mama Wolf sought to calm him. The following morning Papa Wolf went to the goat stall and paid Nanny Goat back in kind. Here begins the story of "Wolf and the Seven Kids" that you all know.

Translated by Martha Humphreys

ACKNOWLEDGMENTS

Every reasonable effort has been made to locate the parties who hold rights to previously published translations reprinted here. We gratefully acknowledge permission to reprint the following:

Fifty-seven tales from *The Complete Grimm's Fairy Tales,* translated by Margaret Hunt. Copyright 1944 by Pantheon Books. Copyright renewed 1972 by Random House, Inc. Reprinted by permission of Pantheon Books, A Division of Random House, Inc., and Routledge & Kegan Paul Ltd.

"The Goat and the Seven Small Wolves" by Iring Fetscher, translated from *Wer hat Dornröschen wachgeküsst? Das Märchen Verwirrbuch.* Claasen Verlag, Hamburg and Düsseldorf, 1972. Translated by permission of Claassen Verlag.

THE GERMAN LIBRARY
in 100 Volumes

Edited by Helmut Brackert and Volkmar Sander
Foreword by Bruno Bettelheim
Illustrations by Otto Ubbelodhe

Volume 30
German Literary Fairy Tales
Edited by Frank G. Ryder and Robert M. Browning
Introduction by Gordon Birrell
Foreword by John Gardiner

Volume 32
Heinrich Heine
Poetry and Prose
Edited by Jost Hermand and Robert C. Holub
Foreword by Alfred Kazin

Volume 39
German Poetry from 1750 to 1900
Edited by Robert M. Browning
Foreword by Michael Hamburger

Volume 44
Gottfried Keller
Stories
Edited by Frank G. Ryder
Foreword by Max Frisch

Volume 45
Wilhelm Raabe
Novels
Edited by Volkmar Sander
Foreword by Joel Agee

Volume 46
Theodore Fontane
Short Novels and Other Writings
Edited by Peter Demetz
Foreword by Peter Gay